THE

Basic *Basics*

SOUPS

MARGUERITE PATTEN

GRUB STREET · LONDON

This new edition published by Grub Street
4 Rainham Close, London SW11 6SS

Reprinted 2004, 2005, 2007, 2009

British Library Cataloguing in Publication Data
Patten, Marguerite
  The basic basics soups handbook
  1. Soups
  I. Title II. Soups handbook
  641. 8′13

ISBN 1 904010 19 9

Typeset by Pearl Graphics, Hemel Hempstead
Printed and bound by MPG Books Ltd, Bodmin, Cornwall

MEASUREMENTS
All the recipes in this book give metric, imperial and American
weights and measures. Note that American pints and
tablespoons are smaller than the British equivalent.
    Use measures from one column only – do not mix them.
    All spoon measures are level.
    Soups are not like cakes, where strict adherence to a recipe
is important to maintain the balance of ingredients. In a soup
the quantity of each ingredient is very much a matter of
personal taste, but the recipes have been tested with the
quantities given.

Choice of Ingredients
Where recipes give a choice of ingredients, such as butter or
margarine, vegetable or chicken stock, the first-mentioned
ingredient is my preferred choice.

CONTENTS

INTRODUCTION

Soup of the evening, beautiful soup!
Beautiful soup! who cares for fish,
Game, or any other dish?
Who would not give all else for two
Pennyworth only of beautiful soup?

Lewis Carroll (1832-98)

I do not entirely agree with the words spoken in *Alice in Wonderland* about the time to eat 'beautiful soup'. I welcome it in the middle of the day and late at night, as well as in the evening. Many soups are economical dishes, though the cost today may be a little more than two pennyworth. Soup is easy to digest and wonderfully soothing, so it is ideal when you are rather tired and unwilling to eat more solid foods. Hot soups are warming in cold weather and cold soups refreshing in the heat of summer.

Soup has been an important part of family and special occasion meals in many countries of the world for centuries. It is reported that the Ancient Greeks ate black broth (presumably a type of soup), but sadly I do not have a recipe for this. The Romans made soup, known as *polus*, and the historian Apicus records the impressive selection of vegetables, herbs and seasonings they used in cooking them.

The countries occupied by the Romans all have a great tradition of soup-making. Although the word *polus* is not used today, it was undoubtedly the origin of the French word *potage*. In England this became 'pottage', which has been used for centuries to describe some British soups.

The first chapter of this book gives information to help you make soups that have a perfect flavour and consistency. It includes recipes for various stocks – the secret of many good soups – although modern stock (bouillon) cubes can be used as an alternative when home-made stock is not available.

Our approach to stock has changed a great deal: no longer is there a large pot on the kitchen range into which liquid, leftover bones and other foods have to be boiled daily in an effort to stop the contents becoming rancid. Nowadays the stock is kept in the safety of the refrigerator or freezer, awaiting the time when it can be used. There is clear information about freezing stock in Chapter 1 and also at the end of recipes, for it is a great asset to have containers of soup waiting for you to heat as required.

Stock can be prepared in various ways: apart from in a saucepan, in the oven, in a microwave or in a pressure cooker (see pages 11 and 12).

It is a mistake to think one needs a vast selection of ingredients to make a good soup – quite the contrary. If you make a tomato soup, or order it in a restaurant, you expect the soup to have a definite flavour of tomatoes. If, due to an over-long list of other ingredients, the tomato taste has been lost, it is *not* a good soup. Carefully chosen herbs, spices and other suitable ingredients must be chosen to enhance the flavour of the basic ingredient(s). You will find information about these in Chapter 1.

Knowing how many keen cooks are short of time, Chapter 2 is devoted to Quick Soups. Each of the varied recipes can be cooked within 30 minutes. The soups are based on vegetables, fish, meat, chicken, fruit and cheese.

Clear Soups follow in Chapter 3. These will be enjoyed by people who appreciate the flavour of a classic consommé, and are ideal if you want to lose a little weight. There are many suggestions for giving a special touch to consommés, together with other clear soups, including those based on beer or wine. These retain an alcoholic flavour, but the alcohol content is destroyed during cooking.

Chapter 4 includes vegetable soups from around the world, but all have one thing in common – I have kept the cooking times to a minimum to retain the flavour, colour and texture of the ingredients. This is a change from old-fashioned vegetable soups, where the cooking time was so long that the lovely fresh flavour of the vegetables was lost.

Obviously, this chapter will be of special appeal to vegetarians. Although some recipes suggest using chicken stock vegetarians can easily substitute vegetable stock (see page 14) or water with a vegetable stock cube.

Soups based on fish, meat, poultry and game fill Chapters 5, 6 and 7. Many of these soups are sufficiently satisfying to make a complete light meal, particularly the chowders, broths and intriguing sticky gumbo soups.

In many countries soups based upon fruit are traditional favourites. We in Britain, alas, have not established that tradition. Fruit soups can be an appetizing and refreshing start to a meal at any time of the year, but they must be made with a subtle mixture of sweet and sharp or savoury flavours, so it does not appear you are serving a fruit dessert at the start of the meal. My favourite fruit soups are in Chapter 8.

Hot soups far outnumber cold soups in this book, as hot ones are more popular. Sometimes, however, a hot soup can be turned into a cold one by adding a little extra liquid so that the consistency is perfect when the ingredients cool. As a lover of chilled, jellied and even iced soups, I am delighted to find that more and more people are discovering the virtues of cold soups on a warm day. You will find a good selection in Chapter 9.

I hope you will enjoy using this book and, like me, you will extol the virtues of good home-made soups at all times.

MARGUERITE PATTEN

1 PERFECT SOUPS

There is such a wide range of soups, based on an almost endless variety of ingredients and flavours, that it may sound difficult to give a few golden rules about making good ones. In fact, it is relatively simple to summarize these.

Flavour: Generally, soup is the first course of a meal, or the second course if served after an hors d'oeuvre: as such, the flavour must not be so pronounced that it will overwhelm the taste of the foods that are to follow; it should be interesting but not too strong. This point is emphasized in the introduction to the various chapters.

The soup should be well seasoned but never over-seasoned, so it is wise to add relatively little salt, pepper and other flavourings at the beginning of the cooking period. Taste the soup when it is cooked and adjust the seasoning just before serving.

If, by some unlucky chance, you over-salt the soup, see page 198.

Consistency: It is important to get this right. Puréed soups, for example, should be rather like a thickish cream. The correct amount of liquid is given in the recipes but this is a guide only. If your saucepan lid does not fit as well as it should, you may lose more liquid than anticipated during the course of cooking. If a soup is kept heating gently for some time until ready to serve, the liquid will evaporate and the soup will become thicker. Check the consistency as well as the flavour at the last minute; too thick soups are not appealing.

If the soup is thinner than desired, there are various ways of correcting this (see page 8).

Additions: All the recipes in this book can be varied in many ways, so you can enjoy giving your own individual touch, but do not get carried away and add too many extra ingredients. The principal flavour in, say, a tomato soup should be tomatoes, not over-strong stock, herbs or spices. These ingredients should be included to bring out the taste of the tomatoes, not overwhelm them.

Appearance: The look of a soup is important, so choose garnishes that enhance the appearance, as well as the flavour, of the particular mixture of ingredients. Appropriate garnishes are suggested in the recipes, and there are additional suggestions in each chapter and on pages 193 and 194.

Temperature: Make sure soups are served at the right temperature. Hot soups should be piping hot, so warm the bowls or soup plates before serving. Cold soups should be well chilled: a tepid soup is not appealing to most people.

Imagination: Be imaginative in your choice of soups. Nowadays we enjoy ingredients and dishes that come from many different countries, that is why I have included a number of soup recipes from around the world, as well as the much-loved familiar flavours. It is easy to obtain the ingredients in supermarkets or shops specializing in ethnic foods.

TO COOK SOUPS

The cooking time given in the recipes assumes the soup is being cooked in an ordinary saucepan. Choose a good heavy pan so there is no possibility of the ingredients burning, and make sure the lid fits as tightly as possible so that evaporation of the liquid is not more than it should be during the cooking process. If the lid on your pan is a poor fit, place a sheet of foil under it to ensure a tighter fit.

Other ways of cooking soups are outlined below. These may prove more convenient for you.

Oven cooking: If the oven is already being used, cooking soup in it too is a sensible way of saving fuel. It is also a good method if you want to leave the soup unattended for there is no possibility of it sticking to the pan. Make sure you use a covered casserole. I find oven cooking less suitable for vegetable soups because it is slow and therefore you lose the fresh flavour of the vegetables. It is, however, quite a good method for longer-cooking fish and meat soups. Ideally, the ingredients should be brought to the boil on top of the cooker, then transferred to a casserole and covered tightly.

The initial cooking of onions and similar ingredients should be done in an ordinary pan, or in a casserole if made of suitable material, on top of the cooker.

Preheat the oven to 180°C/350°F/gas mark 4. Allow 50 per cent longer cooking time in the oven than when cooking in a saucepan.

Pressure cooking: This is an excellent way of cooking many soups because it saves time and results in an excellent flavour. Do not use the rack in the cooker. As explained in the chapter introductions, less liquid is needed for pressure cooking because the cooking time is shorter.

Use the pressure cooker, without a lid, as an ordinary pan to fry the onions or other ingredients at the beginning, and again at the end when adding egg yolks or cream.

Microwave cooking: This method of cooking soups does not save as much time as you might imagine because liquids are relatively slow to reach boiling point in a microwave. The introduction to each chapter includes specific hints on using a microwave for particular soups.

The initial frying of onions and suchlike can be done in the container in the microwave. Always chop the ingredients very evenly for this method of cooking.

When you add cream, eggs and other enriching ingredients, cook the soup slowly on a lower setting. Stir or whisk regularly and make sure the liquid does not boil.

Microwave soup in a large, microwave container with a lid, or cover it with cling film or kitchen paper during the cooking period. Use full power until the soup reaches boiling point, or is very hot (according to the instructions in the recipe), then set to defrost for the cooking time. If the soup seems to be cooking too quickly on this setting, turn to an even lower one.

Allow the soup to stand for at least 2 minutes before serving.

MICROWAVE TERMS

Various terms are used to describe the settings on a microwave. On the whole, I tend to use the words *full power*, but many manufacturers simply say *high*, which means exactly the same thing.

Defrost is a term used by most manufacturers of microwaves, and this gives half the full output.

If the recipe states 'turn to a low setting', I suggest you use *warm* or the lowest setting on your dial.

Just like cooking in an oven or a saucepan, you need to check cooking progress, for microwaves vary considerably in their output and therefore their speed of cooking.

As stated above, it is advisable to let microwaved soup stand for 2 minutes before serving because cooking continues during that time.

Safety first

Although microwave containers are specially manufactured, ovenproof glass bowls are ideal for making soup in a microwave; allow a sufficiently large container so there is no possibility of the soup boiling over. Reduce the setting if there is any danger of this happening.

Be very careful when removing hot containers from the microwave. Use oven gloves to protect your hands. If the container is the type that could crack, place the bowl on a *dry* surface in the kitchen: a wooden board is ideal.

COMMON WAYS TO THICKEN SOUPS

There are various ways of thickening soups to give the desired consistency. If you find the soup is thinner than you wish, this can be easily rectified by following steps 3, 4, 5 or 6 before serving.

1) **The ingredients** themselves help to thicken the mixture. Potatoes and other starchy root vegetables are excellent for this purpose, which is why vegetable soups are frequently made with no other thickening agent.

Similarly, when fish, meat, poultry and fruit soups are puréed, you will achieve just the right consistency without adding flour or any other thickener.

2) **Cereals**, particularly rice, are very popular additions to soup. Unless the recipe states to the contrary, you should use round-grain (pudding) rice or the Italian arborio (risotto) rice for thickening purposes, even though they do give a slightly cloudy appearance to the liquid. Long-grain rice gives a clearer liquid, but is not so effective at thickening.

Old-fashioned recipes use tapioca and sago instead of rice. If you would like to substitute these, use exactly the same quantity as stated for rice.

3) **Flour** is another very common thickening agent. Potato flour may be used instead of ordinary flour, and in exactly the same quantity. Cornflour (cornstarch) is another alternative. In this case you require exactly half the amount of cornflour as given for flour in the recipe because it has twice the thickening quality.

All these flours may be used at the last moment if the soup is too thin. Blend 2 tablespoons (2½ tablespoons) flour or 1 tablespoon (1¼ tablespoons) cornflour with a little cold water, stock or milk, depending upon the recipe. Add several ladles of the hot soup to the blended ingredients, return to the pan and whisk or stir briskly for several minutes as the soup boils and thickens. If the recipe advises gentle cooking because of egg, cream or wine content, cook slowly for at least 10 minutes. Always check the flavouring after this to make sure there is no taste of inadequately cooked flour or cornflour.

If the soup is only slightly too thin, reduce the quantities above.

4) **Beurre manié** is a classic method used to thicken liquids. Mix equal amounts of butter and flour together, e.g. 115 g/4 oz (½ cup) butter and 115 g/4 oz (1 cup) flour.

To add beurre manié. Make sure the soup is very hot, then drop small amounts – the size of a large pea – into the soup. Wait until this is absorbed before adding any more. Continue like this until the soup is the right consistency. Store any left-over beurre manié in a covered container in the refrigerator for future use. The addition of butter adds a pleasing richness to the soups.

5) **Eggs** also thicken mixtures, although the yolks alone are better for this purpose. Whisk the eggs or yolks with a little cold water, milk, stock or wine (depending upon the recipe). Carefully spoon a little hot soup over the blended eggs or yolks then return to the pan, whisking over a low heat until the soup is adequately thickened.

6) **Double (heavy) cream** immediately adds a thicker consistency, as well as a richer taste, to soups. Thick yoghurt can also be used for the same purpose, as can fromage frais, but these are less rich in flavour. However, they are much lower in calories than cream.

Take great care the soup does not boil when adding dairy products to a soup that contains wine or acid ingredients like lemon juice. It must simmer gently.

7) **Longer heating** with the lid off the pan during cooking so the liquid evaporates and the soup becomes thicker. This is not an ideal method, as prolonged cooking can obliterate the fresh taste of the ingredients.

UNUSUAL WAYS TO THICKEN SOUPS

All soups can be sieved or liquidized, but if they are not suitable for making into a smooth purée, the following three ingredients will successfully thicken them.

1) **One or two peeled and diced old potatoes** can be added to the other ingredients during the cooking period. If the cooking time of the soup is short, peel and grate the potatoes so they will cook more quickly. Stir the soup briskly with a wooden spoon to ensure the potato has disintegrated.

2) **Oatmeal** is excellent for thickening soups and stews. A little imparts a pleasantly nutty flavour, but too much makes for a sticky and rather cloying texture.

If using very fine pinhead, fine or medium oatmeal (as opposed to rolled oats), mix a few tablespoons with a little water, stock or milk (depending upon the recipe) and add halfway through the cooking period. Stir briskly until the soup reaches boiling point again and starts to thicken. Stir from time to time, as oatmeal or rolled oats tend to stick to the pan. (Sticking is not a problem if the soup is cooked in a microwave.)

If using quick-cooking rolled oats, follow the same procedure but add towards the end of the cooking time.

If using oats to replace flour in a recipe, use approximately half the amount of oatmeal or rolled oats as given for flour.

3) Breadcrumbs are excellent for thickening soups since they do not form lumps or stick to the pan. Add a few tablespoons of fine breadcrumbs to the soup just before the end of the cooking time. Simmer for a few minutes, then stir briskly to blend the crumbs with the other ingredients.

TO PURÉE SOUPS

The ingredients in many soup recipes need to be made into a smooth purée. There are various ways of achieving this.

Sieving: This is the classic way of making sure you have a perfectly smooth mixture, entirely free from small pieces of skin, seeds or particles of meat, fish or vegetables. While a metal sieve can be used for many ingredients, it is advisable to choose a hair or nylon sieve where the ingredients include acid fruits, lemon juice, vinegar or tomatoes because metal can spoil the colour and give a slightly metallic flavour to the soup.

Place the sieve over a large bowl or clean saucepan and rub the ingredients firmly through the mesh with a wooden spoon. Always wash and dry the sieve with great care after use. Allow hair or nylon sieves or those with plastic rims to dry naturally at room temperature.

Liquidizing after cooking: This method of puréeing ingredients involves using a liquidizer (blender) or food processor. In most cases a liquidizer is better than a food processor for preparing a puréed soup since the goblet allows a large amount of liquid to be included with the solid ingredients.

Using a liquidizer: If the soup ingredients are very hot, warm a glass liquidizer goblet before filling it. This ensures it will not crack.

Never fill the goblet more than three-quarters full as the liquid rises dramatically when the machine is switched on. It is better to purée the soup in several batches.

Make sure the lid of the goblet is firmly in position and hold it down as you switch on so it cannot be forced off as the liquid and other ingredients rise in the goblet.

If you find that firm particles of meat are not completely puréed or that skin and pips remain, sieve the mixture after liquidizing it. These two processes are far less time-consuming than simply sieving the ingredients.

Liquidizing before cooking: Raw vegetables for soup can be liquidized to speed up the cooking process. Prepare them as necessary and cut into small chunks; place in the liquidizer with a small amount of water or stock and switch on. The result will be rather like grated vegetables.

The one vegetable I have never found completely satisfactory liquidized in this way is onions: they seem to retain rather a raw taste, even with prolonged cooking. Spring onions or shallots, however, work perfectly well because they have a milder taste.

Processing: While food processors are better than liquidizers at making smooth purées of solid ingredients, such as cooked meat, poultry and firm vegetables, the amount of liquid in most soup recipes means that it may well leak through the centre cavity where the cutting blades fit in the food processor bowl. The solution is to transfer the solid ingredients from the pan to the processor bowl using a perforated spoon, then add only a little of the liquid. The remaining soup can be poured through a strainer.

Never process the ingredients for too long or they become sticky, rather than a smooth purée.

Using a pestle and mortar: This is a traditional method, which involves pressing ingredients by hand to produce a smooth purée. As this method is very slow, it's suitable only if there are few solid ingredients in the soup.

Using a potato masher: If a soup contains potatoes or other root vegetables which have become really soft during cooking, the liquid can be strained into a bowl, and the vegetables mashed separately until smooth. Return the liquid to the purée in the pan and reheat.

Using a vegetable mill: A mouli-grater can be used for puréeing if you have no other utensils. Spoon a small amount of cooked vegetables into the grater cavity and turn the handle to push them through the holes. The purée will not be quite as smooth as when using the other methods described. Note that a mouli-grater is not strong enough to purée cooked meat.

MAKING STOCK

'Stock' is the culinary term given to the liquid produced when the bones, skin and other parts of animals or fish and/or vegetables are simmered in liquid. Do not imagine, however, that home-made stock is essential to successful soups. In some recipes water is perfectly adequate, for the other ingredients have sufficient flavour and the soup could be spoiled by the addition of stock. In other recipes, where stock is specifically mentioned, you would be well advised to give additional flavour to the soup by using stock as the liquid or by adding a commercial alternative (see page 13).

The basic way to make stock is to simmer the ingredients in a saucepan on top of the cooker (see approximate cooking times below). There are, however, alternative ways of preparing stock.

Oven cooking: Instead of using a saucepan, place the ingredients, plus the liquid, in a tightly-covered casserole in the oven. This is a sensible idea if the oven is already being used to cook something else. The ideal temperature should be about 150°C/300°F/gas mark 2. Allow about 50 per cent longer cooking time than when using a saucepan. If the lid of the casserole fits very tightly, you may produce rather more stock than when a saucepan is used since the evaporation will be less.

Pressure cooking: This form of cooking is ideal for making stock and the cooking time is considerably shorter than using a saucepan. As there is also less evaporation, you can be a little more sparing with the water. Use about 450 ml/¾ pint (scant 2 cups) instead of each 600 ml/1 pint (2½ cups) you would use in a saucepan or casserole.

Remove the trivet (rack) from the base of the cooker, then put in the water, vegetables, bones, etc. Never have the pan more than half-full. Fix the lid and bring up to high (maximum) pressure. Maintain this pressure for the time stipulated in the recipe for stock. Allow the pressure to drop steadily at room temperature. Strain the stock and store until needed.

Microwave cooking: This is an excellent way of making stock, although the saving of time is not as great as when using a pressure cooker.
As water takes quite a long time to heat in a microwave, it is usually quicker to boil a kettle.

Place the ingredients for the stock in a large microwave bowl, add the recommended amount of water, then cover the bowl with a lid or plate.

Set the microwave to defrost and leave for 5-10 minutes. If at the end of that time the liquid is boiling rapidly, lower the setting slightly and continue cooking for the time stipulated in the recipe.

Be very careful when removing the hot stock from the microwave, especially if using a ceramic bowl. Place on a dry surface. Strain the stock, allow to cool and store until needed.

REMOVING FAT FROM STOCK

As the stock cools and clears, the fat floats to the top of the liquid. If you are in a hurry to use the stock, you can spoon most of this off. It is, however, far better to allow the stock to become very cold. In the case of meat stocks, the fat will form a fairly solid layer which can be lifted from the liquid with a knife. The fat from poultry and game birds tends to be softer, so this should be spooned off.

Fat from stock can be used instead of the butter, margarine or oil in a soup recipe, provided it is suitable, i.e. use beef dripping in soups where beef stock is used and a strong, meaty flavour is required; use chicken fat in soups based on chicken. Do not use the fat from stock in delicately flavoured vegetable soups for it will give too pronounced a taste.

STORING STOCK

Strain the stock carefully through a fine sieve into a bowl to remove all particles of bone, skin and vegetables. Allow to become quite cold, then cover the bowl and place in the refrigerator.

After some hours you may find that a layer of fat has formed on top of the liquid. It is a good idea to spoon or lift this away as it can cause stock to deteriorate. The fat can be used in various forms of cooking.

The stock can be stored for 3 days in the refrigerator. If you want to store it for up to a week, pour the chilled stock into a saucepan and bring to boiling point. Maintain at this temperature for several minutes, then cool again and replace in the refrigerator.

If you want to store stock for more than a week, even with re-boiling, then it is wise to freeze it (see below).

FREEZING STOCK

All stocks freeze well. Remove any fat from the top of the liquid, as this can become slightly rancid in freezing. Freeze the stock in small containers so you have a reasonable amount for making a particular soup. Mark the containers clearly as all stocks look alike when frozen.

If short of space in the freezer, it is wise to boil the strained stock vigorously in an uncovered pan to reduce the quantity but increase the flavour. One of the most practical ways to freeze stock is to boil it down until very concentrated then pour it into ice-making trays and freeze until firm. Transfer the cubes of stock to clearly marked boxes or bags. When needed, simply add 1 or 2 frozen stock cubes to the other ingredients in a soup. This very strong stock should be diluted with water.

Frozen stock should be used within 3 months.

USING WINES IN STOCK

As the stocks in this book are to be used for a wide variety of soups, I prefer to make them with water rather than wine. Water produces a stock that will not overwhelm the flavour of the other ingredients in a soup. It is very simple to add a little wine to the soup itself if you feel that it will improve the flavour; in fact, the addition of alcohol is suggested in a number of recipes.

COMMERCIAL STOCKS

Home-made stock takes time and effort to prepare, so you might prefer to use ready-made stock cubes and flavourings. These are available in many varieties, but they often have a high salt content. Take care, therefore, when adding extra salt to soup: taste first and add judiciously.

It is also advisable to use rather less commercial flavouring than recommended on the packet in case your basic soup ingredients already have a strong flavour and require very little extra seasoning.

BEEF STOCK

Cooking time: about 3 hours • Makes about 1.2 litres/2 pints (5 cups)

In view of the fairly long time needed to make a good beef stock, it is sensible to prepare a reasonable quantity at one time. The recipe given below is ideal for most soups where a slightly delicate flavour of beef is required. The stock is not sufficiently strong to be termed a Beef Consommé (see page 49). Fresh bay leaves are used below; if substituting dried bay, use just one leaf.

Metric/Imperial	Ingredients	American
1 kg/2¼ lb	beef bones	2¼ lb
1 medium	onion	1 medium
2 medium	carrots	2 medium
2 or 3	celery sticks	2 or 3
2	bay leaves	2
2.4 litres/4 pints	water	10 cups
to taste	salt and freshly ground black pepper	to taste

It is a good idea to crack the bones, or ask the butcher to do this, as cracked bones yield more flavour. Peel and thickly slice the onion and carrots, and chop the celery into small pieces. Put all the ingredients into a large saucepan, bring to boiling point, then remove the scum that floats to the top. Cover the pan, lower the heat and simmer gently for 3 hours.

Strain and use or store as described on page 12.

Variations

Bacon or Ham Stock: Use the liquid from boiling a joint of bacon or ham. If the stock is lacking in flavour, boil it in an open pan until more concentrated in flavour. One or two rashers (slices) of bacon can be cooked in the stock to produce a stronger taste.

Chicken Stock: Use the carcass of a chicken instead of beef bones in the recipe on page 13. If the carcass is rather small, cook a raw joint of chicken in the liquid.
  This stock is not sufficiently strong to use as a **Chicken Consommé** (see page 51).

Game Stock: The bones of game birds or venison make a very rich stock. Use them instead of beef bones in the recipe above. The recipe for **Game Consommé** is on page 52.

Brown Stock: Use the bones of mutton or lamb instead of beef in the recipe above. The flavour is not quite as good, but it is an acceptable alternative.

White or Veal Stock: Use veal bones in the recipe for Beef Stock to produce a really good stock. Failing this, use the carcass of a chicken, turkey or guinea fowl. The recipe for **Veal Consommé** is on page 50.

Vegetable Stock: Use the liquid from cooking vegetables, or make a special stock by peeling and chopping 1 or 2 onions, 2 carrots, a few celery sticks and 2 or 3 cauliflower florets, and simmer in approximately 1.2 litres/2 pints (5 cups) of water for 20 minutes. Season lightly during cooking. Strain and use or store (see page 12).

Freezing: See page 12.

Quick Tip

Allow 45 minutes to 1 hour in a pressure cooker for the Beef Stock and other stocks based upon the same recipe. (For information about pressure cooking stock, see page 11).
  Allow about 10 minutes in a pressure cooker for Vegetable Stock.
  Allow 1 to 1¼ hours in a microwave for the Beef Stock and other stocks based upon the same recipe, and about 15 minutes for the Vegetable Stock. (For details on using a microwave oven to prepare stock, see page 12).

DUCK AND GOOSE STOCK

These stocks are made in the same way as Beef Stock (see page 13). Use the carcass of the birds to make a strongly flavoured liquid. As well as the bay leaves, 2 or 3 sage leaves can be added to the other ingredients.
  Most present-day ducklings and ducks are much leaner than in the past, but they still have an appreciable amount of fat, and geese have considerably more. Much of this fat will have run out when cooking the bird, but the carcass may still have some fat adhering to it. Do not remove this or any particles of skin, for they both add flavour to the stock. It is important, though, to remove all the fat from the top of the cold stock for reasons explained on page 12, and to prevent any soup it is used in becoming over-greasy.

Any fat removed from these stocks should be used in cooking. Goose fat is particularly good for roasting vegetables.

STOCK FOR ORIENTAL SOUPS

Chicken stock is ideal for these soups. Follow the directions for making Beef Stock on page 13, but add 1 teaspoon finely grated root ginger to give a piquant flavour. Do not exceed this amount as the ginger should not be too pronounced. For a more interesting flavour, add 1 or 2 small pork bones to the chicken carcass.

FISH STOCK

Cooking time: 30 to 40 minutes • Makes about 600 ml/1 pint (2½ cups)

A really rich fish stock gives body and flavour to fish soups. The stock is made from the head, skin, bones, tail and fins of the fish, or from the well-washed shells of lobster, prawns or shrimps. The quantity of bay leaves used is a matter of personal taste. The number given here refers to fresh bay leaves; if using the dried variety, use only half the amount for they are very strong. When making stock for delicately flavoured bisques (see page 124), be sparing with the vegetables and herbs.

Metric/Imperial	Ingredients	American
900 ml/1½ pints	water	3¾ cups
	fish head, skin, etc.	
1 medium	onion	1 medium
1 medium	carrot	1 medium
1	celery stick, optional	1
2 fresh	bay leaves	2 fresh
to taste	chervil, parsley or herbs, depending on recipe	to taste
to taste	salt and freshly ground white pepper	to taste
to taste	little lemon zest	to taste

Put the water into a saucepan and add the fish parts: the more you use, the stronger the flavour of the finished stock. Peel the onion and carrot, chop the celery and add to the water with all the other ingredients. Bring the liquid to simmering point, cover the pan and cook steadily for 30 to 40 minutes. Strain and use or store as instructed on page 12.

Variation

Shellfish Stock: Follow the recipe above, but use the shells of lobster or other crustaceans. The shells produce a stock with an attractive pale pink colour. Strain and use or store as instructed on page 12.

Freezing: See pages 12 and 16.

Quick Tip

Allow 10 to 15 minutes in a pressure cooker. (For details on using a pressure cooker to make stock, see page 11).

Allow about 25 minutes in a microwave. (For details on using a microwave to make stock, see page 12).

FREEZING SOUPS

It is extremely useful to have containers of home-made soup in the freezer, ready to defrost and heat quickly. Information about freezing is included in all recipes where it is satisfactory. If a recipe states 'Do not freeze', it is for a very good reason. Either I have found that the flavour of that particular soup deteriorates badly in freezing, or the firm texture of some of the ingredients is lost, or there is an ingredient in the soup that should not be frozen.

Clear soups freeze especially well. The information about storing stocks (see page 12) applies to clear soups too.

Puréed soups, such as the vegetable soups on pages 60 to 115, freeze well, with a few exceptions. When defrosted, you may find that a soup has separated, i.e. there is a layer of clear liquid and a layer of very thick purée. Whisk vigorously as you heat the soup and the original consistency should return. If it is still a little thin, simmering in an uncovered pan for some minutes should restore the original consistency.

Creamy soups, such as those on pages 67 and 124, can be problematic. Clear instructions about freezing these are given wherever it can be done successfully. When reheating a frozen soup that contains cream, eggs, wine or lemon juice, take great care that it does not boil and curdle (separate): simmer gently and whisk continually during the reheating process. Flour-thickened soups have a tendency to separate slightly when frozen. There are two solutions:

• Use cornflour (cornstarch), arrowroot or potato flour (fécule) instead of ordinary wheat flour for thickening the soup. All these ingredients are less likely to cause separation during freezing and defrosting.

If you use cornflour or arrowroot instead of ordinary flour, allow exactly half the amount specified in the recipe as cornflour and arrowroot have twice the thickening ability of flour.

If you use potato flour instead of ordinary flour, allow the same amount specified in the recipe.

• Prepare and cook the soup to the stage where it should be thickened, allow it to cool, then pack and freeze it. Make a note on the label about the amount of thickening and any extra ingredients needed when the soup is reheated.

A good 'safety measure' when freezing puréed, creamy and flour-thickened soups is to sprinkle 1 teaspoon cornflour on top of the soup when it is packed for freezing. When it is reheated, this cornflour can be stirred into the other ingredients and it will cook and add a little thickening as the soup heats.

PACKING SOUPS FOR FREEZING

Use freezer boxes and make sure they are well filled: the less air space, the better the results in freezing. On the other hand though, all soups contain a large amount of liquid and this will expand during freezing. If the box is completely filled the expanded mixture could force the lid right off. Allow about 1.25 cm/¹/₂ inch of space above the level of the soup. Label the box clearly with the type of soup and the date it was made.

If you have no suitable freezer boxes, put large, strong freezer bags into sugar cartons or similar containers. Pour the soup into the bag, which is well supported by the rigid container. Leave until the soup is frozen, then remove the filled bag from the container. You will have a neat package which fits well into the freezer. Seal the bag (allowing 1.25 cm/¹/₂ inch air space) and label.

To save room in the freezer, halve the amount of liquid in the recipes so you have a very concentrated soup. Make a note on the label of the amount of liquid that should be added when reheating the soup.

STORAGE TIMES

Clear soups, such as consommé, should be used within 3 months; soups containing eggs and cream within 2 months; vegetable soups within 4 months; meat, fish and poultry soups within 3 months.

HERBS IN SOUPS

Herbs are one of the ingredients which help to flavour soups. Use fresh rather than dried herbs whenever possible, as their flavour is better and more subtle. If you do not grow herbs, you can buy them from good supermarkets. As only a small amount is used in a soup, you can chop and freeze the surplus for future use. Herbs keep for several days in the salad drawer of the refrigerator.

When substituting dried herbs for fresh ones, always reduce the quantity in the recipe by half, or even less, for dried herbs have a much stronger flavour. Although the recipes suggest the herbs that I feel are ideal for particular soups, you may like to experiment by using others, as listed below.

CHOOSING HERBS FOR SOUPS

If doubtful as to whether you would like the flavour of a particular herb, add a small sprig to the soup at the beginning of the cooking period. Taste the soup after a short while and remove the herb if you feel it has given enough flavour or you do not like the taste. If you do like the herb, you could chop a few leaves and add these to the other ingredients, or use them for garnish.

Arugola (see Rocket).

Balm has a lemony flavour and, while it is rarely used in savoury dishes, you could add a small sprig as an alternative to lemon and remove it before serving the soup.

Basil is a herb associated with tomato dishes, and is excellent in many soups containing tomatoes. Do be sparing with the amount you use, for it has a very strong and pungent taste. **Lemon basil** is particularly good in tomato soups.

Bay leaves are used a great deal in cooking. The large green shiny leaves should be removed before puréeing or serving the soup. Fresh leaves have a delicate taste, but dried ones are very strong.

Borage, although generally associated with drinks, has small blue flowers which can be floated on fruit soups as a colourful garnish (see page 165).

Bouquet garni is a small bunch of fresh or dried herbs which can be removed before making a purée or serving the soup. Tiny sachets of dried bouquet garni can also be added to the soup and removed in the same way as the fresh herbs.

Burnet is a cucumber-flavoured herb and could be used in suitable soups to enhance the cucumber taste.

Chervil tastes like parsley but has a more delicate flavour. It can be used instead of parsley, and its delicate leaves make an attractive garnish.

Chives are an invaluable herb, whether as part of a **bouquet garni**, as a delicate flavouring on their own, or as garnish. Ordinary chives have a mild onion taste, while **garlic chives** give the taste of mild garlic.

Coriander leaves and seeds, which are used a great deal in Oriental cooking, also appear in some recipes in this book. The leaves have a distinctly bitter taste.

Dill has a slight aniseed flavour. Chopped dill is an excellent addition to fish, both in the soup and as a garnish. Use sparingly.

Fennel bulb makes a wonderful soup (see page 30) and the chopped feathery leaves look most attractive as a garnish. The aniseed taste blends well with some fish soups.

Garlic is an invaluable addition to many dishes, and soups are no exception. Use sparingly in delicately-flavoured soups. One or two cloves (segments) from the complete head are generally sufficient. See the recipe for Garlic Soup on page 77.

Marjoram has a slightly sweet taste that blends well with tomato dishes, including soups. With oregano it makes an interesting alternative to basil.

Mint has a very distinctive taste, so use sparingly in soups. It is particularly good in certain chilled soups. There is a range of different mints you may like to try, including apple mint, eau de cologne mint and horse mint.

Oregano is the name given to wild marjoram; it has a slightly stronger flavour than marjoram, so should be used sparingly in soups.

Parsley is undoubtedly the most popular and widely used of all herbs. There are two types – the curly leaf and the flat leaf. The flat leaf parsley has the stronger taste. Do not use too much parsley in a soup. The stalks impart more flavour than the leaves, so tie a few stalks together, add these to the soup and remove them before puréeing or sieving.

Rocket is also known as arugola. The dark leaves are popular in salads, but a few can be floated on top of a soup as a garnish. They are particularly good with tomato and vegetable soups.

Rosemary has a strong aromatic taste. It can be used sparingly in meat and other soups. When dried, the flavour is very pronounced.

Sage leaves enhance some meat soups. When dried, the flavour is ultra strong, so use sparingly.

Savory, also called summer savory, is used too rarely. It is a good herb in bean soups. The flavour is not unlike that of thyme but rather more peppery.

Sorrel has a taste and appearance rather like spinach. There are recipes for sorrel soups on page 99.

Tarragon blends well with many ingredients, particularly chicken, fish and tomatoes. It has a refreshing, aromatic taste.

Thyme is a strongly aromatic herb, available in many varieties. **Lemon thyme** is one of the best, but all kinds of thyme impart an interesting flavour to a range of soups. Do not be too generous with the amount you add as it can become overpowering.

SPICES IN SOUPS

Spices should be used sparingly in soups because their flavour becomes very pronounced when added to a mixture containing a high percentage of liquid.

If you want to extract the utmost flavour from a spice, heat it in a pan with the fat stipulated in the recipe, or with the onions and/or garlic (if these are used). Even if the recipe does not list a spice, you may care to add a little, following the guidelines below. Note that spices deteriorate in flavour with long-term storage.

Allspice, as the name suggests, has the flavour of a mixture of spices. A little combines well with vegetable, fruit and some meat soups.

Anise has a distinctly aniseed flavour and is not suitable for soups. The only occasion when it might be used is to enhance a soup containing fennel, which already has an aniseed flavour (see page 30).

Caraway is obtainable in the form of seeds. A small amount is excellent added to a cabbage soup.

Cardamom is obtainable both in powder and seed form. It is often used to make curries, so any soup with a curry flavour could have a very small amount of this spice added.

Cinnamon is obtainable in the form of ground spice or sticks. It is suitable in fruit soups and is sometimes used in home-made curry powder.

Chilli is obtained from dried chilli peppers. Use very sparingly in soups in place of cayenne pepper.

Cloves are available as a ground spice or whole dried flower-buds. The only soup which would be improved by a very small amount is the Apple Soup on page 167.

Coriander is obtainable as a ground spice, as seeds or as a fresh herb, and is often used in curry powder. The slightly bitter taste is good in Oriental soups, but use very sparingly.

Cumin, in the forms of powder or seeds, is a valuable ingredient in curry powder.

Curry powder and **Curry paste** are both used in certain soups. There is a wide variety on the market, so choose brands that will be the most useful for soup-making, generally those with a fairly mild flavour, as soups should not have an overpowering taste. The paste is easier to blend with other soup ingredients than the powder, and tends to give a more mellow flavour. A recipe for Home-made Curry Powder is on page 21.

Garam masala is another blending of spices, used a great deal in Arab dishes, including the Harira on page 139.

Ginger can be used in soups in the fresh root form or as a ground spice. It gives a pleasant bite to some vegetable soups.

Juniper is sold as dried berries. Use a teaspoonful in game soups, see page 163.

Mace is the outer skin of nutmeg and is obtainable as blades (pieces of skin) or ground. It can be used instead of nutmeg.

Nutmeg is obtainable as a whole dried nut or as a ground spice.
A better flavour is achieved by grating the whole nut when required.
The combination of a sweet and slightly bitter taste is quite pleasant in some vegetable soups, such as Corn Soup (see page 29).

Paprika is a ground spice made from peppers. There are various kinds, but the most popular has a sweetish flavour. Its attractive, deep orange-red colour enhances many soups. If stale, paprika develops a very musty taste.

Saffron, available as strands or a ground powder, comes from a special variety of crocus and is the most expensive of all spices. It is used to give a golden colour, as well as a delicate flavour, to many dishes, including the Harira on page 139.

Turmeric is a spice used a great deal in pickles. It is not of great value in soups unless you want to enhance the golden colour. It has a sweet-savoury taste.

TO EXTRACT THE FLAVOUR FROM SEEDS

Many spices are obtainable in seed form, and these give a better flavour than ground spices. To obtain the very maximum of flavour from seeds, place them in a dry frying pan and heat gently over a low heat for about 2 minutes. The seeds will darken slightly and give off a definite smell. They are then ready to be used.

If you wish to grind the seeds after heating them, use a pestle and mortar or a spice mill. A coffee grinder could be used instead but this must be washed very thoroughly after use otherwise it will affect the flavour of the coffee.

HOME-MADE CURRY POWDER

The following recipe has a good mixture of flavours and produces a moderately hot curry taste.

Blend together:

1 teaspoon	*cardamom seeds,*
	removed from their pods
2 teaspoons	*cumin seeds*
2 teaspoons	*coriander seeds*
1 teaspoon	*mustard seeds*
1 teaspoon	*black peppercorns*

Put the mixture on a baking tray and place in a preheated oven set to 180°C/350°F/gas mark 4 for 9 minutes. Remove and leave until cold.

Add:

2	*dried hot chilli peppers*
½ teaspoon	*ground ginger*
3 teaspoons	*ground turmeric*
½ teaspoon	*ground cinnamon*
¼ teaspoon	*grated or ground nutmeg*

Place all the ingredients in a mortar, liquidizer or food processor and grind to a smooth powder. Store in a covered container and use as required.

Variation

- For a hotter flavour use more chilli peppers or a good pinch ground chilli powder and/or more ground ginger.

SEASONINGS IN SOUPS

Throughout this book you will find the words: to taste, salt and freshly ground black (or white) pepper. This means you add them gradually, tasting as you do so.

Never add too much seasoning at the beginning of the cooking period as the other ingredients will change the flavour as they cook. Vegetables, for example, contain appreciable amounts of mineral salts which contribute to the salt taste.

Freshly ground pepper has a far better taste than ready-ground pepper, which may have been stored for some considerable time and so developed a slightly musty taste. You need to buy black and/or white peppercorns and pepper mills.

Some recipes specify using **white pepper** which is less usual in cooking than **black pepper**, in order to preserve the colour of a soup. White pepper has a stronger flavour than black pepper, so use it sparingly.

Freshly ground **sea salt** or kitchen salt has a better taste than ready-prepared table salt.

In addition to ordinary salt, **celery salt** has a very pleasing flavour and can enhance the taste of many soups, especially those based on vegetables.

Mustard: English mustard can be obtained in powder form, or ready-mixed in tubes or pots. There are also various *herb-flavoured* and *wholegrain* English mustards, which have an exceptionally good flavour. If adding powdered mustard to soup towards the end of the cooking time, mix it with a little water first so that it blends more easily with the liquid.

There are also many French mustards, perhaps the most famous of which is Dijon. All can also be used to season soups.

2 QUICK SOUPS FOR BUSY PEOPLE

Often I have heard people say, 'I love home-made soups but I have no time to make them.' This implies that all soups take a long time to prepare and cook, but in most cases that is not true. On the following pages you will find a selection of appetizing soups which are exceptionally quick and easy to make. They use a range of readily available ingredients.

Although once it was considered right to simmer soup for a long time to give the best result, nowadays we find that in most instances a shorter cooking time is better for retaining the flavour of the ingredients, particularly vegetables.

You may be surprised to see that this chapter starts with a recipe for a basic White Sauce, but this is often an important part of a soup recipe. The sauce can be used as an alternative to cream, but it is also an excellent basis for a number of quick, creamy and nutritious soups.

In order to save time preparing fresh stock, the recipes in this section use water and stock (bouillon) cubes. There is a good range of these on the market, but some are rather salty, so be careful when adding extra seasoning.

A microwave is suitable for cooking many soups, particularly those made with young vegetables (see page 27) and fish. You do not save a great deal of time with this appliance when heating a fairly large amount of liquid, so I suggest you boil the required amount of water in a kettle then add this to the ingredients in the bowl in the microwave. There are brief hints on using the microwave for each group of soups in this chapter, and more information on page 12.

Use a microwave instead of a saucepan for making a White Sauce (see page 24). It is far easier to wash a bowl than a sticky pan.

Pressure cookers have gone rather out of fashion, but if you own one it is certainly useful for making soups, particularly when you are in a hurry (see pages 7, 11 and 27).

As you will find when you use the recipes that follow, home-made soups *can* be made in a very short time and you will be rewarded with excellent results.

WHITE SAUCE

Cooking time: 10 to 15 minutes • Serves 4 to 8, depending on the recipe

A white sauce is an important ingredient in quite a number of soup recipes. In most cases it should have a pouring consistency, as in the recipe below. The quantities given here will make 600 ml/1 pint (2½ cups) of sauce.

Metric/Imperial	Ingredients	American
25 g/1 oz	**butter or margarine**	2 tablespoons
25 g/1 oz	**plain (all-purpose) flour**	¼ cup
600 ml/1 pint	**milk**	2½ cups
to taste	**salt and freshly ground black pepper**	to taste

Heat the butter or margarine until just melted, then remove from the heat and stir in the flour. Return to a low heat and stir for 1 or 2 minutes. Gradually add the milk, stirring all the time, then allow the sauce to boil steadily for about 5 minutes. Reduce the heat and simmer for another 5 minutes. The longer cooking gives a better flavour. Season to taste.

Variations

- Omit 2 or 3 tablespoons (2½ to 3¼ tablespoons) milk and add this amount of single (light) cream to give a richer flavour.
- To add extra flavour to the sauce, add a chopped onion, one or two chopped celery sticks and a small bunch of herbs (parsley, thyme and a little rosemary) to the milk. Bring the milk to boiling point, allow it to stand for as long as possible so that it absorbs the various flavours, then strain and use in the sauce.

Freezing: The sauce is better freshly made, but it freezes well as part of a soup.

Quick Tip

Blending method: put all the ingredients into a saucepan and whisk briskly as the sauce comes to the boil and thickens.

Put all the ingredients into a suitable microwave bowl. Stir or whisk briskly, immediately before starting to cook on full power for approximately 2½ to 3 minutes. Stir or whisk every 30 seconds to ensure a smooth sauce.

VEGETABLE SOUPS
BASED ON WHITE SAUCE

Cooking time: about 20 minutes • Serves 4

One of the easiest and quickest ways to produce a home-made soup is to make a White Sauce (see page 24), then add your chosen ingredients to it and heat for a short time.

Artichoke (Globe) Soup: Finely chop, sieve or liquidize 4 to 5 well-drained cooked or canned globe artichoke hearts. Add to the hot White Sauce together with 3 or 4 tablespoons (3³/₄ or 5 tablespoons) artichoke liquid. Heat thoroughly. Remove from the heat and stir in 1 tablespoon (1¹/₄ tablespoons) lemon juice, 150 ml/1¹/₄ pint (²/₃ cup) single (light) cream, 2 tablespoons (2¹/₂ tablespoons) chopped chives, and 1 tablespoon (1¹/₄ tablespoons) finely chopped parsley.

Artichoke (Jerusalem) Soup: Make 300 ml/¹/₂ pint (1¹/₄ cups) purée by sieving cooked Jerusalem artichokes. Add to the White Sauce, together with 150 ml/¹/₄ pint (²/₃ cup) liquid from cooking the artichokes, 4 tablespoons (5 tablespoons) finely chopped spring onions (scallions) or thinly sliced leeks. Heat thoroughly, then flavour with a little seasoning, including celery salt. Top the soup with cream or yoghurt and finely chopped red pepper or paprika.

Asparagus Soup: Open a 300 g/10 oz can asparagus spears. Drain but reserve the liquid from the can. Cut off about 8 tips for garnish, then liquidize the spears and reserved liquid. Heat the White Sauce and add the asparagus purée with seasoning to taste. Serve topped with a little soured cream or yoghurt and the asparagus tips. Garnish with heart-shaped croûtons (see page 193).

Beetroot Cream Soup: Peel and coarsely grate about 225 g/8 oz (¹/₂ lb) cooked beetroot (weight when peeled and grated). (Use tiny summer beets if possible.) Make the White Sauce, add the beetroot and stir gently over the heat. Pour in 150 ml/¹/₄ pint (²/₃ cup) single (light) cream and 1¹/₂ tablespoons (2 tablespoons) lemon juice. Heat gently without boiling. Serve topped with a thick layer of finely chopped parsley and chives.
  Low-fat yoghurt could be used instead of cream.

Broccoli Cream Soup: Use about 225 g/8 oz (¹/₂ lb) cooked broccoli (weight when cooked). Strain but save 150 ml/¹/₄ pint (²/₃ cup) of the cooking liquid. Cut off a few very small florets for garnish and sieve or liquidize the remainder to make a purée. Add the broccoli stock to the White Sauce, heat thoroughly, then stir in the vegetable purée with 25 g/1 oz (2 tablespoons) butter and a good pinch of grated or ground nutmeg. Heat thoroughly. Top the soup with finely chopped skinned tomatoes and the broccoli florets.
  Cooked cauliflower can be used instead of broccoli.

Carrot Cream Soup: Heat the White Sauce and add 300 ml/¹/₂ pint (1¹/₄ cups) single (light) cream or extra milk. Peel and grate 225 g/8 oz (¹/₂ lb) carrots (weight when peeled and grated). Add to the hot mixture together with 2 tablespoons (2¹/₂ tablespoons) finely chopped spring onions (scallions), 1 teaspoon chopped savory or ¹/₂ teaspoon dried savory and seasoning to taste. (Use marjoram or oregano if savory is not available.) Heat well but do not overcook the soup, for in this recipe the grated carrots should remain firm. Garnish with chopped chives.

Instead of all carrots, use 225 g/8 oz (½ lb) mixed root vegetables such as grated carrots, swede (rutabaga), turnip and parsnip and/or celeriac.

Speedy Chestnut Soup: Heat the White Sauce, add 300 ml/½ pint (1¼ cups) vegetable, ham or chicken stock (see page 14) and 350 g/ 12 oz (¾ lb) canned unsweetened chestnut purée. Stir until very hot and smooth then add a good pinch paprika and/or curry powder. Top with soured cream or yoghurt, or finely chopped crisp bacon.

Speedy Leek Soup: Thinly slice and cook about 350 g/12 oz (¾ lb) leeks in just 150 ml/¼ pint (⅔ cup) of water with seasoning to taste. Make the White Sauce while the leeks are cooking. Blend with the leeks and liquid in the pan, and adjust the seasoning. Top with paprika and chopped parsley or finely chopped crisp bacon.

Spinach Cream Soup: Make the White Sauce. Use approximately 225 g/ 8 oz (½ lb) frozen chopped spinach. Add the block of frozen spinach to the sauce, heating gently and stirring frequently as the spinach defrosts and blends with the sauce. When thoroughly heated, add 300 ml/½ pint (1¼ cups) single (light) cream or extra milk, a little grated or ground nutmeg and a shake of cayenne pepper. Heat and serve the soup topped with blanched flaked almonds.

Use approximately 350 g/12 oz (¾ lb) fresh or frozen leaf spinach, cook and sieve or liquidize to make a purée. Add to the White Sauce, then continue as above.

A purée of cooked young nettle leaves can be used instead of spinach (see page 98).

Freezing: Do not freeze any of these soups: they are better freshly made.

FISH, MEAT AND POULTRY
SOUPS BASED ON WHITE SAUCE

Cooking time: about 20 minutes • Serves 4

Seafood Soup: Make the White Sauce, add 300 ml/½ pint (1¼ cups) Fish Stock (see page 15) or water plus a few drops of anchovy essence and heat thoroughly. Stir 100 g/4 oz (¼ lb) frozen shelled prawns (shrimp) into the hot sauce. Allow to stand for a short time, without cooking, so that they defrost. Add the same weight of flaked, cooked or canned salmon and of chopped smoked salmon or flaked crabmeat. Heat for a few minutes only. Top with chopped fennel leaves.

Use all prawns or all salmon instead of the mixture of fish.

Heat 2 or 3 tablespoons (2½ to 3¾ tablespoons) finely chopped fennel root with the sauce before adding the fish.

Creamy Ham and Mustard Soup: Make the White Sauce. Mix 300 ml/½ pint (⅔ cup) single (light) cream with 2 tablespoons French or ready-made English mustard and add to the sauce and heat. Finely dice or mince 225 g/8 oz (½ lb) cooked ham and add to the sauce with 1 tablespoon (1¼ tablespoons) finely chopped parsley. Heat for a few minutes only and season to taste.

Speedy Chicken Soup: Make the White Sauce and add 150 ml/¼ pint (⅔ cup) chicken stock (see page 14). Finely dice or mince 350 g/12 oz (¾ lb) cooked chicken and add to the other ingredients with 1 teaspoon finely grated lemon zest, 1 teaspoon French or ready-made English mustard and 3 tablespoons (3¾ tablespoons) double (heavy) cream. Heat gently and serve topped with blanched flaked almonds.

Freezing: Do not freeze any of these soups: they are better freshly made.

QUICK VEGETABLE SOUPS

Choose young vegetables whenever possible because they cook in a shorter time than older ones. Frozen vegetables, which have been partly cooked by blanching before freezing, make excellent alternatives to fresh vegetables, especially when time is limited or a particular fresh vegetable is not obtainable.

Microwave cooking is excellent for vegetable soups if the vegetables are young, but less efficient for cooking older vegetables, as they do not become really tender.

You will need to check cooking progress carefully the first time you use the microwave for a particular vegetable soup, but on the whole allow about 25 per cent less cooking time than on a conventional hob. Make sure all the vegetables are cut into small, even-sized pieces and reduce the amount of liquid in the recipe by 150 ml/¼ pint (⅔ cup).

There is more information about using microwaves on page 7.

Pressure cooking provides a good way of cooking vegetables for soup, even when the vegetables are older. Allow half the cooking time given in the recipe when the cooker reaches pressure, and reduce the amount of liquid in the recipe by 25 per cent.

Further information about pressure cookers appears on pages 7 and 11.

CLEAR MUSHROOM SOUP

Cooking time: 20 minutes • Serves 4 to 6

This quickly made soup is ideal for slimmers since it contains no fat.
It has an excellent flavour, but can be made to look more enticing by
topping each portion with a spoonful of lightly whipped cream.
Large open mushrooms or chestnut mushrooms are ideal for this soup.

Metric/Imperial	Ingredients	American
550 g/1¼ lb	mushrooms	1¼ lb
1 small bunch	spring onions (scallions)	1 small bunch
2 tablespoons	finely chopped parsley	2½ tablespoons
1 litre/1¾ pints	water	scant 4½ cups
1	beef, chicken or vegetable stock cube	1
to taste	salt and freshly ground black pepper	to taste

Wipe the mushrooms, cut and discard the ends of the stalks. Chop the
mushrooms roughly. Prepare the spring onions, using only the white
part. Put the mushrooms, onions and parsley into a pan with the water
and stock cube. Bring to the boil and simmer for 15 minutes. Sieve or
liquidize and reheat.

Variation

• I often add a little yeast extract, rather than a stock cube, as this gives
an excellent flavour to the liquid. Take care when adding other
seasonings as yeast extract tends to be very salty.

Freezing: This soup freezes very well.

CORN SOUP

Cooking time: 25 minutes • Serves 4 to 6

This is a soup I first tasted in South Africa, where it is generally called Mealie Soup. It is delicious and ready in minutes. Use fresh corn, if in season, as the flavour is much better than canned or frozen corn.

Metric/Imperial	Ingredients	American
2 medium	onions	2 medium
50 g/2 oz	butter	1/4 cup
25 g/1 oz	plain (all-purpose) flour	1/4 cup
good pinch	grated or ground nutmeg	good pinch
750 ml/1¼ pints	milk	good 3 cups
350 g/12 oz	canned sweetcorn	3/4 lb
to taste	salt and freshly ground black pepper	to taste
	To garnish	
	chopped parsley and/or chives	
	croûtons (see page 193)	

Peel and finely chop the onions. Heat the butter and fry the onions gently for 10 minutes. Do not allow to colour, so stir well during this time. Add the flour and nutmeg, stir to blend with the onions. Pour in the milk. Stir or whisk as the liquid comes to the boil and thickens slightly.

Drain the canned sweetcorn, add to the pan and heat thoroughly. Season to taste, then garnish and serve.

Variations

- Cook 2 large corn cobs in boiling water, adding a little salt towards the end of the cooking period. If salt is added to the corn too early, it toughens the grains. Strip the corn from the cob and add as above. Use 150 ml/¼ pint (⅔ cup) of the liquid in which the corn has cooked instead of that amount of milk.

- Place 350 g/12 oz (¾ lb) frozen sweetcorn in the soup after adding the milk and cook steadily until tender. You may find you need to add a little extra milk towards the end of the cooking period.

Do not freeze.

FENNEL AND TOMATO SOUP

Cooking time: 25 minutes • Serves 4 to 6

The combination of fennel and tomatoes is a very pleasant one. Make sure the white fennel bulbs are firm and that any leaves are bright green. The soup can be served chunky or smooth.

Metric/Imperial	Ingredients	American
2 large	**fennel bulbs**	2 large
4 medium	**tomatoes**	4 medium
50 g/2 oz	**butter**	¼ cup
900 ml/1½ pints	**water**	3¾ cups
to taste	**salt and freshly ground black pepper**	to taste
to taste	**pinch aniseed, optional**	to taste
	To garnish	
	yoghurt	
	fennel leaves	

Remove the fennel leaves, chop them for the garnish and set aside. Wash, dry and finely chop the fennel bulbs. Skin and halve the tomatoes, then remove the seeds. Chop the flesh finely. Heat the butter and cook the fennel and tomatoes for 10 minutes or until softened. Stir well so that the mixture does not brown. Add the water, bring to the boil and cook for 10 minutes. Season to taste. A little aniseed can be added if you want to enhance the fennel flavour.

Serve the soup topped with yoghurt and fennel leaves. If you prefer a smooth soup, sieve or liquidize the ingredients and reheat.

Variations

- A chopped medium onion and/or 2 crushed garlic cloves can be cooked in the butter with the fennel and tomatoes.

Fennel and Shrimp Soup: Follow the recipe above and add about 175 g/ 6 oz (1 cup) peeled shrimps or chopped prawns just before serving. Heat for a few minutes only, as overheating toughens the shellfish.

Freezing: This soup freezes well.

LEMON AND SPINACH SOUP

Cooking time: 20 to 25 minutes • Serves 4 to 6

Metric/Imperial	Ingredients	American
1 medium	onion	1 medium
1 or 2	garlic cloves	1 or 2
25 g/1 oz	butter	2 tablespoons
900 ml/1½ pints	water	3¾ cups
1	vegetable or chicken stock cube	1
350 g/12 oz	frozen chopped spinach	¾ lb
1 teaspoon	finely grated lemon zest	1 teaspoon
2 tablespoons	lemon juice, or to taste	2½ tablespoons
to taste	salt and freshly ground black pepper	to taste
300 ml/½ pint	milk or single (light) cream	1¼ cups
To garnish		
	blanched, flaked (slivered) almonds or lemon slices	

Peel and finely chop the onion and garlic. Heat the butter and cook the onion and garlic for 5 minutes. Add the water and stock cube. Bring to the boil. If you have a microwave, you can defrost the spinach while preparing the onion and garlic and heating the water. If you do not have a microwave, simply add the spinach to the boiling liquid and stir from time to time to break up the block as the soup cooks.

Add the lemon zest, juice and seasoning. When the ingredients are tender, add the milk or cream and heat without boiling. If preferred, the soup can be sieved or liquidized, then reheated with the milk or cream.

If the soup is too thin for your taste, thicken it by adding a little beurre manié (see page 9).

Variations

- Use about 700 g/1½ lb fresh, young leaf spinach, well washed.
  Cook in the water and stock cube, or use fish stock (see page 15).
  Sieve or liquidize, then reheat with the milk or cream.

Freezing: Freeze without adding the milk or cream; these ingredients can be added when reheating.

10-MINUTE TOMATO SOUP

Cooking time: 10 minutes • Serves 4 to 6

Cans of chopped tomatoes are an invaluable ingredient in the store cupboard because tomatoes add flavour to many dishes. As they are already chopped, they cook in a very short time. You can, of course, prepare and freeze chopped tomatoes or tomato purée. If doing this for use in cooked, rather than uncooked dishes, it is advisable to choose plum tomatoes, as they have a better flavour than ordinary tomatoes.

Metric/Imperial	Ingredients	American
450 g/16 oz	**canned tomatoes**	1 lb
900 ml/1½ pints	**water**	3¾ cups
4 tablespoons	**chopped spring onions (scallions)**	5 tablespoons
1 small	**dessert apple**	1 small
to taste	**salt and freshly ground black pepper**	to taste
½ teaspoon	**paprika**	⅓ teaspoon
1 teaspoon	**brown sugar**	1 teaspoon
	To garnish	
	chopped parsley and/or chives	

Put the tomatoes and their liquid into a saucepan with the water and onions. Bring to the boil. Meanwhile, peel and grate the apple, then add to the pan with a little seasoning, the paprika and sugar. Simmer for 10 minutes and serve, or purée the soup, return to the pan and reheat. Garnish and serve.

SPEEDY VEGETABLE SOUP

Cooking time: 25 minutes • Serves 4

Grating the suitable vegetables before use, either by hand or with the attachment on an electric mixer or food processor, shortens the cooking time a great deal.

Softer ingredients, such as onions and tomatoes, are better chopped. Partially cook the onions in a little fat before adding the liquid as this gives them a better flavour.

Metric/Imperial	Ingredients	American
2 medium	onions	2 medium
350 g/12 oz	mixed vegetables, see Note, weight when prepared	³/₄ lb
25 g/1 oz	butter or margarine	2 tablespoons
900 ml/1½ pints	water	3³/₄ cups
2 medium	tomatoes, optional	2 medium
2 tablespoons	chopped parsley	2½ tablespoons
1 teaspoon	chopped thyme or tarragon or ½ teaspoon dried thyme or tarragon	1 teaspoon
to taste	salt and freshly ground black pepper	to taste
	To garnish	
	cream or yoghurt	

Note: Choose vegetables that will give a range of colour and textures, e.g.

Spring: broad (fava) beans, carrots, fennel, early potatoes.

Summer: fresh green beans and peas, young carrots and turnip.

Autumn: broccoli, celery, leeks, sweetcorn (fresh, frozen or canned).

Winter: carrots, celeriac, leeks, turnip, parsnip.

Peel and finely chop the onions. Prepare your other vegetables as necessary. Heat the butter or margarine in a saucepan, add the onions and cook gently for 5 minutes. Pour the water into the pan, bring to the boil and add the vegetables. Boil steadily for 10 minutes. If too thick, add a little extra water. Skin and finely chop the tomatoes, then add to the pan with the herbs and seasoning to taste. Continue cooking for a further 5 minutes, then garnish and serve.

Variations

- Add a vegetable stock cube to the water for extra flavour.

- If fresh tomatoes are not available, add 1 to 2 tablespoons (1¼ to 2½ tablespoons) tomato purée (paste) or use about 300 ml/½ pint (1¼ cups) tomato juice instead of the same amount of water.

Speedy Cream of Vegetable Soup: Follow the recipe on the previous page, but use only 600 ml/1 pint (2½ cups) water.

When the vegetables are tender, blend 1 level tablespoon (1¼ level tablespoons) cornflour (cornstarch) with 150 ml/½ pint (⅔ cup) milk and 150 ml/¼ pint (⅔ cup) single (light) cream. Stir into the vegetable mixture and cook steadily, stirring all the time, until thickened.

Alternatively, purée the vegetables first, then return them to the pan and add the cornflour mixture. In this case, use only 2 level teaspoons cornflour. Cook steadily, stirring all the time, until thickened. Steady, rather than quick cooking is particularly important if tomatoes or tomato juice are in the soup.

Freezing: The basic soup freezes well. If making the Speedy Cream of Vegetable Soup it is better to freeze the cooked vegetables and add the cornflour mixture when the soup has been defrosted and reheated.

QUICK FISH, MEAT AND POULTRY SOUPS

The soups on the following pages can all be cooked quickly, particularly if you use time-saving devices.

Microwave cooking fish works well, and fish soups are no exception. The flavour is excellent, provided the fish is not overcooked. Overcooking in the microwave makes fish dry and hard. When the fish is added to the other ingredients, allow just over half the cooking time that it would need in a saucepan. If the fish does not appear to be quite cooked, allow the soup to stand for 2 or 3 minutes after cooking and check again. You will probably find that during the standing time the cooking has been completed and the fish is perfectly tender. If it is not quite ready, replace the bowl in the microwave and cook for a further 1 or 2 minutes.

The recipes based on canned consommé take about two-thirds of the cooking time needed in a saucepan.

The chicken soups on pages 151 to 159 also take about two-thirds of the ordinary cooking time provided you boil the water before adding it to the other ingredients.

General information about cooking soups in a microwave appears on page 7.

Pressure cooking can be used for fish and chicken soups. They take just under half the ordinary cooking time given in the recipe and require 25 per cent less liquid.

The recipes based on consommé are so quickly cooked in a saucepan that cooking under pressure after the preliminary stages would not save much time.

General information about making soups in a pressure cooker appears on page 7.

ARBROATH SMOKIE BROTH

Cooking time: 25 minutes • Serves 4

Arbroath Smokies are small, delicately flavoured smoked haddock.
As the smoking process cooks them, subsequent heating can be kept to a
minimum. For the best results, use home-made chicken stock (see page 14)
rather than a stock cube. A famous Scottish haddock soup, Cullen Skink,
is on page 118.

Metric/Imperial	Ingredients	American
1 small	**onion**	1 small
1 small	**leek**	1 small
1 medium	**potato**	1 medium
50 g/2 oz	**butter**	1/4 cup
900 ml/1½ pints	**water**	3¾ cups
1	**chicken stock cube**	1
350 to 450 g/12 oz to 1 lb	**Arbroath Smokies**	¾ to 1 lb
to taste	**salt and freshly ground black pepper**	to taste
to taste	**cayenne pepper, optional**	to taste
	To garnish	
	chopped parsley and/or chopped dill	

Peel, then finely and neatly chop the onion, leek and potato. Heat the
butter and cook the vegetables for 10 minutes. Add the water and stock
cube, bring to the boil and simmer for 10 minutes.
    Meanwhile, skin the smokies and divide the fish into neat, bite-sized
pieces. Add to the liquid, simmer for 4 to 5 minutes, then season to taste
(be sparing with the salt). Garnish and serve.

Variations

Smoked Kipper Broth: Cook kippers in a little boiling water, then drain
and use the flaked flesh instead of smokies in the soup above. A few
tablespoons of the liquid in which the kippers were cooked could be used
with the water. In this case, you may have sufficient flavour to omit the
stock cube, or to use only half of it.

Smoked Trout Broth: Use smoked trout instead of smokies. You will
need 2 good-sized trout as there is considerable wastage from the heads,
skins and bones. These could be simmered to make a fish stock, which
could be substituted for the water and chicken stock cube or chicken
stock. This trout soup could be garnished with lightly whipped cream
flavoured with a little horseradish cream.

Do not freeze.

CRAB SOUP

Cooking time: 25 minutes • Serves 4 to 6

The combination of leeks, tomato and crab makes this a particularly interesting soup. If possible, use all white crabmeat, but it can be frozen, canned or fresh. There is a famous crab soup, Partan Bree, on page 122.

Metric/Imperial	Ingredients	American
350 g/12 oz	small leeks, weight when prepared	¾ lb
25 g/1 oz	butter	2 tablespoons
25 g/1 oz	plain (all-purpose) flour	¼ cup
600 ml/1 pint	tomato juice	2½ cups
450 ml/¾ pint	water	scant 2 cups
2 teaspoons	lemon juice, or to taste	2 teaspoons
225 to 350 g/8 to 12 oz	crabmeat	½ to ¾ lb
to taste	salt and freshly ground black pepper	to taste
	To garnish	
	little whipped cream or cream cheese	
	lemon wedges	

Wash the leeks, discard the tough green parts of the stalks, but use a little of the tender green. Slice thinly. Heat the butter in the saucepan, add the leeks and cook for 5 minutes. Stir in the flour, then add the tomato juice, water and lemon juice. Stir as the mixture comes to the boil and thickens slightly. Cover the pan and simmer steadily for 10 minutes. Add the crabmeat and stir into the hot liquid. Heat for a few moments only, then season to taste. Spoon into warmed soup bowls, then garnish and serve.

Variations

- Sieve or liquidize the cooked leeks, then return to the pan, stir in the crabmeat and heat for a few minutes.
- Add half a fish stock cube to emphasize the fish flavour.
- For a more savoury taste, add 1 crushed garlic clove to the leeks.
- If using fresh crabmeat, make stock from the shells and small claws, as described on page 15, and use this instead of water.
- If you have no tomato juice, use about 225 g/8 oz (½ lb) skinned, deseeded and chopped tomatoes, or a small can of chopped tomatoes plus an extra 300 ml/½ pint (1¼ cups) of water or 2 tablespoons (2½ tablespoons) tomato purée (paste) diluted with 600 ml/1 pint (2½ cups) additional water.

Mussel Soup: Use about 225 g/8 oz (½ lb) cooked mussels (weight without shells), prepared as described on page 127, instead of the crabmeat. Take the mussels out of their shells when cooked. (You will need at least 550 g/1¼ lb mussels in their shells to give the required weight.)

Prawn or Shrimp Soup: Use peeled and chopped prawns or shrimps instead of crabmeat.

Do not freeze.

Quick Tip

If using frozen crabmeat, allow it to defrost before using to save time in heating.

SALMON AND GINGER SOUP

Cooking time: 20 minutes • Serves 4 to 6

This is a delicious creamy soup with the delicate flavour of ginger. Adjust the amount of root ginger used to personal taste. Do not pre-cook the salmon: the small dice of fish cook well in the liquid and retain all their flavour.

Metric/Imperial	Ingredients	American
450 g/1 lb	salmon fillet	1 lb
2 cm/³/₄ inch	root ginger	³/₄ inch
900 ml/1¹/₂ pints	milk	3³/₄ cups
100 g/4 oz	frozen peas	³/₄ cup
to taste	salt and freshly ground black pepper	to taste
1 tablespoon	cornflour (cornstarch)	1¹/₄ tablespoons
300 ml/¹/₂ pint	single (light) cream	1¹/₄ cups
1 oz/25 g	butter	2 tablespoons
	To garnish	
	lemon wedges	

Skin the salmon fillet and cut the flesh into 1.25 to 2 cm/¹/₂ to ³/₄ inch dice. Peel and grate the ginger. Bring nearly all the milk to the boil with the ginger, add the salmon and frozen peas (there is no need to defrost them) together with a little seasoning. Simmer for 10 minutes. Blend the cornflour with the rest of the milk, tip into the soup and stir briskly as it thickens. Lastly, add the cream and butter and heat. Taste the soup and adjust the seasoning. Garnish and serve.

Do not freeze.

SEAFOOD BISQUE

Cooking time: 20 minutes • Serves 4 to 6

A traditional bisque recipe appears on page 124 and describes how to make a fish stock from the shells of lobsters, crabs or prawns, or the bones of fish. In the speedy recipe below, water, milk and cream are used, plus a few drops of anchovy essence, to give more flavour to the trio of fish used. The bread thickens the soup.

Metric/Imperial	Ingredients	American
3 level tablespoons	**soft white breadcrumbs**	3¾ level tablespoons
300 ml/½ pint	**water**	1¼ cups
1	**lemon**	1
600 ml/1 pint	**milk**	2½ cups
few drops	**anchovy essence**	few drops
175 g/6 oz	**peeled prawns or shrimps**	1 cup
175 g/6 oz	**fresh, frozen or canned white crabmeat**	1 cup
100 g/4 oz	**canned salmon, weight without bones or skin**	¾ cup
300 ml/½ pint	**single (light) cream**	1¼ cups
to taste	**salt and freshly ground black pepper**	to taste

Put the breadcrumbs into a saucepan with the water. Heat for a few minutes until the water reaches boiling point, then remove from the heat and allow to stand for 5 minutes. Pare the zest from half the lemon and squeeze out the juice. Put the zest into the pan with the breadcrumbs. Cut the other half of the lemon into wafer-thin slices and set aside for garnish.

Pour the milk over the breadcrumbs and liquid in the pan, heat gently. Add the anchovy essence, the fish, cream, lemon juice and seasoning, heat steadily for 5 to 10 minutes. Stir once or twice to break up the salmon. Serve topped with the lemon slices.

Variations

• Use just one kind of fish; in this case, you need at least 350 g/12 oz (2 cups).

Seafood and Fennel Bisque: Simmer 3 tablespoons (4 tablespoons) finely chopped fennel root for a few minutes in the water before adding the breadcrumbs. Omit the lemon zest and juice in the recipe above but add 2 teaspoons chopped fennel leaves. Garnish with lemon slices and sprigs of fennel leaves.

Do not freeze.

Quick Tip

This is an ideal soup to cook in a microwave. Follow the recipe above, but cook the fish only until it is heated; do not overcook.

SOUPS BASED ON CONSOMMÉ

The following soups are all based on consommé, either canned or home-made (see pages 49 to 55). If you have no consommé, dissolve a stock (bouillon) cube in water; this will make a less rich soup than consommé.

SPEEDY MULLIGATAWNY SOUP

Cooking time: 20 to 25 minutes • Serves 4

This soup has a refreshing and well-spiced flavour. It is equally good made with a chicken, or meat-flavoured stock cube, and excellent with canned consommé.

Metric/Imperial	Ingredients	American
1 tablespoon	sunflower oil	1¼ tablespoons
4 tablespoons	chopped spring onions (scallions)	5 tablespoons
3 teaspoons	curry paste or powder	3 teaspoons
3 tablespoons	grated cooking apple	4 tablespoons
1.2 litres/2 pints	water	5 cups
1	chicken, beef or lamb stock cube, or to personal taste	1
2 tablespoons	seedless raisins	2½ tablespoons
2 tablespoons	long-grain rice	2½ tablespoons
to taste	salt and freshly ground black pepper	to taste

Heat the oil, add the onions and curry paste or powder and cook for 2 minutes. Stir the apple into the curry mixture, then add the water. Bring to the boil, add the stock cube with the remaining ingredients and cook until the rice is tender.

Variation

• Use canned consommé instead of the water and stock cube, or use half consommé and half water.

Freezing: While this soup can be frozen, it is so quickly prepared that it hardly seems worthwhile.

CHICKEN BROTH

Cooking time: 25 minutes • Serves 4 to 6

This is a very satisfying soup which could be served as a light main dish. Make sure the chicken flesh is very finely chopped, minced or processed in order to cook the soup quickly. If speed is not too important, cut the chicken into small, neat dice. As the soup is not sieved or liquidized, chop all the vegetables finely and neatly.

Metric/Imperial	Ingredients	American
225 to 350 g/8 to 12 oz	**chicken breast**	1/2 to 3/4 lb
2 medium	**onions**	2 medium
2 medium	**tomatoes**	2 medium
100 g/4 oz	**button mushrooms**	1/4 lb
2 tablespoons	**sunflower oil**	2 1/2 tablespoons
1 litre/1 3/4 pints	**water**	scant 4 1/2 cups
1	**chicken stock cube**	1
1 tablespoon	**chopped parsley**	1 1/4 tablespoons
to taste	**salt and freshly ground black pepper**	to taste

Mince or finely chop the chicken. Peel and finely chop the onions and tomatoes (these can be deseeded if desired). Wipe and thinly slice the mushrooms. Heat the oil in a pan, add the chicken and vegetables and cook gently for 10 minutes, stirring all the time.

Boil the water in a kettle, then add to the pan with the stock cube. Bring to simmering point, add the parsley and a little seasoning. Cover the pan and cook for another 10 minutes. Check the chicken is cooked. Taste the soup, add additional seasoning if required and serve.

Variation

• Add 1 tablespoon (1 1/4 tablespoons) long-grain rice. Blend this with the vegetables and chicken after these have been cooked in the oil and before adding the water. If using rice the cooking time must be a little longer than given in the recipe above.

Do not freeze.

ORIENTAL CHICKEN SOUP

Cooking time: 25 minutes • Serves 4 to 6

The combination of chicken with water chestnuts, bamboo shoots and soy sauce makes this soup both interesting and satisfying. In order to cook the chicken within the time given, the breast should be finely chopped or minced. If you have a little more time, choose chicken legs rather than breasts as they have more flavour, but allow an extra 10 minutes' cooking time.

Metric/Imperial	Ingredients	American
225 to 350 g/8 to 12 oz	**chicken breast**	½ to ¾ lb
1 small	**carrot**	1 small
1 small	**leek**	1 small
1 small bunch	**spring onions (scallions)**	1 small bunch
1½ tablespoons	**sunflower oil**	scant 2 tablespoons
2 teaspoons	**grated root ginger**	2 teaspoons
1 litre/1¾ pints	**water**	scant 4½ cups
1	**chicken stock cube**	1
6 to 8	**canned water chestnuts**	6 to 8
¼ to ½	**canned bamboo shoot**	¼ to ½
1 tablespoon	**soy sauce**	1¼ tablespoons

Mince or finely chop the chicken. Peel and grate or finely dice the carrot. Wash and thinly slice the white part of the leek. If the spring onions (scallions) are small, cut them in half; if larger, cut into slices.

Heat the oil in a saucepan, then add the chicken and prepared ingredients together with the root ginger. Stir over a low heat for 10 minutes. Meanwhile, boil the water, add to the pan with the stock cube and simmer for 5 minutes.

Drain the water chestnuts and bamboo shoots and cut into fine strips. Add to the soup with the soy sauce and heat for 5 to 8 minutes. No extra seasoning should be needed in this soup, but taste just before serving and add a little salt and pepper if required.

Variations

- When time permits, use home-made Chicken or Oriental Stock (see pages 14 and 15) instead of water and a stock cube.
- Add a few tablespoons of finely chopped fresh or canned beansprouts.

Oriental Duck Soup: Use finely diced duck, free from skin and fat, instead of chicken. The cooking time for the soup will then be about 35 minutes. Use a chicken stock cube with the water, or better still, use home-made Chicken or Duck Stock (see page 14).

Freezing: The soup should not be frozen, but you can transfer the remaining water chestnuts and bamboo shoot(s) with their liquid to suitable containers and freeze for future use.

CHICKEN AND BACON CHOWDER

Cooking time: 25 minutes • Serves 4 to 6

Although it is ideal to use uncooked chicken in a soup, this particular dish has such a lot of flavour from bacon, vegetables and herbs that cooked chicken can be used. In fact, this soup is a good way of using the small pieces of chicken left on a carcass. You will find the timing for making the soup with uncooked chicken under Variation.

Metric/Imperial	Ingredients	American
4 rashers	bacon	4 slices
2 medium	potatoes	2 medium
2 medium	onions	2 medium
100 g/4 oz	button mushrooms	1/4 lb
2	celery sticks	2
25 g/1 oz	butter	2 tablespoons
1 litre/1³/4 pints	water	scant 4¹/2 cups
1	chicken stock cube	1
2 tablespoons	chopped parsley	2¹/2 tablespoons
1 tablespoon	chopped chives	1¹/4 tablespoons
1 teaspoon	chopped thyme	1 teaspoon
to taste	salt and freshly ground black pepper	to taste
1 to 2 teaspoons	ready-made English mustard	1 to 2 teaspoons
350 g/12 oz	cooked chicken	³/4 lb
	To garnish	
	grated or cream cheese	

Derind the bacon and cut the rashers into small pieces. Peel the potatoes and onions, cut the potatoes into 1.25 cm/¹/2 inch dice and finely chop the onions. Wipe and slice the mushrooms. Finely slice the celery.

Heat the bacon rinds with the butter, add the chopped bacon and vegetables and cook steadily over the heat, stirring from time to time, for 10 minutes.

Bring the water to the boil and pour over the ingredients in the pan. Add the stock cube, herbs, a little seasoning and the mustard. Simmer for 5 minutes.

Dice the chicken neatly, add to the soup and heat for 5 minutes. Remove the bacon rinds and serve the chowder topped with the cheese.

Variation

- If using uncooked chicken, cut it into 1.25 cm/¹/2 inch dice. Allow 50 g/2 oz (¹/4 cup) of butter and cook the chicken with the bacon for 5 minutes. Add the vegetables and cook for a further 10 minutes. Add the water and stock cube, or better still, real Chicken Stock (see page 14), plus the remaining ingredients and cook for a further 15 minutes.

Do not freeze.

QUICK FRUIT AND CHEESE SOUPS

AVOCADO SOUP 1

Cooking time: 5 or 10 minutes • Serves 4 to 6

This soup is based upon the well-known spiced dip guacamole, and can be served hot or cold. When serving it cold, I prefer to use ripe, ordinary tomatoes; if serving it hot, I would choose plum tomatoes.

Metric/Imperial	Ingredients	American
900 ml/1½ pints	water	3¾ cups
1	vegetable or chicken stock cube	1
2	garlic cloves	2
6 tablespoons	chopped spring onions (scallions)	7½ tablespoons
350 g/12 oz	tomatoes	¾ lb
3 medium	avocados	3 medium
1 tablespoon	lemon juice	1¼ tablespoons
to taste	salt and freshly ground black pepper	to taste
to taste	Tabasco sauce	to taste
	To garnish	
	lemon slices	

If serving cold: put about 150 ml/¼ pint (⅔ cup) of water into a pan, add the stock cube and heat until dissolved. Remove from the heat, add the cold water and mix together.

Peel and crush the garlic cloves, add to the onions. Skin, deseed and chop the tomatoes. Halve the avocados, remove the stones and skin, chop the flesh and sprinkle with the lemon juice immediately.

Sieve or liquidize all the ingredients with some of the stock. Blend with the remaining stock, then add salt, pepper and Tabasco to taste. Chill well and garnish with the lemon before serving.

If serving hot: heat all the water with the stock cube. Prepare the ingredients as above, then sieve or liquidize with a little of the stock. Return to the pan, add the seasoning and Tabasco sauce, heat for a few minutes only, then garnish and serve.

Do not freeze.

GOLDEN CHEDDAR SOUP

Cooking time: 15 minutes • Serves 4 to 6

Cheese soups make an excellent light meal; if served as a first course, be fairly sparing with the portions as the soup is very satisfying. Never overcook a cheese soup; when the cheese has melted the soup is ready to serve; long cooking makes the cheese stringy. The addition of firm ingredients, such as sweetcorn and carrots, gives an interesting appearance and texture. Soups are a good way of using up cheese that has become dry; grate or dice it finely so that it melts quickly.

Metric/Imperial	*Ingredients*	*American*
1 or 2	**garlic cloves**	*1 or 2*
175 g/6 oz	**mature Cheddar cheese**	*1½ cups, when grated*
25 g/1 oz	**butter**	*2 tablespoons*
25 g/1 oz	**plain (all-purpose) flour**	*¼ cup*
900 ml/1½ pints	**milk**	*3¾ cups*
2 medium	**carrots, grated**	*2 medium*
100 g/4 oz	**canned sweetcorn**	*¼ lb*
to taste	**salt and freshly ground white pepper**	*to taste*
1 teaspoon	**ready-made English or French mustard**	*1 teaspoon*

Peel the garlic cloves but leave them whole. Grate the cheese. Melt the butter in a saucepan, add the garlic and turn in the butter until pale golden. Stir in the flour, then add the milk. Bring to the boil and stir until thickened. Add the carrots and simmer for 2 or 3 minutes (they should remain fairly firm). Add the sweetcorn, then stir in the cheese until melted. Add salt, pepper and mustard to taste. Remove the garlic and serve.

Variations

- For a more savoury flavour, increase the amount of butter to 50 g/2 oz (¼ cup). Peel and finely chop 1 medium onion and cook with the garlic cloves.
- Use half milk and half chicken stock.
- Diced celery or finely grated celeriac could be used in place of the sweetcorn.
- Choose other good cooking cheeses, such as Double Gloucester, Cheshire or Stilton (see below).

Golden Stilton Soup: Use diced Stilton cheese in place of the Cheddar.

Stilton Soup: Omit the carrot and corn in the first recipe and use Stilton instead of Cheddar cheese. Heat 50 g/2 oz (¼ cup) butter and cook 2 finely chopped medium onions and 2 crushed garlic cloves until tender. Add the flour, as in the first recipe, but with 450 ml/¾ pint (scant 2 cups) of chicken stock and only 300 ml/½ pint (1¼ cups) of milk. When thickened, sieve or liquidize. Return to the pan with the cheese and seasoning to taste, and heat until the cheese has melted. Continue as the recipe. Garnish with croûtons before serving.

Freezing: All these cheese soups freeze well, but take care when defrosted that they are heated for the minimum time.

PASTA AND CHEESE SOUP

Cooking time: 15 to 20 minutes • Serves 4

This is a very satisfying soup, which lends itself to many variations (see below). The actual cooking time depends upon the kind of pasta used. Short-cut, quick-cooking macaroni or small shells are an ideal choice, but long pasta, such as spaghetti, can be broken into small pieces before cooking. Soup noodles could be used if you prefer. Do not overcook the pasta: while it can be served softer in a soup, it retains more flavour if slightly al dente (firm to the bite).

Metric/Imperial	Ingredients	American
1 small	onion	1 small
900 ml/1½ pints	canned consommé or water with 1 chicken, meat or vegetable stock cube	3¾ cups
75 g/3 oz	pasta, see above	⅔ cup
300 ml/½ pint	milk	1¼ cups
2 tablespoons	chopped parsley	2½ tablespoons
1 tablespoon	chopped chives	1¼ tablespoons
to taste	salt and freshly ground black pepper	to taste
3 tablespoons	grated Parmesan cheese	3¾ tablespoons

Peel and chop or thinly slice the onion. Bring the consommé or water and stock cube to the boil, add the onion and pasta. Cook in an uncovered pan until nearly tender, then add the milk, herbs and any seasoning required. Heat well then stir in the cheese and serve.

Variations

- Instead of Parmesan cheese, use about 100 g/4 oz (¼ lb) grated Gruyère, Cheddar or other good cooking cheese.
- For a richer soup use half milk and half single (light) cream.
- Add 1 or 2 finely chopped hard-boiled eggs to the soup.
- Add a little finely chopped crisp bacon or cooked ham or chicken to the soup with the milk and herbs.
- Add finely diced cooked vegetables to the soup just before serving.
- Vegetarians could use all water and omit the milk, or use soya milk.
- Rice and Cheese Soup: Use 75 g/3 oz (scant ½ cup) long-grain rice instead of the pasta. Any of the variations work well with rice.

Freezing: Do not freeze. The first soup is inclined to lose both texture and flavour. The variation with rice freezes better.

EASY GARNISHES

The following suggestions are based on ingredients you probably already have in your kitchen.

Cheese: Top vegetable and other soups with a little grated cheese or with a small spoonful of cream or curd cheese.

Cream, etc: A spoonful of cream turns a soup into a more luxurious dish and adds a richer flavour. Yoghurt, soured cream, crème fraîche or fromage frais are other alternatives. Add any creamy topping immediately before serving the soup so that it does not dissolve in the hot liquid.

If you draw a knife through thick cream or yoghurt, you can create an interesting feathered effect. Alternatively, whip the cream and put a blob on top of the soup.

If the recipe requires soured cream and none is available, see below.

Directions for freezing soups containing cream or yoghurt appear at the end of the recipe or in the introduction to that particular chapter.

Croûtons: If you have frozen croûtons, take them out of the freezer shortly before they are required (see page 193). Ready-prepared croûtons are on general sale.

Herbs: Chopped herbs make a soup look colourful and add flavour. It saves time if you chop small batches with a sharp knife or kitchen scissors and store them in covered containers in the refrigerator or freezer.

Nuts: Chopped nuts make an interesting garnish on a number of soups and also add to the food value. Blanched and flaked almonds (obtainable in packets) are a particularly good garnish for chicken or vegetable soups.

SOURED CREAM

This is made commercially from single (light) cream to which a culture has been added, giving it a slightly sharp taste. It gives a subtle flavour to many kinds of dishes, including soup.

To produce the same effect at home, simply add a little lemon juice to fresh cream, tasting as you do so to achieve the desired acidic flavour.

3 CLEAR SOUPS

C lear soups are a wise choice for anyone wanting to retain a slim figure, as, apart from the garnish, they are made without high-calorie ingredients.

The finest of all clear soups is undoubtedly a consommé. To achieve a perfect result, the meat, stock and other ingredients must be given long, slow cooking. After that it is important to clarify the stock so that the consommé is beautifully clear. Recipes for making consommés based on various meats, poultry and game are given on pages 49 to 52.

Having prepared a consommé, you can turn it into a wide range of soups by using different garnishes. The French fill pages and pages of their cookery books with these, and I have selected some of the more practical and interesting ones. In these the garnish gives the soup its name.

This chapter also includes other interesting unthickened soups, including those based on beer and wine.

Clear soups are less satisfying than thicker soups, so you can be more generous with the portions.

Microwave cooking: This method can be used for making a consommé. First make the stock as described on pages 13 to 15, but reduce the amount of liquid by a quarter, e.g. 1.8 litres/3 pints (7½ cups) instead of 2.4 litres/4 pints (10 cups). There is less evaporation in a microwave than in a saucepan, and the total cooking time is shorter.

Having made the stock, prepare the extra ingredients, as described in the recipe, and place them in a very large bowl or casserole suitable for microwave cooking. To save time, bring the stock to the boil in an ordinary pan and pour it over the ingredients in the microwave container. Heat for a few minutes on full power until you see bubbles on the surface of the liquid, then turn to defrost and cook for about 10 minutes. Check the speed of cooking; if the liquid is simmering gently, cover the bowl and continue cooking for 30 minutes. If the liquid is boiling too quickly on defrost, turn to a lower setting.

When cooked, strain the stock. You can then return it to the container for clarifying with egg whites and shells, as described on page 49. Heat for 10 minutes on defrost, then strain.

Pressure cooking: This is a splendid way of making consommé. First make the stock in the pressure cooker, as described on page 11. Put your consommé ingredients in the pressure cooker and add the stock. In the case of Beef Consommé, you will need only 1.2 litres/2 pints (5 cups) of stock, since the total cooking time is short and there is virtually no evaporation of liquid.

Bring the cooker to full pressure (high) and maintain this for 30 minutes only. Allow to drop at room temperature, then strain the stock. Continue as the recipe, using the pressure cooker as an ordinary saucepan if you want to clarify the liquid using egg whites and shells.

Always check on the capacity of your particular pressure cooker if making large amounts of consommé or other soups, and follow the manufacturer's instructions about filling the pan. It should never be more than half full, so if your cooker is small, you may need to prepare the consommé in two batches.

Slow cooking: Electric slow cookers have not been mentioned before in this book, but could be used for making stock and consommé. Always fill the cooker with boiling water or boiling stock before turning down to the recommended position for your particular model. You should allow about 6 to 8 hours to produce a good stock, and the same time for a consommé. At the end of the cooking time, strain the liquid and transfer to an ordinary saucepan if you want to clarify it using egg whites and egg shells, as described on page 49.

Oven cooking: It is also possible to make consommé in a tightly covered casserole in the oven. Follow the instructions about making stocks in the oven on page 7. Use the amount of liquid given in the recipes. In the case of the Beef Consommé on page 49 you need to allow at least 2¼ hours (plus the time to make the stock) in a preheated oven set to 150°C/300°F/ gas mark 2. Strain the cooked consommé into a saucepan if you want to clarify it using egg whites and shells (see page 49) and continue as the recipe on page 49.

BEEF CONSOMMÉ

Cooking time: 1¼ hours plus time to make stock • Serves 6 to 8

A really first-class consommé takes a great deal of time and care. The first stage is to prepare a good beef stock (see page 13). In order to darken the colour of the stock, place the beef bones, with any meat adhering to them, in a roasting tin with about 25 g/1 oz (2 tablespoons) butter and cook for 30 minutes in the oven preheated to 200°C/400°F/gas mark 6. Place the bones and all your other ingredients in a large saucepan, add the water and make the stock as described on page 13. Allow the stock to become cold, then remove the fat (see page 12).

Basic additions to the shin of beef and stock are listed below, but the Variations list a number of other ingredients that add interest and flavour.

Metric/Imperial	Ingredients	American
675 to 900 g/1½ to 2 lb	**shin of beef**	1½ to 2 lb
2.4 litres/4 pints	**good beef stock** (see page 13)	10 cups
to taste	**salt and freshly ground black pepper**	to taste
1 medium to large	**onion**	1 medium to large
1 medium	**carrot**	1 medium
2	**fresh bay leaves or** 1 dried leaf	2
300 ml/1½ pint	**dry sherry**	1¼ cups
	To clarify the consommé	
	3 egg whites and their shells, optional, see method	

Cut the meat into small pieces, then place in a large saucepan with the well-strained stock and a little seasoning. Peel the onion and carrot, but leave them whole to prevent them breaking up in the liquid. Add the vegetables and bay leaves. Bring the liquid to boiling point and remove any scum floating on top with a spoon. Cover the pan, lower the heat and simmer for 1 hour.

Strain the soup, using an ultra-fine strainer or preferably a sieve lined with several layers of fine muslin (chemists sell this as gauze).

If you feel the consommé is sufficiently clear, simply reheat it with the sherry, then taste and adjust the seasoning. If not, add the **egg whites** and **shells** to the boiling consommé and simmer for a further 20 minutes. Any minute particles will adhere to the whites and shells. Strain once more through muslin, as described above, then reheat, add the sherry and serve.

Variations

- Add several chopped celery stalks and their leaves; a small, whole peeled turnip could be added, plus several peeled garlic cloves, sprigs of parsley, and/or thyme or tarragon. A deseeded and halved red pepper may also be added for an interesting taste.

Jellied Consommé: If you want the consommé to become lightly jellied to serve cold, cook a small part of knuckle of veal or 2 pig's trotters with the other ingredients.

Lamb Consommé: This is far less popular than its beef counterpart but is none the less delicious. Follow the recipe for Beef Consommé but use the Brown Stock (see page 14) made with lamb bones and about 900 g/2 lb diced lean lamb, plus the ingredients given on page 49.

Veal Consommé: This is a delicious consommé to have hot or cold. Follow the recipe for Beef Consommé but substitute shin of beef with a knuckle of veal plus 450 g/1 lb diced lean veal and the White Stock (see page 14) made with veal bones. The finished consommé is very pale, so it is advisable to flavour it with Madeira or port instead of sherry.

Freezing: All these recipes freeze perfectly (see the information about freezing stock on page 16). As alcohol tends to lose some flavour in freezing, add it after defrosting the consommé.

CHICKEN CONSOMMÉ

Cooking time: 1¼ hours plus time to make stock • Serves 6 to 8

While the ingredients are different, the method of making Chicken Consommé is exactly the same as Beef Consommé.

Metric/Imperial	Ingredients	American
1	900 g/2 lb chicken or several chicken portions	1
2.4 litres/4 pints	chicken stock (see page 14)	10 cups
to taste	salt and freshly ground black pepper	to taste
1 or 2	lemons, as required	1 or 2
¼	celery heart	¼
1 medium to large	onion	1 medium to large
2	fresh bay leaves or 1 dried leaf	2
1 sprig	thyme	1 sprig
300 ml/½ pint	dry sherry or port	1¼ cups

Skin the chicken and cut into portions if necessary. Remove any giblets or dark parts of the inside, which could spoil the colour of the consommé. Put into a saucepan with the stock and add a little seasoning. Pare the zest from the lemons, take care not to use any bitter white pith. Cut the celery into large chunks. Peel the onion and leave it whole. Put the lemon zest, vegetables and herbs into the pan and continue as for Beef Consommé (see page 49).

Strain through muslin or clarify with egg whites and shells, as described on page 49. Add the sherry and a little lemon juice to taste.

Variations

Duck Consommé: Follow the recipe for Chicken Consommé, but use duck flesh instead of chicken and duck stock as described on page 14. Discard any skin and excess fat. Instead of thyme use a small sprig of sage. You can replace the lemon zest with that of oranges; bitter Seville oranges give a particularly interesting taste to the soup.

Guinea Fowl Consommé: Follow the recipe for Chicken Consommé, or for Game Consommé (see page 52).

Turkey Consommé: Follow the recipe for Chicken Consommé, but use turkey flesh instead of chicken. If you take a mixture of breast and leg meat, you produce a darker-looking consommé, which has a very good flavour.

The stock used in the recipe can be chicken stock (see page 14), or a similar stock produced from turkey bones or the carcass of the bird.

Freezing: All these consommés freeze well. Freeze as Beef Consommé (see page 50).

GAME CONSOMMÉ

Cooking time: 1¼ to 2 hours plus time to make stock • Serves 6 to 8

This consommé has a particularly rich and delicious flavour. You can use stewing venison, jointed rabbit or joints of hare, pheasant or other game birds. The cooking time depends on the tenderness of the game used. Elderly game birds make a first-class consommé; to extract the full flavour cook the flesh until tender.

Metric/Imperial	Ingredients	American
900 g/2 lb	game flesh, see above	2 lb
2.4 litres/4 pints	game stock (see page 14)	10 cups
to taste	salt and freshly ground black pepper	to taste
about 6	juniper berries, optional	about 6
1 medium to large	onion	1 medium to large
–	celery heart or about 100 g/4 oz (¼ lb) celeriac	¼
1 medium	carrot	1 medium
2	fresh bay leaves or 1 dried leaf	2
1 sprig	rosemary	1 sprig
300 ml/½ pint	Madeira or port	1¼ cups

Cut the venison or other game into pieces. Place in a saucepan with the stock, a little seasoning and the juniper berries. Peel the onion but leave it whole. Chop the celery into large pieces but leave the celeriac in one piece. Peel the carrot and leave whole. Put the vegetables and herbs into the pan and follow the directions for Beef Consommé (see page 49).

Strain through muslin or then clear with egg whites and shells, as described on page 49. Add the Madeira or port.

Freezing: As Beef Consommé (see pages 16 and 50).

FISH CONSOMMÉ

Cooking time: 40 minutes • Serves 4 to 6

Fish Consommé is not served as frequently as meat consommés but it is an excellent basis for a clear fish soup to which you can add shellfish or small pieces of prime fish, such as sole or turbot.

There is no need to buy fish to make the consommé if you have sufficient fish heads, bones and trimmings.

This recipe is made in the same way as the Fish Stock on page 15 but with a higher percentage of fish, so giving a stronger flavour to the liquid.

Metric/Imperial	Ingredients	American
1 kg/2¼ lb	fish, see above	2¼ lb
1.8 litres/3 pints	water	7½ cups
to taste	salt and freshly ground white pepper	to taste
1 medium	onion	1 medium
1 medium	carrot	1 medium
1	celery stick	1
2	fresh bay leaves or 1 dried bay leaf	2
1 sprig	chervil or parsley	1 sprig
to taste	little lemon zest	to taste
300 ml/½ pint	dry white wine	1¼ cups

Wash the fish and put into a large saucepan with the water and add a little seasoning. Peel the onion and carrot but leave them whole, add to the water with the chopped celery, herbs and lemon zest. Bring to the boil, remove any scum that may float to the top of the liquid, then cover the pan. Lower the heat and simmer for 35 minutes. Strain through fine muslin (see page 49), then return to the pan with the wine and heat.

Variations

• Add about 150 ml/¼ pint (⅔ cup) dry sherry to the liquid instead of the white wine.

Seafood Consommé: Make the consommé, strain very carefully, then reheat. Add a mixture of flaked crabmeat (preferably white), peeled prawns and finely diced lobster. Heat for a few minutes only so that the shellfish does not become overcooked and tough. Top each portion of consommé with a little cream.

Sole Consommé: Skin fillets of sole and cut the flesh into small goujons (ribbons) about 2.5 cm/1 inch in length. Put into the hot consommé and poach for a few minutes. Top the soup with cream and chopped fennel leaves.

Halibut, turbot or other white fish can be used instead of sole.

Fish and Tomato Consommé: Follow the main recipe, but add 450 g/ 1 lb skinned and deseeded tomatoes to the other ingredients. Strain and return to the pan. Taste the liquid and add a little tomato purée (paste) for a stronger tomato taste. For a more piquant flavour add a few drops of Tabasco sauce.

This soup can be topped with cream and small pieces of sun-dried tomatoes.

Freezing: This consommé freezes well.

TOMATO CONSOMMÉ

Cooking time: 30 minutes • Serves 4

This fresh tomato consommé has a most refreshing flavour. It is ideal to serve hot or cold. Use really ripe tomatoes so you can extract the maximum amount of juice and flavour.

Metric/Imperial	Ingredients	American
1 medium	onion	1 medium
2	garlic cloves	2
675 g/1½ lb	tomatoes	1½ lb
1.2 litres/2 pints	vegetable stock (see page 14)	5 cups
1 tablespoon	lemon juice	1¼ tablespoons
to taste	salt and freshly ground black pepper	to taste
to taste	cayenne pepper, optional	to taste

Peel and finely chop the onion and garlic. Cut the tomatoes into pieces on a plate so no juice is wasted. Put the onion, garlic and tomatoes, with any juice, into a saucepan with the stock, lemon juice and a very little seasoning. Bring the liquid to simmering point. Lower the heat and cook steadily for 30 minutes. Strain carefully through fine muslin (gauze) placed over a sieve. (Use a nylon or hair sieve if possible as metal sieves sometimes give a faint metallic flavour to the liquid.) Reheat and taste the consommé and add any additional seasoning required.

For details of cold, jellied and iced consommés, see pages 50, 178, 189 and 191.

Variations

- If you feel the consommé is lacking flavour before straining, add a little concentrated tomato purée (paste). Heat for a few minutes, then strain as above.
- A red deseeded chilli pepper could be added to the other ingredients but in this case omit the cayenne pepper.

Beetroot and Tomato Consommé: Use 450 g/1 lb tomatoes and 350 g/ 12 oz (¾ lb) skinned and grated cooked beetroot with the other ingredients given above, but omit the cayenne. Cook as before, then strain.

Cucumber and Tomato Consommé: Use 1 large peeled and sliced cucumber with 350 g/12 oz (³/₄ lb) tomatoes, a sprig of mint and the other ingredients given in the recipe above. Omit the cayenne. Cook as before, then strain.

Freezing: All the recipes freeze well.

Quick Tip

Each of these consommés can be cooked in a large bowl in the microwave. Allow about 20 minutes' cooking time.

STRACCIATELLA

Cooking time: 10 minutes plus time to make stock • Serves 4 to 6

This is an interesting way to combine a good beef stock or consommé (pages 13 and 49) with cheese and eggs, thus turning it into a light meal. Where possible, grate the Parmesan just before using – it has much more flavour than when ready-grated.

Metric/Imperial	Ingredients	American
1.2 litres/2 pints	beef stock or consommé (see pages 13 and 49)	5 cups
to taste	salt and freshly ground black pepper	to taste
4 to 6	eggs	4 to 6
100 g/4 oz	Parmesan cheese	¼ lb
	To garnish	
	chopped chives	

Bring the stock or consommé to the boil and season to taste. Lower the heat until the liquid is boiling gently. Beat the eggs. Grate the cheese, blend with the eggs and gradually pour the mixture into the soup, stirring with a fork as you do so. Serve as soon as the eggs form ribbons in the liquid. Top with the chives.

Freezing: While the stock or consommé can be frozen, the soup containing the eggs cannot.

LEMON AND EGG SOUP
(SOUPA AVGOLEMONO)

Cooking time: 25 minutes plus time to make stock • Serves 4

This classic Greek soup is wonderfully refreshing. If using chicken stock cubes rather than real chicken stock (see page 14), do not use too many as the delicate flavour of the eggs and lemon should predominate.

Metric/Imperial	Ingredients	American
1.2 litres/2 pints	chicken stock (see page 14)	5 cups
to taste	salt and freshly ground black pepper	to taste
50 g/2 oz	long-grain rice	1/3 cup
2 or 3	eggs, see method	2 or 3
3 tablespoons	lemon juice, or to taste	3³/₄ tablespoons

Bring the stock to the boil, season lightly if necessary, then add the rice. Cover the pan and simmer for 15 minutes, or until the rice is just tender. Beat the eggs (3 eggs give a richer soup) with the lemon juice in a basin. Gradually whisk in a little of the hot stock from the saucepan until smooth. Tip the egg and lemon mixture into the saucepan and simmer very gently for 3 or 4 minutes only. Do not allow the soup to boil at this stage. Serve at once.

Do not freeze.

Quick Tip

This soup can be cooked in a large bowl in a microwave. Use full power until the rice is cooked. Blend the eggs and lemon juice as above, add a little stock, return to the bowl; place in the microwave on defrost (or a lower setting if your microwave has a high output, see page 7).
Heat for 1 to 2 minutes only, stirring or whisking at 1/2-minute intervals. Allow to stand for 1 to 2 minutes before serving.

BEER AND BREAD SOUP (OLLEBROD)

Cooking time: 20 minutes plus time to make stock • Serves 4 to 6

This Danish soup is made with bread and beer flavoured with cinnamon and lemon rind. Although pumpernickel bread gives a rich colour and flavour, any wholemeal bread can be used instead of the mixture of breads. It is imperative to allow adequate soaking time for the bread. It is best to select a light ale unless you know you would appreciate a richer dark beer.

Metric/Imperial	Ingredients	American
225 g/8 oz	pumpernickel bread	1/2 lb
100 g/4 oz	white or wholemeal (wholewheat) bread	1/4 lb
600 ml/1 pint	chicken stock (see page 14) or water	2 1/2 cups
1.2 litres/2 pints	beer or ale	5 cups
2.5 cm/1 inch or 1 teaspoon	cinnamon stick or ground cinnamon	1 inch or 1 teaspoon
1	lemon	1
4 tablespoons	brown sugar	5 tablespoons
to taste	salt and freshly ground black pepper	to taste

Break the bread, including the crusts, into small pieces. Heat the chicken stock or water, pour over the bread and soak for several hours or even overnight.

Tip the bread mixture into a large pan and stir briskly until smooth. Stir in the beer and cinnamon. Pare the rind from the lemon, avoiding the bitter white pith. Add the rind to the bread mixture. Halve the lemon, squeeze out the juice and add 1 tablespoon (1 1/4 tablespoons) to the pan but retain the remainder in case it is required.

Heat the soup, stirring well, and add the sugar and seasoning. Simmer for about 10 minutes. Remove the cinnamon stick, if using. Taste and adjust the seasoning and add extra lemon juice if necessary.

Freezing: This soup freezes well, but the beer or ale loses some of its flavour. It is better to freeze the soaked bread and lemon mixture, adding the remaining ingredients when defrosted and reheated.

Quick Tip

To shorten the soaking time, make the bread into fine crumbs and soak for about 15 to 30 minutes.

GERMAN BEER SOUP (BIERSUPPE)

Cooking time: 25 minutes • Serves 4 to 6

*This soup should be made with one of the light German beers (lagers).
The addition of cream gives it a surprisingly mellow taste.*

Metric/Imperial	Ingredients	American
50 g/2 oz	butter	¼ cup
50 g/2 oz	plain (all-purpose) flour	½ cup
1 litre/1¾ pints	light beer	scant 4¼ cups
1 tablespoon	lemon juice	1¼ tablespoons
300 ml/½ pint	double (heavy) cream	1¼ cups
to taste	salt and freshly ground black pepper	to taste
¼ to ½ teaspoon	ground cinnamon	¼ to ½ teaspoon
2 teaspoons	brown sugar, or to taste	2 teaspoons

Heat the butter in a saucepan, stir in the flour and continue stirring over a
low heat for 2 to 3 minutes. Gradually add the beer and lemon juice.
Bring to the boil and cook over a medium heat, stirring all the time until
the soup thickens slightly. Lower the heat, cover the pan and continue
simmering for 10 to 15 minutes.

Remove from the heat so the soup is no longer boiling, add the cream,
seasoning and cinnamon. Stir well, then add the sugar. Heat gently,
without boiling, for a further 2 or 3 minutes and serve with crisp toast.
(Sometimes toast is placed in soup bowls and the soup poured over.)

Variations

- Black bread or pumpernickel is an excellent alternative to toast.
- Follow the recipe for Weinsuppe (page 59), but substitute beer for the
  wine, or use half beer and half chicken stock.
- Use single (light) cream instead of double cream and mix it with 2 level
  teaspoons of cornflour (cornstarch). Pour into a small saucepan, stir
  over the heat until thickened, then whisk into the hot, but not boiling,
  beer soup. (Instead of adding cornflour to the cream, use 1 extra level
  tablespoon [1¼ tablespoons] of flour at the beginning of the method.)

Do not freeze.

WINE SOUP (WEINSUPPE)

Cooking time: 15 minutes • Serves 4 to 6

This German soup has a most refreshing flavour. It is excellent made with a sparkling Moselle wine, but other white wines, still or sparkling, can be used instead. Once the egg yolks are added to the hot, but not boiling, liquid, the soup must be cooked very slowly so there is no fear of it becoming overheated and curdling.

Metric/Imperial	Ingredients	American
1	lemon	1
600 ml/1 pint	white wine, see above	2½ cups
600 ml/1 pint	water	2½ cups
5 cm/2 inches	cinnamon stick	2 inches
2	egg yolks	2
to taste	salt and freshly ground black pepper	to taste
1 teaspoon	caster sugar, or to taste	1 teaspoon

Pare the zest from the lemon in fairly wide strips, avoiding the bitter white pith. Put the wine and nearly all the water into a pan with the lemon zest and cinnamon stick and bring just to boiling point. Simmer for 3 minutes.

Mix the egg yolks with the remaining water in a basin. Add 2 tablespoons (2½ tablespoons) of the very hot liquid, mix thoroughly, then pour into the pan. Lower the heat and whisk briskly until the mixture thickens sufficiently to coat the back of a wooden spoon. Remove the lemon zest and cinnamon stick. Add salt, pepper and sugar to taste, then serve with crisp toast or plain biscuits.

Freezing: This soup must be freshly made.

Quick Tip

This soup can be made in a microwave. Use defrost (or a lower setting if your microwave has a high output, see page 7) when the egg yolks are added, and cook for 1 to 2 minutes. Stir or whisk at ½-minute intervals. Allow to stand for 1 to 2 minutes before serving.

4 VEGETABLE SOUPS

The wonderful range of vegetables available today means we have an almost unlimited choice of soups based on them. Many of the recipes in this chapter suggest cooking the vegetables in chicken stock, as this imparts a rich flavour that complements the other ingredients. If you are a vegetarian, simply substitute fresh vegetable stock (see page 14), or use a stock cube dissolved in water. Never overcook vegetable soups, as it is important to retain the flavour and texture of fresh vegetables.

There are several different types of vegetable soup. The first is a *clear liquid soup* in which diced vegetables add interesting flavour and colour. The soup can be exotic, like Beansprout Soup on page 63, or homely, as the Farmhouse Soup on page 76. Always cut the vegetables into a sensible size, as it is difficult to cope with oversized pieces of food on a soup spoon.

Puréed soups, where the vegetables, sometimes mixed with a little flour or other thickening, create a smooth, creamy texture, are easily and quickly prepared thanks to modern liquidizers (blenders) and food processors (see page 10). When using a food processor, remember to remove the blades before pouring out the soup as the blades can easily drop out and create a mess or even damage.

In these weight-conscious times try to use the vegetables themselves as the main thickening agent rather than introducing flour or similar ingredients.

Creamed or velouté soups include cream or a similar alternative. As stressed in the recipes, do take care when heating a soup that includes cream, wine or lemon juice: if allowed to boil rapidly, it will curdle (separate).

Low-fat alternatives to cream include yoghurt and fromage frais, both of which give an excellent flavour to soups. However, both need just the same care in heating as cream. Soured cream and crème fraîche have slightly acid flavours, so you may find them more interesting additions than cream.

Do try some of the less usual vegetable soups, such as Bortsch on pages 64 and 65, which is made with beetroot or a combination of cranberries and beetroot, or Vegetable Gumbo (see page 104), based on the vegetable sometimes known as ladies fingers. These soups are sufficiently satisfying to form a complete light meal.

Microwave cooking: Soups can be cooked very successfully in a microwave, saving time and retaining a lot of flavour. Use this appliance if the vegetables are young and tender. As large amounts of liquid are slow to heat in a microwave, boil it by conventional means and then add to the other ingredients.

It is not possible to give exact microwave timings as soups vary so much, but once they come to simmering point, they will cook in about half the time stated in the recipes. Use 10 per cent less liquid than indicated and cook on the defrost setting. Check and stir the soup from time to time, just as you would do if using a saucepan. General hints about microwaving soups are on page 7.

Pressure cooking: This is an excellent way to soften vegetables and other ingredients in a soup, particularly if they are not particularly young and tender. Check in your manufacturer's book to find the timing for vegetable soups. Onion Soup, for example, takes about 3 minutes under pressure. Use full pressure (high) and never have the cooker more than half filled. Always allow the pressure to drop at room temperature. General hints about pressure cooking soups are on page 7.

GARNISHES FOR VEGETABLE SOUPS
In most recipes an appropriate garnish is recommended, but if this is not the case, the soup can be topped with cream, soured cream, crème fraîche, yoghurt or fromage frais. Chopped herbs also complement vegetable soups. A generous topping of grated cheese, cream cheese or dumplings turns the soup into a more satisfying dish.

AUBERGINE SOUP

Cooking time: 35 minutes • Serves 4 to 6

Aubergines, or eggplants as they are also called, form the basis of many dishes and are excellent in soups. In the past aubergines were salted to remove their slightly bitter taste, but modern varieties do not seem to have this problem. If you fear they may have a bitter flavour, simply peel off the skin, or salt the vegetable before cooking, as described below.

Metric/Imperial	Ingredients	American
450 g/1 lb	aubergines, see method	1 lb
to taste	salt and freshly ground black pepper	to taste
2	garlic cloves	2
1 small bunch	spring onions (scallions)	1 small bunch
225 g/8 oz	tomatoes	½ lb
2 tablespoons	olive oil	2½ tablespoons
1 litre/1¾ pints	chicken or vegetable stock (see pages 13 to 14)	scant 4½ cups
1 tablespoon	lemon juice	1¼ tablespoons
1 teaspoon	chopped oregano or marjoram	1 teaspoon
1 tablespoon	chopped parsley	1¼ tablespoons
150 ml/1¼ pint	white wine	⅔ cup
	To garnish	
	yoghurt, fromage frais or cream cheese	

If you are confident that your aubergines are not bitter, wipe them and cut into 1.25 cm/½ inch dice. If not, peel them and weigh to ensure you have 450 g/1 lb. Alternatively, score the skin(s), sprinkle with salt and leave to stand for 30 minutes. Rinse in cold water, then dice. The advantage of retaining the skin is that it gives more flavour and colour to the soup.

Peel and crush the garlic, skin and chop the white part of the spring onions and a very little of their tender green stems. Skin and finely chop the tomatoes. Heat the oil, add the garlic, onions, aubergine(s) and tomatoes and cook gently, stirring, for 5 minutes.

Add the stock, lemon juice, herbs and seasoning. Bring the liquid to the boil, cover the pan and lower the heat. Simmer for 20 minutes.

Pour in the wine, heat for 2 or 3 minutes. Taste the soup and add more seasoning if required. Garnish with yoghurt, fromage frais or small spoonfuls of cream cheese.

Variation

Purée of Aubergines: cook the soup as above, then sieve or liquidize. Return to the pan, add the wine and heat for a few minutes. Garnish as above.

Freezing: This soup freezes well.

BEANSPROUT SOUP (KONG NA-MOOL KOOK)

Cooking time: 20 minutes plus time to make stock • Serves 4

This Korean soup is most interesting. The mild flavour of chicken stock forms a pleasing contrast to the stronger flavour of the beef and the delicate beansprouts.

Metric/Imperial	Ingredients	American
1 to 2	garlic cloves	1 to 2
100 g/4 oz	beef fillet steak	1/4 lb
900 ml/1½ pints	chicken stock (see page 14)	3¾ cups
2 tablespoons	sliced spring onions (scallions)	2½ tablespoons
2 tablespoons	soy sauce, or to taste	2½ tablespoons
350 g/12 oz	beansprouts	¾ lb
to taste	salt and freshly ground black pepper	to taste

Peel and crush the garlic; cut the meat into 6 mm/¼ inch dice. Pour the stock into a saucepan, add the garlic, beef and spring onions and bring to the boil. Add most of the soy sauce and the beansprouts (chopped, if desired). Simmer for 10 minutes, then add seasoning to taste and the rest of the soy sauce if necessary. Serve hot with crisp biscuits.

Variations

- If using canned beansprouts, drain carefully and add to the soup after it has been cooking for 5 minutes.
- Use only half the amount of beansprouts and stir in 4 or 5 tablespoons (5 or 6¼ tablespoons) cooked, long-grain rice.
- For a vegetarian soup, use vegetable stock and diced water chestnuts instead of beef.

Freezing: This soup is better freshly made.

Quick Tip

A chicken stock cube and water can be used instead of fresh chicken stock.

This soup is ideal for making in a microwave. Cook for only about 2 minutes on full power once the liquid comes to the boil to make sure the meat is not overcooked.

BORTSCH

Cooking time: 1¼ hours plus time to make stock • Serves 4 to 6

There are almost as many variations in the spelling of bortsch as there are recipes for making this Russian soup. The name indicates that it originally included blood as one of the ingredients. Nowadays, most recipes are based on beetroot. Although the cooking time is longer with uncooked beetroot, it gives a better flavour than cooked beetroot. Beef stock adds a richer taste, but chicken stock produces a brighter colour to the soup.

Metric/Imperial	Ingredients	American
450 g/1 lb	raw beetroots (beets)	1 lb
1 medium	onion	1 medium
1 medium	carrot	1 medium
2	celery sticks	2
3 medium	tomatoes	3 medium
1.2 litres/2 pints	beef or chicken stock (see pages 13 and 14)	5 cups
1 tablespoon	lemon juice or white wine vinegar	1¼ tablespoons
to taste	salt and freshly ground black pepper	to taste
2 teaspoons	sugar, or to taste	to taste
To garnish		
soured cream or yoghurt		
chopped dill		

Peel the beetroots, onion and carrot, then either cut them into fine shreds or grate coarsely. Cut the celery into small dice. Skin and halve the tomatoes, remove the seeds and chop the pulp.

Put all the vegetables into a saucepan with the stock, lemon juice or vinegar and a little seasoning. Bring to the boil, lower the heat and cover the pan. Simmer for 1¼ hours, or until the beetroot is very tender. Adjust the seasoning and stir in the sugar. Top each serving with a generous amount of soured cream or yoghurt and dill.

Variations

- This version of Bortsch is excellent served cold. Chill the cooked soup then garnish as above.
- Many other ingredients can be added to the basic soup, including 1 or 2 teaspoons caraway seeds; a little finely shredded cabbage; a thinly sliced leek; about ¼ peeled and shredded small cucumber.
- For a richer flavour, toss the vegetables in 50 g/2 oz (¼ cup) heated butter before adding the stock. This should not be done if serving the soup cold.
- **Using cooked beetroot:** Dice or grate a generous 450 g/1 lb cooked beetroot instead of the raw vegetable, and shorten the cooking time to 30 minutes.

Freezing: The cooked soup freezes well.

CRANBERRY BORTSCH

Cooking time: 30 minutes plus time to make stock • Serves 4 to 6

Cranberries have so much flavour that this soup can be made with water, rather than stock, if desired. Always keep the lid on the pan when cooking, for cranberries pop so violently that they could spray out hot liquid.

Metric/Imperial	Ingredients	American
1 medium	onion	1 medium
1 large	carrot	1 large
225 g/8 oz	cooked beetroot (beets)	½ lb
2	celery sticks	2
1 litre/1¾ pints	beef or chicken stock (see pages 13 and 14) or water	scant 4½ cups
175 g/6 oz	cranberries	1½ cups
2 teaspoons	lemon juice or white wine vinegar	2 teaspoons
to taste	salt and freshly ground black pepper	to taste
1 tablespoon	sugar, or to taste	1¼ tablespoons
To garnish		
	soured cream or yoghurt	

Peel and finely dice or coarsely grate the onion, carrot and beetroot. Cut the celery into small dice. Put these ingredients into a saucepan with the stock or water and bring to the boil. Add the cranberries, lemon juice and a little seasoning, then cover the pan, lower the heat and simmer for 20 to 25 minutes, or until all the ingredients are tender. Taste the soup and add the sugar and any extra seasoning required. Serve hot or cold, topped with soured cream or yoghurt.

Variation

- Omit the beetroot and use 350 g/12 oz (¾ lb) cranberries. As the fruit is so sharp, you will need to use at least twice the amount of sugar.

Freezing: This soup freezes well.

RUSSIAN CABBAGE SOUP (SCHI)

Cooking time: 45 minutes plus time to make stock • Serves 4 to 6

This sustaining soup depends a great deal on the strong flavour of the stock. While beef stock, or even a stock cube and water, could be used, the classic recipe for the stock is made from beef bones (see page 13), but with the addition of a small amount of lean pork and the carcass of a duck to give a subtle taste.

Metric/Imperial	Ingredients	American
2 medium	**onions**	2 medium
3 medium	**carrots**	3 medium
1 very small	**turnip**	1 very small
2	**celery sticks**	2
1 medium	**leek**	1 medium
2 tablespoons	**olive or sunflower oil**	2½ tablespoons
1.2 litres/2 pints	**stock, see above**	5 cups
to taste	**salt and freshly ground black pepper**	to taste
1 medium	**crisp young cabbage**	1 medium
300 ml/½ pint	**soured cream**	1¼ cups

Peel and neatly dice the onions, carrot and turnip. Cut the celery and leek into thin slices. Heat the oil in a pan, add all the vegetables and stir over a low heat for 10 minutes. Add the stock and a little seasoning. Cover the pan and simmer for 25 minutes.

Meanwhile, finely shred the cabbage, tip into a small quantity of boiling water and cook for 3 to 5 minutes only, until slightly softened. Drain carefully. Add the cabbage to the hot soup together with half the soured cream. Heat for 5 minutes. Serve the soup topped with the remaining soured cream.

Note: In old recipes for this soup the cabbage is added and the soup cooked for about 30 minutes. Nowadays, we have developed a taste for lightly cooked cabbage and I find the soup much nicer with the shorter cooking time given above.

Variations

- To make an even more satisfying soup, finely dice about 225 g/8 oz (½ lb) tender beef or lean pork and simmer this with the vegetables. Diced beef steak should be given only about 10 minutes' cooking time.

Russian Nettle Soup: Prepare the mixed vegetables as above but omit the cabbage and use about 225 g/8 oz (½ lb) young nettle tops plus the same amount of sorrel leaves instead. If you have no sorrel, double the amount of nettle leaves. Blanch in the same way as the cabbage, then add to the soup and cook for 10 minutes.

Do not freeze.

CAULIFLOWER AND POTATO SOUP
(CRÈME DUBARRY)

Cooking time: 40 minutes • Serves 4 to 6

Cauliflower makes a delicious and economical soup because it uses mainly the leaves and stalks; most of the florets can be served as a separate vegetable. This recipe is a classic version of the French soup. If you omit the potatoes, you will need all the cauliflower florets to thicken the soup.

Metric/Imperial	Ingredients	American
1 medium to large	**cauliflower**	1 medium to large
750 ml/1¼ pints	*water*	good 3 cups
to taste	**salt and freshly ground black pepper**	to taste
50 g/2 oz	**butter or margarine**	¼ cup
1 medium	**onion**	1 medium
1 medium	**leek**	1 medium
2 medium	*potatoes*	2 medium
600 ml/1 pint	**milk**	2½ cups
150 ml/¼ pint	**single (light) cream**	⅔ cup
	To garnish	
	cauliflower florets, see method	
	paprika	

Discard any imperfect leaves from the cauliflower, then cut the remaining leaves, stalks and base into small pieces. Bring the water to the boil with a little seasoning, add the chopped leaves and stalks, then cover the pan and cook briskly for 15 minutes. Strain the stock and reserve it. Set aside a few tender cooked stalks and leaves to liquidize with the other ingredients. Divide about 175 g/6 oz (2 cups) of the cauliflower into small florets. Put these into the hot cauliflower stock and cook for 5 minutes, or until tender. Strain and put a few florets on one side to garnish the soup. Save the stock.

Peel and finely chop the onion, wash and slice the white part and a very little of the tender green stalk of the leek; peel and finely dice the potatoes. Heat the butter or margarine and cook the onion, leek and potatoes for 5 minutes. Add the cauliflower stock, bring to the boil, lower the heat and cover the pan. Simmer for 15 minutes, then sieve or liquidize the soup with the cooked florets, stalks and leaves.

Return to the pan, add the milk and cream and heat. Taste and adjust the seasoning. Garnish with the reserved florets and paprika.

Variations

- Heat the milk with the puréed ingredients. Blend 1 or 2 egg yolks with the cream in a basin, then spoon a few tablespoons of the hot soup over the egg mixture. Return to the pan, lower the heat and cook gently, whisking briskly, for 5 minutes.

Cauliflower Soup: Follow the main recipe but omit the potato and use all the cauliflower florets. When sieving or liquidizing the soup, you can also add a more generous quantity of the cooked stalks and leaves to give body to the soup.

Broccoli Soup: Use broccoli instead of cauliflower in the main recipe or the variations.

Freezing: The puréed soup freezes well.

CELERIAC SOUP

Cooking time: 30 minutes plus time to make stock • Serves 4

Celeriac is a vegetable about the size of a large turnip with a flavour similar to celery. It is often known as celery root. Under the brown skin the flesh is white, it discolours easily when peeled, so should be placed immediately in a bowl of cold water containing at least 1 tablespoon (1¼ tablespoons) lemon juice or white wine vinegar until needed.
A little celeriac is an excellent alternative to celery in any vegetable soup.

Metric/Imperial	Ingredients	American
2 tablespoons	lemon juice	2½ tablespoons
225 g/8 oz	celeriac, prepared weight	½ lb
2 medium	onions	2 medium
1	garlic clove, optional	1
1 teaspoon	finely grated lemon zest	1 teaspoon
40 g/1½ oz	butter	3 tablespoons
900 ml/1½ pints	white stock (see page 14)	3¾ cups
to taste	salt, celery salt and freshly ground white pepper	to taste
	To garnish	
	paprika or finely diced red pepper	
	chopped parsley	

Fill a bowl with cold water, add half the lemon juice. Peel the celeriac, cut into 1.25 cm/½ inch dice, then place in the lemon-flavoured water.
Peel and finely chop the onions and garlic. Heat the butter in a saucepan, add the onions and garlic and cook gently for 5 minutes. Drain the celeriac and sprinkle with the remaining lemon juice and the lemon zest. Tip into the pan and cook gently for 5 minutes; take care the vegetables do not brown.

Add the stock with salt, celery salt and pepper to taste. Bring to the boil, cover the pan and simmer steadily for 20 minutes.

Sieve or liquidize the soup, return to the pan and reheat. Garnish and serve.

Variations

- Omit the lemon juice and zest in the main recipe and flavour the soup with 2 to 3 teaspoons English or French mustard. Add this to the stock.
- Add a few tablespoons cooked rice to the cooked soup or any of the variations that follow.

Cream of Celeriac Soup: Follow the main recipe, but use only 600 ml/ 1 pint (2½ cups) stock. Cook the soup, then sieve or liquidize. Return to the pan with 300 ml/½ pint (1¼ cups) single (light) cream and reheat gently without boiling.
   Instead of cream use 300 ml/½ pint (1¼ cups) thin White Sauce (see page 24).

Celeriac and Apple Soup: Follow the main recipe, but cook a small, peeled and diced cooking apple with the celeriac.

Celeriac and Leek Soup: Omit the garlic in the main recipe or in the Cream of Celeriac Soup and use only 1 medium onion. Cut 2 medium leeks into thin slices, using a little of the tender green part as well as the white. Heat the onions and leeks in the butter then continue as the recipe.

Celeriac and Orange Soup: Follow the main recipe, but omit the lemon zest and use only 600 ml/1 pint (2½ cups) of stock. Add 1 tablespoon (1¼ tablespoons) finely grated orange zest with the stock. Sieve or liquidize the cooked soup, then return to the pan with 300 ml/½ pint (1¼ cups) orange juice and reheat. Garnish with orange segments.
   This soup is equally good served cold or lightly frozen (see page 191).

Celeriac and Tomato Soup: Follow the main recipe, but omit the lemon juice and rind in the soup and use 4 medium tomatoes (these should be peeled, deseeded and chopped, as explained on page 101). Add the tomatoes with the celeriac and continue as the main recipe. This soup is equally good served cold.

Viennese Celeriac Soup: Known as Selleriesuppe in Austria, this soup is often mistakenly translated as celery soup, but it is actually based on celeriac. Prepare the 225 g/8 oz (½ lb) celeriac and cook in boiling water flavoured with 1 tablespoon (1¼ tablespoons) lemon juice and a little seasoning. When tender, strain and sieve the celeriac, then liquidize or mash until smooth.
   Make 600 ml/1 pint (2½ cups) White Sauce (see page 24), add the celeriac and heat. Blend 2 egg yolks with 150 ml/¼ pint (²⁄₃ cup) soured cream and gradually whisk into the hot, but not boiling, soup.
Cook slowly for about 6 to 8 minutes. Serve topped with julienne strips of cooked celeriac, i.e., cut into matchstick shapes.

Freezing: All versions of this soup freeze well, but omit the egg yolks and soured cream in Viennese Celeriac Soup; add these to the hot soup and cook quietly for 6 to 8 minutes.

Quick Tip

Celeriac softens quite easily, so the main recipe on page 68 and all the variations can be cooked in a microwave.

CORN CHOWDER

Cooking time: 25 minutes • Serves 4

Sweetcorn is a favourite vegetable in North America, and in chowders it adds flavour and food value as well as colour. The corn must be cooked or canned before use. In this recipe the potatoes are diced, but they can also be mashed to thicken the liquid. Instead of relatively thin slices of bacon you could have one thick slice and cut it into small cubes. The bacon rind is an important garnish.

Metric/Imperial	Ingredients	American
2 medium	**onions**	2 medium
3 medium	**potatoes**	3 medium
3 or 4 rashers	**streaky bacon**	3 or 4 slices
25 g/1 oz	**butter, optional**	2 tablespoons
450 ml/³/₄ pint	**water**	scant 2 cups
to taste	**salt and freshly ground black pepper**	to taste
600 ml/1 pint	**milk**	2¹/₂ cups
350 g/12 oz	**cooked or canned sweetcorn**	2¹/₄ cups
6 to 8	**plain crackers**	6 to 8
	To garnish	
	paprika	

Peel the onions and cut into 6 mm/¹/₄ inch dice. Peel the potatoes and cut into 1.25 cm/¹/₂ inch dice. Remove the rind from the bacon and dice the rashers. Heat the rinds for 2 minutes, then add the bacon and cook slowly for a further 2 minutes. If lots of fat runs out, omit the butter. Add the onions and potatoes and cook steadily, stirring from time to time, until they are pale golden. Remove the bacon rinds and set aside. Add the water, bring to the boil and season to taste. Cover the pan and simmer steadily for 10 to 15 minutes. Pour in the milk, then add the hot, well-drained sweetcorn and heat for 5 minutes.

Crumble the crackers into soup bowls, spoon the hot soup on top and garnish with crushed bacon rinds and paprika.

Variations

- If using frozen sweetcorn, allow it to defrost, then add to the water 5 minutes before the end of cooking time.
- **With creamed potatoes:** instead of diced potatoes use 450 g/1 lb (2 cups) of smooth mashed potatoes mixed with a little butter. Cook the bacon and onions as above, then add the water and simmer until the onions are soft. Add the mashed potatoes. Mix well, then gradually stir in 900 ml/1¹/₂ pints (3³/₄ cups) milk. When hot, add the sweetcorn and continue as above.

Chicken and Corn Chowder: Chicken and sweetcorn are perfect partners. Cut 225 g/8 oz (¹/₂ lb) cooked chicken breast or leg into neat dice. Follow the main recipe, but use only 225 g/8 oz (1¹/₂ cups) sweetcorn. Add the chicken to the hot soup a few minutes before adding the sweetcorn.

Crabmeat and Corn Chowder: Follow the main recipe or the variation with creamed potatoes. Use only 225 g/8 oz (1½ cups) sweetcorn with 175 g/6 oz (1 cup) flaked white crabmeat. Add the crabmeat after the sweetcorn.

Do not freeze.

CREAM OF COURGETTE (ZUCCHINI) SOUP

Cooking time: 35 minutes • Serves 4 to 6

Courgettes make an excellent soup. Choose small vegetables with unmarked skins, as they are not peeled.

Metric/Imperial	Ingredients	American
450 g/1 lb	courgettes, prepared weight	1 lb
2 medium	onions	2 medium
2	garlic cloves	2
50 g/2 oz	butter	¼ cup
25 g/1 oz	plain (all-purpose) flour	¼ cup
600 ml/1 pint	vegetable stock (see page 14)	2½ cups
300 ml/½ pint	milk	1¼ cups
to taste	salt and freshly ground black pepper	to taste
1 tablespoon	chopped parsley	1¼ tablespoons
1 teaspoon	chopped oregano or marjoram	1 teaspoon
300 ml/½ pint	single (light) cream	1¼ cups

Wash and dry the courgettes, cut away the tough ends then weigh the vegetables. Cut into 1.25 cm/½ inch slices. Peel and finely chop the onions and garlic. Heat the butter, add the onions and garlic and cook gently for 5 minutes. Add the courgettes and cook for a further 5 minutes. Stir in the flour and mix thoroughly.

Add the stock and bring just to the boil. Cover the pan and simmer for 15 minutes. Sieve or liquidize the soup. Return to the pan, add the milk, seasoning, herbs and cream, then heat and serve.

Variation

Cream of Asparagus Soup 1: Use 450 g/1 lb asparagus instead of the courgettes and omit the herbs. Cut 12 tender tips from the asparagus and set aside. Trim the asparagus stalks, discard the tough ends, then chop into 2.5 cm/1 inch lengths. Follow the method given above. If the asparagus is very young and thin, the simmering time should be only 10 minutes; if thicker, allow 15 to 20 minutes.

Sieve or liquidize the soup then return to the pan with the milk, seasoning and cream. Meanwhile, simmer the tips in a very little lightly salted water, drain and add to the soup just before serving.

Freezing: Both these soups freeze well, although they have a tendency to separate (see page 16). It is better to freeze the courgette or asparagus purée, then add the milk and other ingredients when reheating.
The asparagus tips should be cooked, then frozen separately. Pack in a small container when frozen to avoid damaging them.

CUCUMBER SOUP

Cooking time: 35 minutes • Serves 4 to 6

Cucumbers have an excellent flavour when cooked, and this recipe is ideal for really large, mature vegetables. I leave about 5 cm/2 inches of skin on one of the cucumbers to give a delicate colour; any more than that gives a bitter taste to the soup.

The main recipe is very simple, without flavourings to detract from the taste of the cucumber. It makes an excellent basis for the variations that follow.

Metric/Imperial	Ingredients	American
2 large	cucumbers	2 large
50 g/2 oz	butter or margarine	1/4 cup
25 g/1 oz	plain (all-purpose) flour	1/4 cup
600 ml/1 pint	water	2 1/2 cups
1 tablespoon	chopped parsley	1 1/4 tablespoons
1 tablespoon	chopped chives	1 1/4 tablespoons
1	dried bay leaf	1
to taste	salt and freshly ground black pepper	to taste
600 ml/1 pint	milk	2 1/2 cups
150 ml/1/4 pint	single (light) cream	2/3 cup
	To garnish	
	croûtons or cheese croûtons (see page 193)	

Peel the cucumbers, retain a small amount of skin in one piece (see above); this makes it easy to remove from the soup.

Grate the cucumbers or cut into 1.25 to 2 cm/1/2 to 3/4 inch dice. Heat the butter or margarine and toss the cucumber in this for 5 minutes. Stir in the flour, then add the water with the herbs and a little seasoning. Bring to the boil, stirring or whisking until thickened. Lower the heat and simmer for 20 minutes, then remove the skin and bay leaf and add the milk and cream.

Heat thoroughly, taste and adjust the seasoning then serve topped with the croûtons.

Variations

- For additional flavour, add 1 or 2 medium onions to the ingredients above. Peel and chop very finely, then cook in the butter or margarine with the cucumber.
- A few strips of lemon zest could be added to the water and herbs.
- Use only 300 ml/½ pint (1¼ cups) milk and the same amount of dry white wine. Heat very gently with the cream, taking care the soup does not boil.

Puréed Cucumber Soup: For a fairly thick soup, retain the flour, as in the main recipe; for a thinner soup, omit the flour. When the cucumber has been cooked, remove the bay leaf but retain the skin, if you like, for extra flavour. Sieve or liquidize, then return to the pan with the milk and cream and reheat.

Cucumber and Cheese Soup: Use the main recipe or the recipe for puréed soup. Add 75 g/3 oz (¾ cup) grated Gruyère, Cheddar, Cheshire or any good cooking cheese to the hot soup immediately before serving. Heat for a very short time only.

Cucumber and Chicken Soup: Use the main recipe or the puréed soup recipe. Substitute good chicken stock (see page 14) for the water. About 100 g/4 oz (¼ lb) finely chopped or minced uncooked chicken breast could be cooked with the cucumber.

Cucumber and Crabmeat Soup: Use the main recipe or the puréed soup recipe. Add about 100 g/4 oz (¼ lb) flaked white crabmeat to the soup with the milk and cream, together with a good shake of paprika and a squeeze of lemon juice. Heat gently, without boiling, then serve.

Other shellfish, such as prawns or shrimps, could be used instead of crabmeat.

Cucumber and Potato Soup: Add onion(s), as suggested in the first Variation, and about 225 g/8 oz (½ lb) grated or diced potato to the cucumber. (This is the weight of potato when peeled.) The soup can be served with or without sieving or liquidizing.

Freezing: The main recipe, using grated or diced cucumber, does not freeze well: it loses texture and flavour. The puréed version of the soup freezes well, although it is advisable to add the milk and cream when reheating.

CUCUMBER AND MINT SOUP

Cooking time: 30 minutes plus time to make stock • Serves 4 to 6

The combination of cucumber and mint is a very happy one. This soup is equally good hot or cold, although I make some slight adaptations when it is served cold (see below). To enhance the colour of the soup leave about 5 cm/2 inches of skin on the cucumber; this softens during cooking and loses any bitter taste.

Metric/Imperial	Ingredients	American
1 very large	**cucumber**	1 very large
1 medium	**onion**	1 medium
1 small	**sprig mint**	1 small
600 ml/1 pint	**chicken stock (see page 14)**	2½ cups
to taste	**salt and freshly ground white pepper**	to taste
300 ml/½ pint	**single (light) cream**	1¼ cups
	To garnish	
	chopped mint and chopped chives	
	croûtons (see page 193)	

Peel the cucumber, as instructed above, then cut into slices. Peel and chop the onion. Put the cucumber, onion and mint into a saucepan with the stock and a little seasoning. Simmer for 15 to 20 minutes, or until the vegetables are tender. Sieve or liquidize and return to the pan with the cream. Heat and adjust the seasoning. Garnish with the herbs and croûtons.

Variations

• A thicker soup can be made by adding beurre manié made with 25 g/ 1 oz (2 tablespoons) butter and 25 g/1 oz (¼ cup) plain (all-purpose) flour before adding the cream (see page 9).
• Any of the hot soups given below can be thickened in the same way.

Courgette and Mint Soup: Use 450 g/1 lb small courgettes (zucchini) in place of cucumber. Cut the tough ends from the courgettes, wash well but do not peel. Slice and cook as above.

As courgettes have less flavour than cucumber, you may like to use 2 onions as well.

Pumpkin and Mint Soup: Use 450 g/1 lb peeled pumpkin instead of cucumber. Various kinds of squash or vegetable marrow can be used instead of pumpkin.

Chilled Cucumber and Mint Soup: Use only 450 ml/¾ pint (scant 2 cups) chicken stock in the main recipe. When the soup is cooked, sieve or liquidize it, allow to cool, then stir in 150 ml/¼ pint (⅔ cup) yoghurt, 300 ml/½ pint (1¼ cups) single (light) cream and a little lemon juice. Top the cold soup with chopped chives and chopped walnuts.

Do not thicken this cold soup with beurre manié.

Freezing: It is better to freeze the cucumber, courgette or pumpkin mixture after sieving or liquidizing. Add the cream, yoghurt or lemon juice when the soup is defrosted.

SPICED CUMBERLAND SOUP

Cooking time: 35 minutes plus time to make stock • Serves 4 to 6

This interesting soup, with its combination of savoury ingredients and the sweetness of orange juice and redcurrant jelly, has some of the subtle flavour of Cumberland sauce.

Metric/Imperial	Ingredients	American
1 small	onion	1 small
1 small	carrot	1 small
3 medium	mushrooms	3 medium
2 small	tomatoes	2 small
1 rasher	streaky bacon	1 slice
25 g/1 oz	butter	2 tablespoons
600 ml/1 pint	beef stock (see page 13)	2½ cups
3 tablespoons	red wine	3¾ tablespoons
1 teaspoon	allspice	1 teaspoon
to taste	salt and freshly ground black pepper	to taste
150 ml/¼ pint	orange juice	⅔ cup
3 tablespoons	redcurrant jelly	3¾ tablespoons
	To garnish	
	1 to 2 oranges	

Peel and chop the onion and carrot; wipe and slice the mushrooms. Skin and chop the tomatoes; derind the bacon, save the rind and chop the rasher into small pieces. Heat the butter and bacon rind in a saucepan, add the vegetables and diced bacon. Cook gently for 5 minutes. Remove the bacon rind.

Pour the stock into the pan, cover and simmer steadily for 30 minutes. Sieve or liquidize the ingredients, then return to the pan with the red wine, allspice and seasoning to taste. Simmer for 5 minutes, then add the orange juice and redcurrant jelly. Stir over a low heat until the jelly has dissolved.

To garnish the soup cut away the orange rind and pith, then cut out segments of fruit free from skin and pips. Add to the soup just before serving.

Variations

• Vegetarians should omit the bacon and add an extra onion to give more flavour.

Cold Spiced Cumberland Soup: Chill the soup and the orange segments and add to the soup immediately before serving.

Do not freeze.

FARMHOUSE SOUP

Cooking time: about 45 minutes plus time to make stock • Serves 4 to 6

This is not a classic recipe, but its name describes a homely mixed vegetable soup made with country ingredients. The French make a similar soup called potage paysanne. *The soup is hearty and satisfying, as it is not sieved or liquidized. To turn it into a complete meal, top with crisp chopped bacon, or diced ham, or cooked sliced sausages, or a thick layer of grated cheese.*

Metric/Imperial	Ingredients	American
675 g/1½ lb	mixed vegetables, prepared weight, see method	1½ lb
50 g/2 oz	butter	¼ cup
1.8 litres/3 pints	vegetable, chicken or bacon stock (see page 14)	7½ cups
to taste	salt and freshly ground black pepper	to taste
bunch	mixed herbs, see method	bunch
	To garnish	
	cooked bacon, ham or sausages (optional)	
	chopped parsley	
	grated cheese	

The vegetables should consist of 1 or 2 carrots, a few celery sticks, 1 small turnip, 1 small parsnip, 1 small swede (rutabaga), 1 or 2 small leeks, a few cauliflower florets, a red pepper and a small amount of cabbage.

Peel and dice or slice the vegetables. Divide the cauliflower into small florets, deseed and dice the pepper. Heat the butter in a saucepan and add all the prepared vegetables, except the cauliflower and pepper. Pour the stock into the pan, bring to the boil and add a little seasoning. Take some sprigs of parsley and chives, plus a very little rosemary and thyme and tie in a bunch or place in a muslin bag. Add to the pan, then cover and simmer the soup for 15 to 20 minutes. Add the cauliflower and pepper and continue cooking for 10 minutes. Add the cabbage and cook for 5 to 7 minutes.

Taste the soup and adjust the seasoning. Add any of the meat garnishes and heat for 1 to 2 minutes. Just before serving, top each portion with parsley. Add the cheese when the soup is served.

Variations

- Change the vegetables according to the season: in summertime add shelled peas and diced green beans or fresh broad (fava) beans.
- Add small or diced new potatoes with a sprig of mint instead of thyme.
- Substitute shredded lettuce, cabbage kale or spinach for the cauliflower and small skinned tomatoes for the pepper.

Do not freeze.

FRENCH GARLIC SOUP (SOUPE À L'AIL) 1

Cooking time: 35 to 40 minutes plus time to make stock • Serves 4 to 6

Even if you are a lover of garlic, the thought of including a whole head in a soup may sound a little daunting. In fact, by the time the garlic is cooked and puréed with the other ingredients, it has a wonderfully mellow flavour, particularly if you use chicken stock; beef stock makes a rich, strongly flavoured soup.

The second recipe is a favourite in Provence, and the slight variation shows it is just as popular in Spain.

Metric/Imperial	Ingredients	American
2 medium	**onions**	2 medium
1 medium head	**garlic**	1 medium head
1 tablespoon	**olive oil**	1¼ tablespoons
900 ml/1½ pints	**chicken or beef stock** (see pages 13 and 14)	3¾ cups
1	**fresh bay leaf or** ½ **dried leaf**	1
1 tablespoon	**chopped parsley**	1¼ tablespoons
1 teaspoon	**chopped thyme or** ½ **teaspoon dried thyme**	1 teaspoon
to taste	**salt and freshly ground black pepper**	to taste
2	**egg yolks**	2
1 tablespoon	**lemon juice**	1¼ tablespoons

Peel and chop the onions. Peel the garlic, remove the skin around the cloves, but do not chop them. Heat the oil in a saucepan, add the onions and cook for 5 minutes. If using chicken stock, do not allow them to brown. If using beef stock, cook for 10 minutes, or until the onions are golden brown.

Add most of the stock. Put the herbs and garlic into the pan with a little seasoning. Bring to the boil, lower the heat and simmer for 25 minutes. Remove the bay leaf, then sieve or liquidize the soup, return to the pan and bring almost to boiling point. Blend the egg yolks with the reserved stock and lemon juice. Whisk into the hot soup and cook without boiling for 5 minutes, whisking or stirring constantly. Add extra seasoning if required. Serve with crusty French bread.

Variations

• For a thicker soup blend 25 g/1 oz (¼ cup) plain (all-purpose) flour with the onions before adding the stock.

French Garlic Soup 2: Use a large head of garlic. Peel the cloves. These can be chopped, if desired, but generally they are served whole. Bring 900 ml/1½ pints (3¾ cups) of water to the boil, add the garlic with a little seasoning, then cover the pan and simmer for 15 to 20 minutes, or until the garlic is tender. Blend 2 egg yolks with a little cold water or milk, whisk into the pan and simmer steadily for 5 minutes, whisking or stirring to keep the soup smooth.

Cut thin slices of French bread, spread with extra virgin oil, then place in heated soup bowls. Ladle the soup over the bread and serve.

This soup is often known as *àgua bolido*, which means **boiled water soup**. A more interesting version is made if a small sprig of sage, 1 or 2 dried whole cloves or a good pinch of ground cloves and 2 tablespoons (2½ tablespoons) olive oil are added to the water and garlic cloves. Remove the sage and whole cloves before serving the soup. Spread slices of bread with olive oil and grated Gruyère cheese. Place under a preheated grill until the cheese melts. Put into heated soup bowls, then add the soup.

Spanish Garlic Soup (Sopa De Ajo): This is cooked in a similar manner to French Garlic Soup 2, but is enriched by adding 1 tablespoon (1¼ tablespoons) olive oil and 4 whole eggs instead of 2 egg yolks. After thickening with the eggs, the liquid is strained over the bread spread with olive oil. This gives a creamy soup with the flavour of garlic, but without the cloves.

Do not freeze: The garlic tends to develop an unpleasant flavour in freezing.

ITALIAN GLOBE ARTICHOKE SOUP
(VELLUTTATA DI CARCIOFI)

Cooking time: 35 minutes • Serves 4 to 6

Italians love globe artichokes – indeed, I remember seeing piles of freshly prepared artichoke hearts in the market at Padua. The vegetable is so plentiful in Italy that the leaves seem to be discarded quite happily. The fresh hearts (bottoms of the artichokes) are used in this soup but, since they are not prepared in this manner in Britain, I have based the recipe on whole artichokes.

Metric/Imperial	Ingredients	American
6 medium	artichokes	6 medium
to taste	salt and freshly ground black pepper	to taste
	Velouté base	
50 g/2 oz	butter	1/4 cup
50 g/2 oz	plain (all-purpose) flour	1/2 cup
750 ml/1 1/4 pints	chicken or white stock (see page 14)	good 3 cups
300 ml/1/2 pint	single (light) cream	1 1/4 cups
	To garnish	
	diced artichoke heart	

Trim away any tough outer leaves from the artichokes and cut out the centre chokes (hairy middles). Bring a pan of water to the boil, add a little salt and the artichokes. Cover the pan and simmer steadily for 20 to 25 minutes or until tender. To check if ready pull away a leaf and see if the base of this is really soft.

If short of time, cut the hearts out of the artichokes. Dice part of one heart finely to use for garnish. Sieve the remaining hearts or liquidize them with 3 tablespoons (3 3/4 tablespoons) of stock. If you have time, scrape the soft pulp from the base of the leaves and sieve or liquidize this with the hearts.

While the artichokes are cooking, prepare the velouté base. Heat the butter in a saucepan, stir in the flour, then gradually add the stock. Stir constantly as the liquid comes to the boil and thickens, then lower the heat and simmer very gently for 10 minutes. Add the cream and the artichoke purée and heat gently. Adjust the seasoning and garnish with the diced artichoke heart.

Variations

- Use about 8 small canned artichoke hearts instead of fresh ones. Drain and sieve or liquidize them.

Italian Asparagus Soup (Velluttata Di Asparagi): This recipe is ideal for the asparagus that has white rather than green stalks. Cut away the very tough ends of the stalks from 450 g/1 lb asparagus. Cut off 8 to 12 tips and cook these separately in a little salted water or stock to use as garnish. Simmer the rest of the asparagus in the same way as the globe artichokes above, then sieve or liquidize.

To make the velouté base, add the cream and asparagus purée, reheat gently and add seasoning to taste. Top the soup with the asparagus tips.

Freezing: Both these soups freeze well, but it is best to do so without the cream; add that when reheating the soup. To save space in the freezer, prepare the artichoke or asparagus purée when the vegetables are in season and freeze until needed. Make the velouté base when required. The diced artichoke heart and delicate cooked asparagus tips should be packed and frozen separately.

MINESTRONE

Cooking time: 2 hours • Serves 4 to 6

Meaning literally 'big soup', traditional minestrone is certainly a satisfying dish. Different regions of Italy have their own versions of this famous soup and some are given on page 81. The method of cooking retains the texture of the various ingredients.

Metric/Imperial	Ingredients	American
225 g/8 oz	dried borlotti or cannellini beans	good 1 cup
1.8 litres/3 pints	water	7½ cups
to taste	salt and freshly ground black pepper	to taste
1 large	onion	1 large
1	garlic clove	1
1 large	carrot	1 large
2 medium	courgettes (zucchini)	2 medium
2	celery sticks	2
225 g/8 oz	tomatoes	½ lb
2 to 4 slices	prosciutto or unsmoked bacon	2 to 4 slices
2 tablespoons	olive oil	2½ tablespoons
100 g/4 oz	pasta, see method	¼ lb
225 g/8 oz	cabbages or other greens	½ lb
3 tablespoons	chopped parsley	3¾ tablespoons
	For the topping	
	grated Parmesan cheese	

Place the beans in a pan, cover with cold water and leave to soak for several hours. Discard the soaking water, then add the amount of water stated above. Bring to the boil and boil briskly for 10 minutes. Add a little seasoning, then cover the pan and lower the heat. Simmer for 1¼ hours or until the beans are nearly tender.

Meanwhile, peel and chop the onion and garlic, peel and dice the carrot. Do not peel the courgettes, but discard the tough ends, wipe the vegetables and cut into small dice. Chop the celery, skin and chop the tomatoes. Cut the prosciutto or bacon into neat pieces, reserving the bacon rinds if possible.

Heat the olive oil with the bacon rinds (if you have them), add the onion and garlic and cook for several minutes, then tip into the pan containing the beans and liquid. Continue cooking for 10 minutes, then remove the bacon rinds and add the carrot, courgettes, celery and tomatoes. Cook for a further 10 minutes. Taste the soup and add more seasoning if required.

If using long pasta, break this into small pieces; small pasta shapes can be left whole. Shred the cabbage or greens finely. Put the prosciutto or bacon, pasta and cabbage into the soup together with half the parsley and cook for a further 10 minutes. Top each serving with chopped parsley and cheese. Serve more bowls of cheese with the soup.

Variations

- The proportions and variety of vegetables can be changed according to personal preference and what is in season: 1 or 2 peeled diced potatoes can be added to the soup above. Cook them in the oil with the onions.
- Use vegetable or chicken stock instead of water (see page 14).

Minestrone Alla Borghese: Follow the main recipe but omit the carrot. Add rather more celery plus 2 or 3 medium peeled and diced potatoes and 2 roasted and diced yellow peppers (see page 97). This soup is generally flavoured with basil, a bay leaf and parsley.

Minestrone Alla Genovese: Follow the main recipe but use both shredded cabbage and the same amount of shredded young spinach leaves. Flavour the soup with chopped basil as well as parsley.

Minestrone Alla Milanese: Substitute 100 g/4 oz (good ½ cup) Italian long-grain rice for the pasta. Add a few sliced green beans and peas to the other vegetables and omit the cabbage or other greens.

Freezing: This soup freezes well but it is better if the ingredients are not completely cooked before freezing.

Quick Tip

Use canned beans and a selection of frozen vegetables to save time in cooking and preparation.

MUSHROOM SOUPS

Mushrooms form the basis of a number of excellent soups. Their flavour is delicate, so do ensure that the other ingredients added to the soup do not overwhelm them. I prefer to use shallots instead of onions for this reason.

When cooking the Cream of Mushroom Soup as described below, you make a paler-coloured soup if you use button mushrooms and stir the cooked mushroom purée into the creamy mixture just before serving (see method 1). For a darker soup use large open mushrooms and follow method 2.

The wide selection of mushrooms on the market means that you can vary the flavour of soups by mixing two or three kinds, or choosing one of the lesser known varieties. I am particularly fond of a soup made with chestnut mushrooms.

CREAM OF MUSHROOM SOUP

Cooking time: 30 minutes • Serves 4 to 6

The skin of cultivated mushrooms adds flavour to soups, so do not peel it off. Simply wipe the mushrooms with damp kitchen paper, or wash in cold water if badly soiled. Always trim and discard the ends of the stalks, but use the remainder with the caps in the recipe.

Metric/Imperial	Ingredients	American
3 medium	**shallots or small onions**	3 medium
50 g/2 oz	**butter or margarine**	¼ cup
25 g/1 oz	**plain (all-purpose) flour**	¼ cup
600 ml/1 pint	**chicken stock (see page 14) or water**	2½ cups
450 g/1 lb	**mushrooms**	1 lb
300 ml/½ pint	**double (heavy) cream**	1¼ cups
to taste	**salt and freshly ground white pepper**	to taste
	To garnish	
	croûtons (see page 193)	

Method 1: Peel and finely chop the shallots or onions. Heat half the butter or margarine in a saucepan, add the shallots or onions and cook gently for 10 minutes, stirring constantly so that they do not discolour. Mix the flour in carefully, then gradually pour in the stock or water. Whisk or stir as the mixture comes to the boil and thickens. Cover the pan and simmer gently for 15 minutes. Sieve or liquidize the mixture and return to the pan.

Meanwhile, heat the remaining butter or margarine in a separate saucepan and cook the mushrooms gently for 10 minutes. Liquidize or process briefly so you have small pieces of mushroom left. If you do not have the necessary equipment, finely dice the mushrooms before cooking. Add the cooked mushrooms to the stock mixture together with the cream and seasoning. Reheat and serve garnished with croûtons.

Method 2: Cook the shallots or onions in 50 g/2 oz (¼ cup) of butter or margarine; add the roughly chopped mushrooms and cook for a further 5 minutes. Stir in the flour then add the stock or water and simmer for 15 minutes. Liquidize or process the soup, then add the cream and seasoning. Reheat, garnish and serve.

Variations

- Use 1.2 litres/2 pints (5 cups) milk and omit the cream. Add an extra 2 teaspoons of flour so that the mixture is adequately thickened. This less rich soup can be topped with a little yoghurt or single (light) cream, chopped parsley and a few sliced mushrooms instead of the croûtons.

Brown Mushroom Soup: Use the main recipe, but substitute good brown stock (see page 14) for the chicken stock or water. A slightly stronger taste can be given to the soup if clarified beef dripping is used instead of butter or margarine. Add the cream as before.

Freezing: This soup freezes well, but do not add the cream until you reheat the soup.

NETTLE SOUP

Cooking time: 15 minutes plus time to make stock • Serves 4 to 6

While nettles may be an enemy to keen gardeners, good cooks regard them with respect as they make a traditional and delicious soup. Choose only young nettle leaves from the tips of plants not exposed to traffic fumes.

The following verse, apparently written on a window, is by Aaron Hill (1685-1750).

> Tender-handed stroke a nettle,
> And it stings you for your pains;
> Grasp it like a man of mettle,
> And it soft as silk remains.

Even if you follow this advice, it is wise to wear rubber gloves when picking and preparing nettles: after cooking they do not sting. The quantity of leaves in the recipe below can be varied according to how strong you want the flavour. Never use old, tough leaves.

Metric/Imperial	Ingredients	American
225 to 350 g/8 to 12 oz	**young nettle leaves**	½ to ¾ lb
1 litre/1¾ pints	**beef stock or Beef Consommé** (see pages 13 and 49)	scant 4½ cups
to taste	**salt and freshly ground black pepper**	to taste
	To garnish	
	soured cream or yoghurt	

Wash the nettle leaves in plenty of cold water, do not drain them. Place in a saucepan with the water adhering to the leaves and cover tightly. Cook for 8 to 10 minutes, then sieve or liquidize the leaves. Return the nettle purée to the pan with the stock or consommé, heat and season to taste. Top each portion with soured cream or yoghurt.

Variations

- Substitute sorrel or spinach purée for the nettle purée in the main recipe.
- Use 225 g/8 oz (½ lb) nettle leaves instead of the sorrel leaves in the first recipe on page 99.
- Use 300 ml/½ pint (1¼ cups) nettle purée instead of spinach purée in the recipe on page 26.

Creamy Nettle Soup: Peel and finely chop 2 medium onions and 2 garlic cloves. Heat 50 g/2 oz (¼ cup) butter and add the onions and garlic. Stir over a low heat for 10 minutes so that they do not colour. Stir in 25 g/1 oz (¼ cup) plain (all-purpose) flour, then add 900 ml/1½ pints (3¾ cups) chicken stock (see page 14). Stir as the soup comes to the boil and thickens slightly. Add 225 g/8 oz (½ lb) young nettle leaves and cook for 15 minutes. Sieve or liquidize the soup. Return to the saucepan with 300 ml/½ pint (1¼ cups) single (light) cream and heat gently. Serve with croûtons (see page 193).

Freezing: All versions of this soup freeze well, but the Creamy Nettle Soup may separate a little (see page 16).

FRENCH ONION SOUP (SOUPE À L'OIGNON)

Cooking time: 30 minutes plus time to make stock • Serves 4 to 6

Onion soup is wonderfully warming for a cold day. The first recipe does not include the familiar cheese topping, but this appears in the Variations. Onions have a very definite flavour which I feel is enhanced by adding 2 or 3 cloves of garlic. I like strongly flavoured onions but that is a matter of personal choice. Use small onions or cut large ones into manageable pieces so they are easy and elegant to eat with a soup spoon.

Metric/Imperial	Ingredients	American
675 g/1½ lb	onions	1½ lb
2 or 3	garlic cloves	2 or 3
50 g/2 oz	butter	¼ cup
1.2 litres/2 pints	beef stock (see page 13) or water	5 cups
to taste	salt and freshly ground black pepper	to taste
	To garnish	
	chopped chervil or parsley	

Peel the onions, slice thinly and separate into rings. Peel and crush the garlic. Heat the butter, add the onions and garlic and cook over a low heat until the onions are delicately browned. Add the stock or water with seasoning to taste. Bring to the boil, lower the heat and cover the pan. Simmer steadily for about 20 minutes or until the onions are tender. Garnish and serve.

Variations

- More flavour can be given to the soup by adding a little cayenne pepper or grated nutmeg, a few drops of Worcestershire sauce or a dash of brandy.
- For a richer taste add 1 tablespoon (1¼ tablespoons) olive oil to the butter.

Soupe à L'Oignon Gratinée: Make the soup as above, then pour into warm bowls. Top with sliced and toasted French bread and cover with grated Gruyère cheese. Place under a preheated grill until the cheese melts. If your bowls are not flame proof (suitable for use under a hot grill), toast the cheese-covered bread separately, then put on the hot soup.

Creamy Onion Soup: Use 900 ml/1½ pints (3¾ cups) of chicken stock or water instead of beef stock in the main recipe. Blend 25 g/1 oz (¼ cup) plain (all-purpose) flour with the cooked onions. Continue as the recipe, but add 300 ml/½ pint (1¼ cups) single (light) cream or half milk and half cream to the cooked soup. Heat gently, garnish and serve.

Onion and Cheese Soup: Follow the recipe for Creamy Onion Soup above and serve it topped with thin slices of Gruyère or Cheddar cheese.

Thickened Onion Soup: Follow the main recipe but blend 25 g/1 oz (¼ cup) plain (all-purpose) flour with the cooked onions. Add the stock and stir as the soup comes to the boil and thickens slightly.

Freezing: All these soups freeze well, but those containing flour may separate when frozen; read the hints about counteracting this on page 16.

Quick Tip

All the soups can be cooked in a microwave. Grated or finely chopped onions, although not classically correct for French Onion Soups, cook more quickly than sliced onions.

CREAM OF PARSNIP SOUP

Cooking time: 30 to 40 minutes • Serves 4 to 6

Parsnips are so sweet that other flavourings are needed to prevent them becoming cloying. The lemon in the soup below and the curry paste in the recipe overleaf turn this vegetable into delicious soups.

Metric/Imperial	Ingredients	American
450 g/1 lb	parsnips, weight when peeled	1 lb
2 medium	onions	2 medium
50 g/2 oz	butter or margarine	¼ cup
25 g/1 oz	flour	¼ cup
750 ml/1¼ pints	vegetable or chicken stock (see page 14)	good 3 cups
2	lemons, rind only	2
to taste	salt and freshly ground black pepper	to taste
300 ml/½ pint	milk	1¼ cups
300 ml/½ pint	single (light) cream	1¼ cups
	To garnish	
	lemon segments	
	chopped chives	

Peel and slice the parsnips and onions. Heat the butter or margarine in a saucepan, add the onions and cook gently for 5 minutes, stirring well so they do not brown. Stir in the flour, then add the stock and bring to the boil. Add the parsnips.

Pare the top zest from the lemons, avoid any bitter white pith, add to the pan with a little seasoning. Cover and simmer for 15 to 25 minutes, depending on the age of the parsnips.

Remove most of the lemon zest; you could retain 1 or 2 small strips for extra flavour. Sieve or liquidize the soup, then return to the pan with the milk and reheat; add the cream and any extra seasoning necessary and continue heating.

Cut a few segments from the lemons and add to the soup with the chives immediately before serving.

Variations

- Use veal stock to give extra flavour.
- Add a pinch of saffron powder or turmeric to the stock to enhance the colour.

Creamed Root Vegetable Soup: Use a mixture of carrots, celeriac, swede (rutabaga) and parsnips.

Freezing: The puréed soup freezes well, but only add the milk and cream when reheating.

CURRIED PARSNIP SOUP

Cooking time: 30 to 40 minutes plus time to make stock • Serves 4 to 6

The amount and strength of curry flavouring used in this recipe is a matter of personal taste, but it is better to have a relatively mild flavour for a dish served at the beginning of a meal so that it does not spoil your palate for the food that follows. A recipe for making curry powder appears on page 21.

Metric/Imperial	Ingredients	American
450 g/1 lb	parsnips, prepared weight	1 lb
2 medium	onions	2 medium
2	garlic cloves	2
50 g/2 oz	butter	1/4 cup
1 tablespoon	curry paste or powder, to taste	1 1/4 tablespoons
1.2 litres/2 pints	vegetable or chicken stock (see page 14)	5 cups
1 tablespoon	grated or diced creamed coconut	1 1/4 tablespoons
to taste	salt and freshly ground black pepper	to taste
	To garnish	
	double (heavy) cream	
	chopped red pepper	
	chopped chives	

Peel and slice the parsnips; peel and chop the onions and garlic. Heat the butter in a saucepan, add the onions and garlic and cook gently for 5 minutes, stirring well so they do not discolour. Blend in the curry paste or powder with the onions.

Add the stock, bring to the boil, then add the parsnips and creamed coconut together with a little seasoning. Cover the pan and simmer for 15 to 25 minutes, or until the parsnips are tender.

Sieve or liquidize the mixture, return to the pan and heat thoroughly. Taste and adjust the seasoning. Garnish the soup with the cream, red pepper and chives.

Variations

- Follow the main recipe, but use 350 g/12 oz (³/₄ lb) carrots and 100 g/ 4 oz (¹/₄ lb) potatoes.
- Use swedes (rutabagas) instead of parsnips.
- Use turnips in place of parsnips or half turnips and half potatoes.

Curried Parsnip and Apricot Soup: To emphasize the sweetness of parsnips, add 100 g/4 oz (¹/₄ lb) tenderized apricots to the other ingredients. Increase the amount of stock by 150 ml/¹/₄ pint (²/₃ cup). Slice and soak the apricots in the stock for 1 hour before making the soup.

If using non-tenderized apricots, slice and soak overnight in cold water (sufficient to cover them), then simmer in the same water for 1 hour, or until tender. Add the apricots plus 150 ml/¹/₄ pint (²/₃ cup) of the cooking liquid to the boiling stock and the other ingredients. Proceed as the recipe on page 87.

Freezing: All these soups freeze well.

FRENCH PEA SOUP (POTAGE ST GERMAIN)

Cooking time: 35 minutes • Serves 4 to 6

The availability of frozen peas means that this soup can be made throughout the year, but it is at its best with young fresh peas. Thrifty cooks can use some of the tender green pods to add body, as well as extra flavour, to the soup (see Variations).

I like this soup made with stock from boiled bacon, but it has a more delicate taste if chicken stock is used. For a subtle taste use half bacon and half chicken stock.

Metric/Imperial	Ingredients	American
3 medium	shallots or small onions	3 medium
350 g/12 oz	peas	³/₄ lb
25g/1 oz	butter	2 tablespoons
900 ml/1¹/₂ pints	bacon or chicken stock (see page 14)	3³/₄ cups
small bunch	mint	small bunch
to taste	salt and freshly ground black pepper	to taste
1 teaspoon	caster sugar	1 teaspoon
1 tablespoon	plain (all-purpose) flour, optional	1¹/₂ tablespoons
150 ml/¹/₄ pint	milk	²/₃ cup
150 ml/¹/₄ pint	single (light) cream	²/₃ cup
	To garnish	
	chopped chervil or parsley	
	croûtons (see page 193)	

Peel and chop the shallots or onions; shell and weigh the peas. If using frozen peas, allow them to defrost slightly so the soup cooks more quickly.

Heat the butter, add the shallots or onions and cook gently for 5 to 8 minutes, stirring well so they do not discolour. Pour the stock into the pan, bring to the boil, then put in the peas, mint, a very little seasoning and the sugar. Cover the pan, lower the heat and cook for 15 minutes.

Remove the mint, sieve or liquidize the soup, then return to the saucepan. If the purée seems rather thin, mix the flour with the milk, add to the soup and stir as it comes to the boil. If sufficiently thick for your taste, omit the flour and simply add the milk. Cook steadily for 5 to 6 minutes. Add the cream and heat for 1 or 2 minutes. Taste and add extra seasoning if required. Serve garnished with the chervil or parsley and the croûtons.

Variations

- Take a few cooked peas from the soup before sieving or liquidizing it, and add them to the soup just before serving.
- Use about 350 g/12 oz (³/₄ lb) tender fleshy pea pods, wash then top and tail. The amount of peas could then be reduced to 225 g/8 oz (¹/₂ lb) if desired. When using pea pods, the soup must be sieved, not liquidized, for a smooth texture. Cook the pods with the peas.
- For extra richness add about 25 g/1 oz (2 tablespoons) butter to the very hot soup just before serving.
- The addition of mint is very much a British taste. The French version of the soup uses chervil or parsley instead.

Green Pea and Mushroom Soup: Follow the recipe for Potage St Germain on page 88. Slice 100 g/4 oz (¹/₄ lb) small button mushrooms or chestnut mushrooms and cook gently in 25 g/1 oz (2 tablespoons) butter until tender. Stir into the soup with the cream and heat.

Green Pea and Tomato Soup: This is a very happy marriage of flavours. Omit the flour, milk and cream in the main recipe, but add 450 g/1 lb chopped tomatoes. The mint can be retained or omitted. If omitted add 2 or 3 basil leaves instead.

Sieve or liquidize the soup, return to the pan and heat. Top with a little soured cream or yoghurt and croûtons before serving.

Freezing: All these versions of pea soup freeze well.

FRENCH POTATO SOUP
(POTAGE PURÉE DE PARMENTIER)

Cooking time: 35 minutes • Serves 4 to 6

The word Parmentier *indicates that a recipe should contain potatoes. This very simple soup is delicious and also forms the basis of other puréed soups (see Variations).*

Metric/Imperial	Ingredients	American
2 medium	leeks	2 medium
50 g/2 oz	butter	1/4 cup
350 g/12 oz	floury potatoes, prepared weight	3/4 lb
1.2 litres/2 pints	white stock (see page 14)	5 cups
2	fresh bay leaves or 1 dried leaf, optional	2
to taste	salt and freshly ground white pepper	to taste
	To garnish	
	chopped chervil or parsley	
	cayenne pepper or paprika	

Wash and slice just the white part of the leeks. Heat half the butter, add the leeks and cook gently for 5 minutes. Dice the potatoes. Pour the stock over the leeks, bring just to boiling point, then add the potatoes, bay leaves and a little seasoning. Cover the pan, lower the heat and cook gently for 20 minutes, or until the potatoes are just soft.

Remove the bay leaves, sieve or liquidize the soup and return to the pan. Heat thoroughly, add any extra seasoning required and the remaining butter just before serving. Garnish with the herbs and cayenne or paprika.

Variations

• You could top each serving of the soup with a small knob of butter before adding the garnish.

Cream of Potato Soup: Reduce the stock by 150 ml/1/4 pint (2/3 cup) and add this amount of single (light) cream before serving.

Jerusalem Artichoke Soup (Potage Purée de Topinambours): This soup is also known as Potage à la Palestine. Follow the main recipe or the variation above, but use Jerusalem artichokes instead of potatoes. You can also use shallots or onions instead of leeks.

Turnip Soup (Potage Purée à la Freneuse): Substitute very young turnips for the potatoes in the main recipe or Cream of Potato Soup variation. Turnips develop a stronger flavour as they age, so use only 225 g/8 oz (1/2 lb) older turnips with 100 g/4 oz (1/4 lb) peeled potatoes.

Leek, shallots or onions can be used to flavour this soup.

Freezing: All these soups freeze well, but add the cream only when reheating.

ROAST GARLIC

Garlic is used in a number of recipes in this book. If you find its flavour too pronounced, simply roast it before using.

Preheat the oven to 190°C/375°F/gas mark 5. If roasting 8 to 10 garlic cloves, heat 1 tablespoon (1¼ tablespoons) olive or sunflower oil in a baking dish. Peel each garlic clove, toss in the hot oil, then cook for 20 minutes or until golden in colour.

POTATO CREAM SOUP

Cooking time: 30 minutes plus time to make the stock • Serves 4 to 6

Do not imagine that a potato soup is dull – that's far from the case. It is full of flavour, particularly if based on ham stock. Alternatives to ham stock appear in the variations.

Metric/Imperial	Ingredients	American
300 g/10 oz	floury old potatoes, prepared weight	1⅔ cups when diced
600 ml/1 pint	ham stock (see page 14)	2½ cups
2 medium	onions	2 medium
1 fresh	bay leaf or ½ dried leaf	1 fresh
to taste	salt and freshly ground black pepper and/or cayenne pepper	to taste
15 g/½ oz	plain (all-purpose) flour	2 tablespoons
300 ml/½ pint	single (light) cream or half cream and half milk	1¼ cups
25 g/1 oz	butter	2 tablespoons
	To garnish	
	chopped chives and/or parsley	
	croûtons (see page 193)	

Peel and dice the potatoes and place in the ham stock so they do not discolour. Peel and finely chop the onions, then add to the stock with the bay leaf. Taste and add whatever seasoning is necessary; you may not need extra salt.

Bring the liquid to the boil, cover the pan and lower the heat. Cook steadily for 15 minutes or until the vegetables are tender. Sieve or liquidize the mixture and return to the pan. Blend the flour with half the cream, add to the soup and stir over the heat until boiling. Whisk in the remaining cream, or milk and cream, add the butter and any extra seasoning required. Heat thoroughly and top with the herbs and croûtons.

Variations

• Use water with 2 bacon rashers (slices) instead of ham stock. Dice the cooked bacon and use as a garnish on the soup.

- Use chicken stock instead of ham stock.
- Use water with vegetable stock cubes.
- Cook 1 or 2 chopped onions with the diced potatoes.

Potato and Celery Soup: Use only 225 g/8 oz (1¼ cups) diced potatoes plus ½ medium-sized heart of celery. Chop the celery and cook with the potatoes. Season the soup with celery salt rather than ordinary salt. Garnish with croûtons and small celery leaves.

Potato and Mushroom Soup: Follow the main recipe, but omit butter, cook 1 chopped onion with the potatoes. Dice 100 g/4 oz (1 cup) mushrooms, fry in a little butter and add to the soup just before serving. This method of incorporating the mushrooms does not spoil the colour of the potato mixture.

Potato and Watercress Soup: Follow the basic recipe but add a small bunch of watercress (tied securely) to the other ingredients; the stalks impart a good flavour. Remove the watercress before sieving or liquidizing the ingredients. Reheat as the recipe, adding about 6 tablespoons (7½ tablespoons) coarsely chopped watercress leaves with the butter.

Freezing: These soups tend to separate in freezing, so whisk or liquidize before reheating.

Quick Tip

Use dried (dehydrated) potato powder instead of ordinary potatoes. Blend 5 tablespoons (6¼ tablespoons) of the powder with the ham stock. Heat and continue as the main recipe.

SWEET POTATO SOUP

Cooking time: 25 to 30 minutes plus time to make stock • Serves 4 to 6

Sweet potatoes and yams (a similar vegetable) have become increasingly popular during the last few years. They can be used in place of ordinary potatoes in many vegetable soups. I like to add a small amount of sharp cooking apple to counter-balance their sweet taste, but tomatoes can also be used.

Metric/Imperial	Ingredients	American
2 medium	**onions**	2 medium
1 medium	**carrot**	1 medium
450 g/1 lb	**sweet potatoes or yams, unprepared weight**	1 lb
2	**celery sticks**	2
1 litre/1³/₄ pints	**chicken stock (see page 14)**	scant 4¹/₂ cups
100 g/4 oz	**cooking apple, prepared weight**	¹/₄ lb
to taste	**salt and freshly ground black pepper**	to taste
	To garnish	
	croûtons (see page 193)	

Peel the onions, carrot and sweet potatoes or yams and cut into small dice. Keep the potatoes or yams in water until ready to cook to prevent them from discolouring. Chop the celery finely. Bring the stock to the boil and add all the vegetables. Peel, core and dice the apple, then add to the other ingredients with a little seasoning. Cover and simmer for 25 minutes. Check the seasoning, then sieve or liquidize the soup. Return to the pan and reheat. Top with croûtons.

Variations

- The soup can be topped with a little soured or fresh cream.
- It is excellent made with bacon stock rather than chicken stock.

Sweet Potato and Tomato Soup: Omit the apple and carrot in the main recipe. Add 3 medium tomatoes, skinned, deseeded and chopped, together with 1 tablespoon (1¹/₄ tablespoons) tomato purée (paste) and 1 teaspoon finely chopped tarragon. Cook as before, then sieve or liquidize.

Yam Soup: Cook yams in exactly the same recipes as sweet potatoes. Although from a different family of vegetables, they have a similar flavour.

Freezing: All these soups freeze well.

CREAM OF ASPARAGUS SOUP 2

Cooking time: 25 to 30 minutes • Serves 4 to 6

Metric/Imperial	Ingredients	American
450 g/1 lb	asparagus	1 lb
900 ml/1½ pints	water	3¾ cups
2	roasted garlic cloves (see page 91)	2
to taste	salt and freshly ground black pepper	to taste
300 ml/½ pint	single (light) cream	1¼ cups

Wash the asparagus and cut off a few tips for garnish. Trim off the tough ends of the stalks, place these in the water with the garlic cloves. Simmer for 15 minutes to make stock. Strain the liquid and return most of it to the pan. Cook the tips in the small amount of reserved liquid until just soft. Chop the rest of the asparagus into small pieces; cook in the pan of stock for 10 minutes or until tender. Season to taste.

Sieve or liquidize the soup, add the cream and reheat or chill well. Top with the asparagus tips just before serving.

Freezing: Freeze the asparagus purée and tips, but add the cream only when defrosted.

There is another asparagus soup recipe on page 71.

PUMPKIN SOUP

Cooking time: 35 minutes plus time to make stock • Serves 4 to 6

Pumpkins, like all squashes, can be used in both sweet and savoury dishes; they make delicious soups. Since these vegetables do not have a great deal of flavour, they require generous amounts of added spices and herbs. If, however, you prefer a less strongly flavoured soup, you will find this under Variations. Although chicken stock can be used for this soup, I prefer it made with vegetable stock.

Metric/Imperial	Ingredients	American
1 medium	onion	1 medium
2	garlic cloves	2
1 medium	carrot	1 medium
550 g/1¼ lb	pumpkin, prepared weight, see method	1¼ lb
50 g/2 oz	butter	¼ cup
¼ teaspoon	ground ginger, or to taste	¼ teaspoon
¼ teaspoon	ground coriander	¼ teaspoon
1.2 litres/2 pints	vegetable or chicken stock (see page 14)	5 cups
1 teaspoon	chopped sage	1 teaspoon
1 tablespoon	finely chopped parsley	1¼ tablespoons
to taste	salt and freshly ground black pepper	to taste
	To garnish	
	1 red pepper (optional)	
	cream or yoghurt	

Peel and finely chop the onion, garlic and carrot. Peel the pumpkin, remove all the seeds and stringy bits. In order to have 550 g/1¼ lb pumpkin you will need to buy a good 900 g/2 lb of the vegetable. A few seeds can be retained and cooked as an unusual garnish (see Variations).

Heat the butter in a pan, add the onion and garlic and cook gently for 5 minutes. Add the carrot, pumpkin and spices and stir over a low heat for another 5 minutes. Add the stock with the herbs and a little seasoning. Cover the pan and simmer for 20 minutes, then sieve or liquidize the soup. Reheat before serving.

To prepare the garnish, halve and deseed the red pepper and place rounded side uppermost under a preheated grill until the skin turns black. Cool slightly, then remove the skin and dice the flesh very finely. Spoon cream or yoghurt over the soup, then top with the diced pepper.

Variations

• The seeds of pumpkin and other squashes may be separated and dried on kitchen paper, then cooked slowly in a little oil or butter until golden brown and slightly crisp. They make a pleasing garnish on the soup.

- Instead of ground ginger, peel and grate about 2.5 cm/1 inch fresh root ginger.
- A hotter flavour can be given to the soup if 1 deseeded, chopped red chilli is added to the other ingredients, or a good pinch of chilli powder added to the spices.
- Use peeled and deseeded squash or marrow in place of pumpkin, adding a pinch of turmeric with the other spices to enhance the colour.

Pumpkin and Sesame Soup: Follow the main recipe but use 2 tablespoons (2½ tablespoons) sesame seed oil instead of the butter. Omit the red pepper and garnish the soup with cream or yoghurt and sesame seeds.

Creamy Pumpkin Soup: Use the main recipe but add just 600 ml/1 pint (2½ cups) stock to the other ingredients. The spices can be reduced to just a pinch of each. The sage can be replaced with 2 teaspoons chopped thyme. Sieve or liquidize the soup then return to the pan with 300 ml/ ½ pint (1¼ cups) milk and 300 ml/1 pint (1¼ cups) single (light) cream. Heat and garnish with crisp pumpkin seeds and/or chopped parsley.

Instead of all single cream, use half single cream and half soured cream.

If the soup looks a little pale, mix a good pinch of turmeric with the milk before adding it to the puréed soup.

Freezing: The main recipe freezes well. The prepared and diced red pepper can also be frozen. When making Creamy Pumpkin Soup, it is better to freeze the puréed pumpkin mixture and add the milk and cream when reheating.

RED PEPPER BROTH

Cooking time: 35 minutes plus time to make stock • Serves 4 to 6

This very colourful soup is made with finely diced vegetables. Although it is not essential to skin the sweet (bell) peppers, they are more tender if this is done.

Metric/Imperial	Ingredients	American
2 large or 3 medium	red peppers	2 large or 3 medium
2 medium	onions	2 medium
1 or 2	garlic cloves	1 or 2
3 medium	tomatoes	3 medium
2 tablespoons	sunflower or olive oil	2½ tablespoons
900 ml/1½ pints	chicken or vegetable stock (see page 14)	3¾ cups
1 teaspoon	chopped basil	1 teaspoon
to taste	salt and freshly ground black pepper	to taste
To garnish		
chopped parsley and chopped basil		

Preheat the grill. Cut the peppers in half lengthwise, then remove the seeds and cores. Place the peppers under the heat, rounded sides uppermost, until the skins turn black. Allow to cool slightly, then peel off the skin.

If more convenient the whole peppers can be baked for approximately 30 minutes, or until the skins darken, in an oven preheated to 190°C/375°C/gas mark 5. Brush the peppers with a little oil before baking. When sufficiently cool to handle, peel off the skin, then halve and remove the cores and seeds.

Cut the flesh of the peppers into very small dice. Skin and finely chop the onions, garlic and tomatoes. Heat the oil in a pan, add the onions and garlic and cook gently for 10 minutes, stirring constantly so they do not brown. Add the peppers, tomatoes, stock, basil and seasoning. Bring to the boil, then cover the pan and simmer for 15 to 20 minutes. Adjust the seasoning, garnish and serve.

Variations

- Use 1 red, 1 yellow and 1 green pepper instead of 3 red peppers.
- Add a few finely chopped mushrooms to the other ingredients.
- Garnish the broth with small pieces of crisply cooked bacon.

Red Pepper Soup: Use the same ingredients as above, but sieve or liquidize the cooked vegetables. Reheat, then stir in about 150 ml/¼ pint (⅔ cup) single (light) cream or fromage frais. Heat gently, without boiling, then top with more cream or fromage frais and the chopped herbs.

Freezing: This soup freezes well.

Quick Tip

This is an excellent soup to cook in the microwave.

SPINACH AND ALMOND SOUP

Cooking time: 35 minutes plus time to make stock • Serves 6

This is a somewhat unusual soup from Yugoslavia, having an interesting taste and texture. As the soup is neither sieved nor liquidized, the onion should be finely chopped and the spinach cut into very thin shreds; use a stainless steel knife to do this so the vegetable does not discolour.

Metric/Imperial	Ingredients	American
1 medium	**onion**	1 medium
1 tablespoon	**olive oil**	1¼ tablespoons
450 g/1 lb	**young spinach leaves**	1 lb
3 tablespoons	**ground almonds**	3¾ tablespoons
100 g/4 oz	**long-grain brown or white rice**	¼ cup
1 litre/1¾ pints	**chicken stock (see page 14)**	scant 4½ cups
to taste	**salt and freshly ground black pepper**	to taste
1 to 2 tablespoons	**chopped dill, or to taste**	1¼ to 2½ tablespoons
300 ml/½ pint	**yoghurt**	1¼ cups
	To serve	
	3 large slices toast	
75 g/3 oz	**cottage or feta cheese**	3 tablespoons

Peel and finely chop the onion. Heat the oil in a really large saucepan, add the onion and gently cook for 5 minutes. Wash, drain and shred the spinach, discarding any stalks. Add the ground almonds to the onion and continue cooking until both ingredients are golden brown. Stir the rice into the onion mixture and add the stock. Bring to the boil, season to taste, then tip in the spinach. Cover the pan and cook steadily for 15 to 20 minutes, or until the rice is cooked.

Stir in half the dill and half the yoghurt and heat gently for 2 or 3 minutes.

Cover the toast with the cheese, cut into fingers or triangles and place on individual plates. Garnish the bowls of soup with the remaining yoghurt and dill.

Freezing: This soup is better freshly made.

SORREL SOUP 1

Cooking time: 30 minutes plus time to make stock • Serves 4 to 6

Sorrel is one of the early summer herbs that is often sadly neglected. The leaves look very like those of young spinach, and the flavour is not dissimilar. In this recipe the sorrel is used uncooked, but a variation follows which uses rather more cooked sorrel. Always shred sorrel and spinach with a stainless steel knife to avoid discoloration.

Metric/Imperial	Ingredients	American
1 medium	**onion**	1 medium
25 g/1 oz	**butter**	2 tablespoons
1 litre/1¾ pints	**chicken stock (see page 14)**	scant 4½ cups
225 g/8 oz	**sorrel leaves**	½ lb
to taste	**salt and freshly ground black pepper**	to taste
225 ml/7½ fl oz	**double (heavy) cream**	scant 1 cup
	To garnish	
	croûtons (see page 193)	

Peel and finely chop the onion. Heat the butter in a pan and cook the onion gently for 10 minutes, stirring from time to time so it does not discolour. Add the chicken stock, cover the pan and simmer for about 15 minutes.

Meanwhile, wash and dry the sorrel, shred and add to the hot liquid. Sieve or liquidize the soup. Return to the pan, add seasoning to taste and reheat. Whisk the cream into the hot, but not boiling, soup. Reheat gently for a few minutes then serve topped with the croûtons.

Variations

- Use vegetable stock instead of chicken stock.
- A few tablespoons of cooked rice can be added to the hot soup with the cream. In this case, omit the croûtons.

Sorrel Soup 2: Cook the onion in 50 g/2 oz (¼ cup) butter, then add 450 g/1 lb washed and shredded sorrel. Stir in 1 to 2 teaspoons finely chopped rosemary. Pour 1.2 litres/2 pints (5 cups) boiling water or chicken stock over the ingredients. If using water, add 2 teaspoons lemon juice to give more flavour. Season the soup, cover the pan and simmer for 15 to 20 minutes, or until the sorrel is tender. Sieve or liquidize the mixture and return to the saucepan.

Blend 2 egg yolks and 150 ml/¼ pint (⅔ cup) single (light) cream with a few tablespoons of the hot soup. Stir into the purée and simmer gently for a few minutes. Serve garnished with croûtons.

Cabbage Soups: Follow either of the recipes for Sorrel Soup, but use 2 onions. If using recipe 1, use half the heart of a small, firm green cabbage. If using recipe 2, use a whole small cabbage heart. Cabbage has less flavour than sorrel, so it is advisable to use either chicken or vegetable stock rather than water.

Chopped tarragon, parsley or chives complement cabbage better than rosemary.

Spinach Soups: Follow either of the recipes for Sorrel Soup, but use spinach instead of sorrel.

In recipe 2 tarragon is a better herb to use than rosemary.

Freezing: All the above soups freeze well.

TOMATO AND MUSHROOM SOUP

Cooking time: 30 minutes plus time to make stock • Serves 4 to 6

This soup combines two favourite ingredients. It is important not to exceed the weight of mushrooms as this will spoil the tomato flavour. This soup is generally served without sieving or liquidizing the ingredients, so do ensure they are chopped evenly and finely.

Metric/Imperial	Ingredients	American
2 medium	onions	2 medium
675 g/1½ lb	ripe tomatoes	1½ lb
100 g/4 oz	small button mushrooms	¼ lb
50 g/2 oz	butter	¼ cup
600 ml/1 pint	chicken stock (see page 14)	2½ cups
1 to 2 teaspoons	Worcestershire sauce	1 to 2 teaspoons
to taste	salt and freshly ground black pepper	to taste
1 to 2 teaspoons	sugar, preferably brown	1 to 2 teaspoons
To garnish		
chopped basil, tarragon or parsley		

Peel and finely chop the onions. Skin and halve the tomatoes, remove the seeds and chop the pulp neatly: this process is known as concassing. Wipe and dice the mushroom caps; the stalks can be trimmed and finely chopped too.

Heat the butter in a saucepan, add the onions and cook gently for 5 minutes. Add the tomatoes and mushrooms and cook for a further 5 minutes, stirring frequently so they do not discolour. Add the stock and remaining ingredients. Bring just to boiling point, then cover the pan and lower the heat. Simmer for 15 minutes, check the seasoning, then garnish and serve.

Variation

• The soup can be sieved or liquidized but it then has rather a thin consistency. To overcome this, blend 3 tablespoons (3¾ tablespoons) plain (all-purpose) flour with 4 tablespoons (5 tablespoons) cold stock or sherry, add to the soup and stir over a moderate heat until thickened and smooth. Garnish with soured cream, yoghurt or cream cheese and chopped herbs.

Freezing: Both versions of this soup freeze well.

Quick Tip

This is an ideal soup to make in the microwave.

TOMATO SOUP

Cooking time: 30 minutes • Serves 4

In spite of the great variety of soups that can be made at home, or purchased in diverse forms, there is no doubt that tomato soups still head the list of favourites for most people, especially children. There are so many ways of making this soup that I have given a selection of recipes. The first is a very basic one, which is better made with water rather than stock.

In all the recipes the tomatoes, preferably the plum variety, should be fully ripe to give the maximum flavour. Do not overcook the soup, for this will destroy the fresh tomato taste.

The amount of sugar added depends upon personal taste and the season. Freshly picked tomatoes generally have a much sweeter flavour than imported winter produce. Canned plum tomatoes or containers of Italian pomodori make a good soup (see Variations).

In the recipes where stock is mentioned, choose one with a mild taste or dilute strong stock with water (unless stated otherwise); or use half the normal amount of stock cubes.

Metric/Imperial	Ingredients	American
675 g/1½ lb	tomatoes	1½ lb
1 medium	onion	1 medium
1	garlic clove	1
2 rashers	lean bacon	2 slices
25 g/1 oz	butter or margarine	2 tablespoons
300 ml/½ pint	water	1¼ cups
1 tablespoon	tomato purée (paste)	1¼ tablespoons
1	bouquet garni*	1
to taste	salt and freshly ground black pepper	to taste
1 teaspoon	sugar, preferably brown, or to taste	1 teaspoon
	To garnish	
	cream, yoghurt or fromage frais	
	chopped parsley or chives	

*Small sprigs of basil, parsley and thyme are ideal for this soup.

Chop the tomatoes into small pieces. If you intend to liquidize rather than sieve the soup and want it to be completely smooth, skin, halve and deseed the tomatoes first.

Peel and chop the onion and garlic, derind the bacon and chop the rashers. Heat the butter or margarine with the bacon rinds in a saucepan, add the onions, garlic and bacon. Cook over a low heat for 5 minutes. Do not allow to brown. Add the remaining ingredients and bring the soup to simmering point. Cover the pan, cook for 20 minutes, then remove the bacon rinds and bouquet garni.

Sieve or liquidize the soup, return to the pan and reheat. You may need to add additional seasoning and sugar. Top with cream, yoghurt or fromage frais and herbs before serving. This soup is also good cold (see page 178).

Variations

- Vegetarians can omit the bacon and use 40 g/1½ oz (3 tablespoons) margarine plus an extra onion and/or garlic clove to give more flavour.
- Use 550 g/1¼ lb canned chopped tomatoes or pomodori instead of fresh tomatoes.
- **For a thicker soup,** mix 25 g/1 oz (¼ cup) flour with the cooked onion mixture.

Herb-Flavoured Tomato Soups: Many herbs combine well with tomatoes, so you may like to omit the bouquet garni, which gives a delicate taste, and emphasize just one herb, such as **basil, fennel leaves, oregano, rosemary, tarragon or thyme**.

Chop enough herbs to give up to 4 teaspoonfuls. Add gradually to the other ingredients until you achieve the desired flavour. Garnish the soup with the herb used in cooking. Be very sparing if using dried herbs – ½ to 1 teaspoon is generally sufficient.

Cream of Tomato Soup 1: Follow the main recipe, then sieve or liquidize the mixture and return to the saucepan.

In another saucepan make a White Sauce (see page 24) with 25 g/1 oz (2 tablespoons) butter or margarine, 25 g/1 oz (¼ cup) plain (all-purpose) flour and 300 ml/½ pint (1¼ cups) milk. When thickened, add 150 ml/ ¼ pint (⅔ cup) of single (light) cream. Whisk the very hot sauce into the very hot, but not boiling, tomato soup and stir over a low heat until well blended. Check the seasoning and serve. This variation serves 6.

Cream of Tomato Soup 2: Mix 25 g/1 oz (2 tablespoons) butter with 25 g/1 oz (¼ cup) plain (all-purpose) flour to make a beurre manié. Gradually drop small amounts of this (see page 9) into the basic hot tomato soup. When absorbed, make sure the soup is no longer boiling, then whisk in 150 to 300 ml/¼ to ½ pint (⅔ to 1½ cups) single (light) or double (heavy) cream, depending on how rich you want the soup to be. Stir until heated and serve topped with croûtons (see page 193). This variation serves 4 to 6.

Tomato and Beef Soup: Use fairly strongly flavoured beef stock (see page 13) instead of water in the main recipe, and stir in approximately 6 tablespoons (7½ tablespoons) minced or finely diced cooked beef. Heat for a few minutes before serving.

Tomato and Chicken Soup: Use chicken stock (see page 14) instead of water in the main recipe. Stir approximately 8 tablespoons (10 tablespoons) minced or finely diced cooked chicken breast and 4 tablespoons (5 tablespoons) neatly diced raw mushrooms into the soup just before serving. Heat for a few minutes. In this variation the chicken stock can be quite strongly flavoured.

Tomato and Lemon Soup: Follow the main recipe, but omit the bacon and bouquet garni. Add 1 teaspoon finely grated lemon zest, 2 tablespoons (2½ tablespoons) lemon juice plus 2 stems finely chopped lemon grass to the other ingredients. This soup is equally good hot or cold. Garnish with lemon slices.

Tomato and Potato Soup: Follow the main recipe but use chicken stock (see page 14) instead of water and add 2 medium peeled and diced potatoes to the other ingredients. Sieve or liquidize the ingredients to make a thick purée, then add extra stock, milk or cream to produce the right consistency. Heat carefully if using milk or cream and do not allow to boil. This variation serves 5 or 6.

This soup can be served without sieving or liquidizing, but all the ingredients should be neatly and finely diced.

Tomato and Vegetable Soup: Use about 350 g/12 oz (¾ lb) root vegetables (unprepared weight), such as **carrots, celeriac, swede (rutabaga), turnips** or chopped **celery heart** in place of the potatoes above, and adjust the amount of liquid as suggested.

Bulgarian Tomato Soup with Cheese: Follow the main recipe, omitting the bacon if you wish. Add salt and 1 to 2 teaspoons paprika for flavour. Sieve or liquidize the soup, then return to the pan and reheat. Add about 5 tablespoons (6¼ tablespoons) soft cream cheese or grated cheese and stir until just melted. Do not overcook at this stage or the cheese becomes stringy.

Austrian Tomato Soup: A typical Austrian tomato soup depends very much on generous amounts of vegetables and herbs. Chop enough parsley, young spinach leaves, celery and carrot to give 2 tablespoons (2½ table-spoons) of each ingredient. Peel and finely chop 1 medium onion. Heat 50 g/2 oz (¼ cup) butter in a saucepan and gently cook the onion, vegetables and parsley for 10 minutes, taking care they do not discolour. Add 675 g/1½ lb chopped tomatoes with 300 ml/½ pint (1¼ cups) water, 150 ml/¼ pint (⅔ cup) red wine and seasoning to taste. Cook for approximately 25 minutes in a covered pan, then sieve or liquidize, return to the saucepan and reheat. This soup can also be served without sieving.

Just before serving 3 tablespoons (3¾ tablespoons) cooked long-grain rice can be added to the soup, and I often add 1 teaspoon caraway seeds at the same time. Top the hot soup with soured cream before serving.

Italian Tomato Soup: Follow the main recipe, but omit the bacon and use 750 ml/1¼ pints (good 3 cups) chicken or other white stock (see page 14). Fry the onion and garlic in the butter or margarine, add the tomatoes and liquid with 3 tablespoons (3¾ tablespoons) arborio (Italian risotto) rice. Cook as the recipe. This soup can be sieved or liquidized if you wish. An extra 25 g/1 oz (2 tablespoons) butter should be stirred into the soup just before serving to enrich it.

A few pieces of finely chopped sun-dried tomatoes (preferably those bottled in olive oil) may be added to the soup just before serving, or before sieving or liquidizing if you prefer a smooth puréed soup. These add a particularly interesting flavour.

Freezing: Most of these tomato soups freeze well, the exceptions being the cream soups, which tend to separate during freezing. (See page 16 for hints on returning them to their original smooth texture.) To avoid this problem, freeze the basic tomato purée and combine with the white sauce or cream *after* defrosting. Always reheat creamed soups gently as the acid content of the tomatoes could cause the soup to curdle if allowed to boil vigorously.

VEGETABLE GUMBO

Cooking time: 30 minutes plus time to make stock • Serves 4 to 6

A gumbo is a soup that contains okra, sometimes called ladies' fingers because of their shape. As these give a slightly odd colour to the soup, I like to add tomatoes for a pleasantly reddish appearance. This recipe uses chicken stock, which I find enhances the flavour of the okra, but vegetable stock could be used instead.

Metric/Imperial	Ingredients	American
350 g/12 oz	okra	³/₄ lb
2 medium	onions	2 medium
1	garlic clove	1
3 medium	tomatoes	3 medium
2 tablespoons	olive or sunflower oil	2¹/₂ tablespoons
1.2 litres/2 pints	chicken stock (see page 14)	5 cups
1 tablespoon	chopped parsley	1¹/₄ tablespoons
to taste	salt and freshly ground black pepper	to taste
To garnish		
4 tablespoons (5 tablespoons) cooked rice		
chopped parsley		

Wipe and slice the okra. Peel and chop the onions, garlic and tomatoes. Heat the oil and cook the onions and garlic gently for 5 minutes, stirring well so they do not brown. Stir in the tomatoes and okra and cook for 5 more minutes.

Pour in the stock, bring to the boil, then stir in the parsley and seasoning. Cover the pan and simmer for 15 to 20 minutes.

Stir in the rice and heat for 1 or 2 minutes. Top the soup with the parsley.

Variation

• Before slicing the okra it can be blanched by cooking it for 2 minutes in boiling salted water.

Do not freeze.

CHEDDAR AND POTATO CHOWDER

Cooking time: 30 minutes plus time to make stock • Serves 4 to 6

This is a very satisfying soup and is suitable for vegetarians. Other chowders appear on pages 42, 70 and 122 to 124.

Metric/Imperial	Ingredients	American
4 medium	potatoes	4 medium
3 medium	onions	3 medium
50 g/2 oz	butter or margarine	¼ cup
900 ml/1½ pints	vegetable stock (see page 14)	3¾ cups
to taste	salt and freshly ground black pepper	to taste
1 teaspoon	ready-made English or French mustard	1 teaspoon
1	bouquet garni*	1
150 ml/¼ pint	single (light) cream or milk	⅔ cup
225 g/8 oz	Cheddar cheese	½ lb
	To garnish	
	chopped parsley	

* Small sprigs of savory, thyme and parsley should be tied together or placed in muslin.

Peel the potatoes and cut into 1.25 cm/½ inch dice. Peel the onions and cut into 6 mm/¼ inch dice. Heat the butter or margarine in a saucepan, add the onions and cook slowly for 5 or 6 minutes. Put in the potatoes and cook, stirring constantly, until both vegetables are a delicate golden colour.

Pour in the stock, bring just to boiling point, then add the seasoning, mustard and bouquet garni. Cover the pan, lower the heat and simmer for approximately 10 minutes or until the vegetables are just tender.

Meanwhile, grate half the cheese and cut the rest into 1.25 cm/½ inch dice. Remove bouquet garni, add cream and grated cheese and stir over the heat until the cheese has just melted – do not overcook. Top with the diced cheese and parsley immediately before serving.

SOUPS WITH PULSES

All the pulses – beans, peas and lentils – make excellent soups. Their food value is high, being excellent sources of protein and fibre.

Check the consistency of soups made with *dried pulses* because they require long, slow cooking and may become too thick, especially if the lid of the pan is not a good fit and too much liquid has evaporated. It is, however, quite easy to add a little extra stock or water at the end of the cooking time so that the soup has the consistency of thick cream.

Microwave cooking: Although this method can be used to cook these soups, dried beans never become quite as soft as when cooked by other means.

The amount of liquid given in the recipe can be reduced by 10 per cent. As large quantities of liquid take a long time to heat in the microwave, save time by bringing the pulses, their soaking water and any other ingredients to the boil in a saucepan. Allow the soup to boil for several minutes (10 minutes in the case of dried beans to make sure harmful enzymes are destroyed). Transfer the very hot mixture to a heated microwave bowl, cover and continue cooking on defrost setting for approximately half the time it would take in a saucepan. The time will vary slightly according to the output of the microwave being used.

Pressure cooking: Dried pulses cook quickly and easily in a pressure cooker. Soak them as directed in the recipes, then place in the pressure cooker with the liquid and other ingredients. Fix the lid and bring up to full pressure (high). Maintain at this pressure throughout the cooking time. It is essential that the pressure cooker is never more than half filled with the ingredients. Always allow the pressure to drop to room temperature.

Dried bean soup takes about 20 minutes at pressure, or a little longer if the beans are large. Dried pea soup takes 15 minutes at pressure, and lentils 10 to 15 minutes, depending upon the type.

You can reduce the amount of liquid given in the recipe by 25 per cent.

If milk or cream is added to the soup, this must be done after the pressure has dropped. Use the cooker like an ordinary saucepan at this stage.

Slow cooking: The soaked pulses with the stock and other ingredients must be brought to the boil in an ordinary saucepan first. When using dried beans, boil for 10 minutes to kill harmful enzymes. Transfer the soup to the heated container in the slow cooker and allow to cook for 5 to 6 hours, or even more if convenient. The pulses will then be very tender.

Use the same amount of liquid as given in the recipes.

ARABIC WHITE SOUP

Cooking time: 1¼ hours • Serves 4

It may seem strange that this soup with its generous amount of beans should be served cold, but it is traditional. It is also sustaining and refreshing.

Metric/Imperial	Ingredients	American
175 g/6 oz	haricot (navy) beans	⅔ cup
to taste	salt and freshly ground white pepper	to taste
100 g/4 oz	almonds	scant 1 cup
1	garlic clove	1
1 to 2 tablespoons	virgin olive oil	1¼ to 2½ tablespoons
as required	ice-cold water	as required
3 tablespoons	soft breadcrumbs	3¾ tablespoons
1 tablespoon	chopped parsley	1¼ tablespoons
2 teaspoons	chopped mint	2 teaspoons

Soak the beans in cold water for several hours. Drain, then cover in fresh cold water. Bring to the boil and boil briskly for 10 minutes. Lower the heat and add a little seasoning. Cover the pan and simmer until the beans are tender. Strain and allow to become cold.

Blanch and chop the almonds. Peel and crush the garlic. Mix the almonds, garlic and olive oil into the beans and gradually add enough water to make the consistency of a thick soup. Stir in the breadcrumbs, parsley and mint and season well. Chill before serving.

Do not freeze.

Quick Tip

Use canned beans, drained and rinsed in cold water.

BUTTER BEAN SOUP

Cooking time: 2 hours • Serves 4 to 6

This dried bean soup is ideal for a light main meal and lends itself to many variations. The other ingredients included add a great deal of flavour and colour to the beans.

Metric/Imperial	Ingredients	American
225 g/8 oz	dried butter (lima) beans	½ lb
1.8 litres/3 pints	bacon or chicken stock (see page 14)	7½ cups
2 medium	onions	2 medium
2	garlic cloves	2
2 medium	carrots	2 medium
2	celery sticks	2
350 g/12 oz	tomatoes	¾ lb
to taste	salt and freshly ground black pepper	to taste
1 teaspoon	chopped savory leaves or pinch dried savory	1 teaspoon
1 tablespoon	chopped parsley	1¼ tablespoons
1 teaspoon	finely grated lemon rind	1 teaspoon
	To garnish	
	soured cream	

Wash the beans, place in the stock and soak overnight, or bring just to the boil and simmer steadily for 10 minutes. Cover the pan and allow to stand for 2 or 3 hours.

Peel and finely chop the onions and garlic; peel and slice the carrots; chop the celery and tomatoes. Add to the pan of beans and stock with some seasoning, be sparing with the salt if using bacon stock. Add the herbs and lemon rind. Cover the pan, bring to the boil and boil briskly for 10 minutes. Lower the heat and simmer gently for 1½ to 1¾ hours or until the beans are tender.

Sieve or liquidize the soup, add a little additional stock if it is rather thick, then return to the pan and reheat. Check the seasoning and serve topped with soured cream.

Variations

- Substitute basil for savory in the main recipe.
- Use white or red haricot (navy) beans instead of butter (lima) beans.

Butter (Lima) Bean Broth: Do not sieve or liquidize the soup above. Top with plenty of freshly chopped parsley and the soured cream.

Adzuki Bean Soup: These dried reddish beans make a delicious soup. They are more expensive than other beans and have a distinctly sweet taste, so you might like to add a little lemon juice to the main recipe.

Follow the main recipe on page 108 but use only 2 medium tomatoes and 1 garlic clove.

Prepare the adzuki beans in the same way as the butter beans, but simmer with the other ingredients for only 45 minutes to 1 hour. Check the seasoning and serve.

Black Bean Soup: If possible, always use bacon stock (see page 14) for a soup based on these excellent black beans. Add several chopped bacon rashers (slices) to the other ingredients listed in the main recipe, and use 1 teaspoon ground cumin instead of the savory.

If you like a hot flavour, add ½ to 1 teaspoon chilli powder with the other seasoning, or include 1 deseeded and chopped red chilli pepper with the rest of the ingredients. Garnish this soup with sliced lemon instead of soured cream.

Cannellini Bean Soup: Follow the main recipe, but use only 1 medium tomato and 1 garlic clove as cannellini beans have a very delicate flavour. Prepare the cannellini in the same way as butter beans, but simmer with the other ingredients for only 45 minutes.

This soup is delicious topped with cream cheese.

Vegetarian Dried Bean Soups: Use vegetable stock (see page 14) instead of bacon or chicken stock in any of the recipes on pages 107 to 110.

Freezing: All the puréed bean soups freeze well. The beans in Butter (Lima) Bean Broth are inclined to become over-soft with freezing, so undercook the soup slightly if you intend to freeze it.

HARICOT BEAN SOUP

Cooking time: 25 minutes • Serves 4

This is a good soup to make from store-cupboard ingredients when time is short. The various ingredients give such a good flavour that there is no need to make stock.

Metric/Imperial	Ingredients	American
2 medium	potatoes	2 medium
2 medium	onions	2 medium
2 or 3 rashers	bacon	2 or 3 slices
1 x 450 g/1 lb can	chopped tomatoes	1 x 1 lb can
600 ml/1 pint	water	2½ cups
1 x 225 g/8 oz can	baked (navy) beans in tomato sauce	1 x ½ lb can
to taste	salt and freshly ground black pepper	to taste
1 teaspoon	chopped fresh oregano or marjoram or ½ teaspoon dried herbs	1 teaspoon
To garnish		
chopped chives		

Peel and grate or finely dice the potatoes and onions. Cut the rinds from the bacon and chop the rashers into bite-sized pieces. Put the vegetables, bacon rinds and rashers and the canned tomatoes into a saucepan with the water. Bring to the boil, lower the heat and cover the pan. Simmer for 15 minutes or until the onions and potatoes are just soft.

Add the baked beans, seasoning and herbs. Simmer for 5 minutes, then remove the bacon rinds. Serve topped with chives.

Variations

- Vegetarians can omit the bacon and add a little finely chopped celery instead.
- Use cooked haricot (navy) beans or other varieties of beans plus 1 tablespoon (1¼ tablespoons) tomato purée (paste) to give extra flavour.

Do not freeze.

LENTIL SOUP

Cooking time: 1 hour plus time to make stock • Serves 4 to 6

This is the soup I make when I have some stock left from boiling a piece of bacon. In my opinion the two flavours – bacon and lentils – are a perfect partnership. I generally use the small orange lentils, although for a more delicate flavour I sometimes substitute the delicious French lentilles de Puy. These green lentils do take about 50 per cent longer to cook, so increase the amount of stock to 900 ml/1½ pints (3¾ cups).

Metric/Imperial	Ingredients	American
2 medium	onions	2 medium
1	garlic clove	1
1 medium	carrot	1 medium
1 small	dessert apple	1 small
600 ml/1 pint	bacon stock	2½ cups
1 bunch	bouquet garni*	1 bunch
225 g/8 oz	lentils	1 cup
to taste	salt and freshly ground black pepper	to taste
1 tablespoon	cornflour (cornstarch)	1¼ tablespoons
300 ml/½ pint	milk	1¼ cups
50 g/2 oz	butter	¼ cup
	To garnish	
	chopped parsley	
	croûtons (see page 193)	

* In this recipe tie together a small bunch of parsley, 1 sprig of thyme and 1 sprig of sage, or use ¼ teaspoon of each of these dried herbs.

Peel and finely chop the onions and garlic; peel and thinly slice the carrot and the apple (discard the core). Bring the stock to the boil, add the vegetables, plus the apple, bouquet garni and lentils. Lower the heat and season to taste, being sparing with the salt at this stage. Cover the pan and simmer for 45 minutes. Remove the bunch of fresh herbs.

Blend the cornflour with the milk, add to the hot soup and stir as it thickens. Sieve or liquidize the mixture, then return to the pan and heat thoroughly. If the soup is a little thick, add more stock or milk to give the perfect consistency. Stir in the butter just before serving and adjust the seasoning. Top with parsley and croûtons.

Variations

American Lentil Soup: Large American green and brown lentils give a wonderful flavour to soups. It is important to soak them in the stock (or other liquid) overnight. Use 1.2 litres/2 pints (5 cups) bacon stock (or half stock and half water for a milder flavour) to 225 g/8 oz (1 cup) lentils. You can use water or chicken stock, in which case add 2 to 3 diced uncooked rashers (slices) of bacon to the other ingredients when cooking the soup for a richer taste.

Put the lentils and their soaking liquid into a saucepan, add 2 medium sliced carrots, 2 chopped celery sticks, 2 medium chopped onions and 2 medium diced potatoes. Cook for 1½ to 2 hours, or until the lentils are tender. Season well and add 2 tablespoons (2½ tablespoons) dry sherry. Sieve or liquidize the mixture, then return to the pan and reheat. Stir 5 tablespoons (6¼ tablespoons) soured or fresh double (heavy) cream into the soup just before serving. Do not allow to boil.

This soup can be turned into a complete meal if about 350 g/12 oz (¾ lb) sliced cooked sausages or frankfurters are heated in the soup.

Austrian Lentil Soup (Linsensuppe): This is made in a similar way to the main recipe, but the lentils are cooked in 900 ml/1½ pints (3¾ cups) water rather than bacon stock. Omit the apple. The soup is given a sharp flavour by adding 1 tablespoon (1¼ tablespoons) red wine vinegar towards the end of the cooking time. Sieve or liquidize the soup. Heat 50 g/2 oz (¼ cup) butter in a saucepan, stir in 50 g/2 oz (½ cup) plain (all-purpose) flour and the lentil purée. Stir over the heat until thickened.

Lentil and Tomato Soup: Follow any of the three recipes on pages 111 and 113, using half stock or water and half tomato purée made with fresh or canned plum tomatoes. Where milk or cream are included, it is important that the soup is stirred well and heated thoroughly but not allowed to boil: this ensures it will not curdle.

Freezing: All versions of this soup freeze well.

INDIAN LENTIL SOUP

Cooking time: 45 to 55 minutes • Serves 4 to 6

In this recipe the tiny red or orange lentils, known as dhal *in India, are ideal. It is not essential to soak them before cooking, but if you do so, it shortens the cooking time by about 10 minutes. To bring out the maximum flavour of the spices, heat them in a dry frying pan. If you do not have the varieties mentioned, use curry powder (see Variations).*

Metric/Imperial	Ingredients	American
2 medium	**onions**	2 medium
2	**garlic cloves**	2
1 tablespoon	**ground cumin, or to taste**	1¼ tablespoons
2 teaspoons	**ground coriander, or to taste**	2 teaspoons
2 teaspoons	**ground ginger, or to taste**	2 teaspoons
½ teaspoon	**turmeric**	½ teaspoon
50 g/2 oz	**ghee* or butter**	¼ cup
1.2 litres/2 pints	**water**	5 cups
225 g/8 oz	**lentils, preferably red or orange**	1 cup
150 ml/¼ pint	**coconut milk****	⅔ cup
to taste	**salt and freshly ground black pepper**	to taste

* **To make ghee,** cover a quantity of butter with water and heat gently until the butter melts. Allow to become quite cold, then lift the clarified butter from the top of the water. It is possible to buy ghee from Indian shops and good supermarkets.

** **To make coconut milk,** cover 2 tablespoons (2½ tablespoons) desiccated coconut with 225 ml/7½ fl oz (scant 1 cup) boiling water. Allow to cool then strain and use the liquid. Another method is to heat 25 g/1 oz (good tablespoon) coconut cream with 150 ml/¼ pint (⅔ cup) water until dissolved.

It is possible to buy ready-made coconut milk.

Peel and finely chop the onions and garlic. Put the four spices into a dry frying pan and heat gently, stirring well, for 4 minutes. Add the ghee or butter, heat until melted, then tip in the onions and garlic. Cook over a low heat for 5 minutes, stirring well. Pour in the water, bring to the boil, then add the lentils, coconut milk and seasoning to taste. Bring just to boiling point, stir briskly, then cover the pan and lower the heat. Simmer gently for 30 to 40 minutes, or until the lentils are soft.

Serve the soup with the whole softened lentils or sieve or liquidize. Reheat before serving.

Variations

- Omit the four spices and use 1 to 2 tablespoons (1¼ to 2½ tablespoons) curry powder. The amount and strength of this depends upon personal taste.
- Many Far Eastern lentil recipes include tamarind purée. This comes

from a very acid-flavoured fruit shaped like a broad bean and is sometimes available canned: add 1 tablespoon (1¼ tablespoons) with the seasoning. If you find it in powder form, add ½ to 1 teaspoon. If you can't find it at all, add a little lemon or lime juice to give a sharper flavour.

Lentil and Vegetable Soup: Follow the main recipe but add 3 small, thinly sliced carrots, 1 diced aubergine and small pieces of peeled, diced marrow or 2 unpeeled, sliced courgettes (zucchini) to the liquid with only 175 g/6 oz (¾ cup) of lentils.

Freezing: This soup freezes well in any form.

DUTCH DRIED PEA SOUP (ERWTENSOEP)

Cooking time: 1¾ hours • Serves 4 to 6

This soup has a very meaty flavour because it includes brown stock, pork, frankfurters and bacon.

The British version (see Variations) has a different, but equally good, taste. It was given the name of 'London Particular' by the author Charles Dickens, who felt it resembled a real 'pea souper' the term used to describe London fogs in his day.

Metric/Imperial	Ingredients	American
300 g/10 oz	**dried split peas**	1¼ cups
2 litres/3½ pints	**brown stock (see page 14)**	8¾ cups
2	**fresh bay leaves or**	2
	1 dried leaf	
225 g/8 oz	**lean pork, weight without bone**	½ lb
2 medium	**onions**	2 medium
2 medium	**leeks**	2 medium
2	**celery sticks**	2
to taste	**salt and freshly ground**	to taste
	black pepper	
2 or 3	**frankfurter sausages**	2 or 3
	To garnish	
	2 or 3 bacon rashers (slices)	

Wash the peas in cold water, drain and place in the pan with the stock. Leave to soak overnight, or bring to the boil, simmer for 10 minutes, then allow to stand in the covered pan for 2 or 3 hours before cooking.

Add the bay leaves or leaf to the soup. Chop the pork very finely. Peel and chop the onions; wash and slice the white part of the leeks and a small part of the tender green stems; chop the celery. Add the meat and vegetables to the pan with a little seasoning.

Bring the stock to the boil, lower the heat, cover and simmer for approximately 1½ hours, or until the peas are tender. Sieve or liquidize the soup and return to the pan. If the soup is too thick, add a little more stock. Slice the frankfurters and simmer in the soup for 5 minutes.

Meanwhile, grill or microwave the bacon until crisp, then chop into small pieces. Check the seasoning in the soup and serve topped with the bacon.

Variations

- Salted pork is often used instead of fresh pork.
- Substitute the pork with 225 g/8 oz (½ lb) chopped bacon rashers.

Dried Pea Soup: Place 225 g/8 oz (1 cup) split dried peas in 1.8 litres/ 3 pints (7½ cups) bacon or chicken stock (see page 14) and soak overnight, or bring to the boil, cook for 10 minutes and allow to stand for 2 to 3 hours in the covered pan.

Add 2 chopped bacon rashers, 2 chopped medium-sized onions, 2 chopped large carrots, 1 or 2 sprigs of mint leaves or ½ to 1 teaspoon dried mint. Season with freshly ground black pepper, but be sparing with the salt if using bacon stock. Cover the pan and simmer for 1½ hours or until the peas are tender. Sieve or liquidize the mixture, then return to the pan. Add a little milk to thin slightly, check the seasoning and reheat. Garnish with croûtons (see page 193) and serve.

Vegetarian Dried Pea Soup: Omit the pork and bacon in the main recipe and the bacon in the second recipe, and use vegetable stock (see page 14).

To compensate for the lack of meat fat and for a stronger flavour add 2 or 3 chopped garlic cloves to the chopped onions in the main recipe and cook in 2 tablespoons (2½ tablespoons) olive or sunflower oil for 10 minutes. Add to the peas and stock.

Cooked vegetarian sausages could be added to the main recipe instead of frankfurters.

Chickpea Soup: Follow any of the pea soup recipes, substituting chickpeas for dried peas. When following either of the variations add 2 chopped garlic cloves to give a more pronounced flavour to the chickpeas.

Freezing: All the dried pea soups freeze well. Use within 4 to 6 weeks if including bacon in the ingredients.

The bacon garnish in the main recipe should be cooked just before serving the soup.

5 FISH SOUPS

S ome of the most luxurious and delicious soups are based on fish, and
a selection appears in the following pages. When preparing fish
soups, as with all fish dishes, it is absolutely essential to use really
fresh fish. Look for bright eyes, firm body and scales and absolutely no
smell of ammonia.

Shellfish keeps less well than white fish, so check the freshness
particularly carefully. You can tell if a lobster is fresh by pulling the tail: if
it springs back, you have no worry; if it is limp, the lobster is not fresh.
Crabs should smell pleasant and feel heavy for their size; if surprisingly
light, they are watery. Mussels have to be inspected carefully when
preparing and cooking (see page 127). Small shellfish, such as prawns
(shrimp) and scallops, should be firm, bright in colour and smell pleasant.

COOKING SHELLFISH

Most people like to buy shellfish ready-cooked, but it is quite easy to
cook them yourself.

Lobsters and crabs may be cooked in two ways. The method
considered most merciful is to put the shellfish into warm water and
gradually bring this to the boil. The alternative is to plunge the shellfish
into boiling water. With either method, lobsters and crabs change colour
when they are cooked.

Prawns are sold fresh or frozen. They can be defrosted at room
temperature or in a microwave oven.

The golden rule with seafood is not to overcook it: this results in loss
of flavour and texture in white fish and toughness in shellfish.

Microwave cooking: A microwave is splendid for cooking fish dishes,
but I have some reservations about using it for fish soups. It is so difficult
to assess the cooking time to the exact minute. Fish overcooked in a
microwave does not become dry, as it can in a conventional oven – it
becomes very hard and tough, really inedible. You must therefore be
prepared to check the cooking process continually or not use this
method.

Pressure cooking: Again, I would stress that cooking has to be done with
the utmost care, otherwise the fish in the soup will break badly. That may
not matter if the soup is sieved or liquidized, but in a chowder the
appearance is very important.

As cooking times for most fish soups are fairly short, I would be inclined
to rely on a good old-fashioned method, using a saucepan.

ABERDEEN SOUP

Cooking time: 25 minutes • Serves 4 to 6

I first made this soup many years ago when I had a portion of uncooked smoked haddock left. It is not only quick and easy to make, but is also very sustaining, especially if milk alone is used as the liquid. The slight curry flavour gives a piquancy to the soup.

Metric/Imperial	Ingredients	American
2	*eggs*	2
1 medium	*onion*	1 medium
1 to 2 teaspoons	*curry paste*	1 to 2 teaspoons
1.2 litres/2 pints	*milk or milk and water*	5 cups
50 g/2 oz	*long-grain rice*	⅓ cup
to taste	*salt and freshly ground black pepper*	to taste
225 g/8 oz	*smoked haddock, weight without bone*	½ lb
25 g/1 oz	*butter*	2 tablespoons
	To garnish	
	croûtons (see page 193)	

Hard-boil the eggs. Shell them and chop the yolks and whites separately. Peel and finely chop the onion. Blend the curry paste with a little of the milk or milk and water until smooth, then add to a large pan with the onion and remaining liquid. Bring just to boiling point, then add the rice plus a very little salt and pepper.

Bring the liquid to the boil, put in the smoked haddock. Cover the pan and simmer for 8 to 10 minutes, or until the fish is just cooked. Transfer the fish to a plate and continue simmering the rice for a further 5 minutes. Meanwhile, flake the fish, return to the pan with the egg whites. Taste the soup, adjust the seasoning and continue cooking for a further 3 to 4 minutes. Serve topped with the egg yolks. Add the crisp croûtons at the last minute.

Freezing: This soup freezes reasonably well. If possible, undercook the rice so that it does not become too soft on reheating. Omit cooked eggs until soup is defrosted. These become leathery in freezing.

CULLEN SKINK

Cooking time: 1 hour • Serves 4 to 6

This rather extraordinary name is given to a soup made from smoked haddock – finnan haddie as it is called in Scotland. There are many versions, depending on where in Scotland you are offered the soup. The version below is homely and very satisfying because a generous amount of mashed potatoes is mixed with the other ingredients.

Metric/Imperial	Ingredients	American
350 g/12 oz	potatoes, unpeeled weight	3/4 lb
to taste	salt and freshly ground black pepper	to taste
1 large	finnan haddock or 350 g/ 12 oz (3/4 lb) smoked haddock fillet	1 large
1 or 2 medium	onions, amount depends on personal choice	1 or 2 medium
750 ml/1¼ pints	milk	good 3 cups
25 g/1 oz	butter	2 tablespoons
4 tablespoons	double (heavy) or single (light) cream	5 tablespoons
	To garnish	
	chopped parsley	

Peel the potatoes and cook in a little salted water until just soft. Strain and mash until very smooth. Remove the skin from the haddock and set aside with the fins and tail. Cut the haddock into pieces. Peel the onion(s) but leave them whole. Place the haddock in a large pan, cover with water and cook until just tender. Remove from the liquid, flake the fish and take out all bones. Put these with the skin, fins and tail back into the liquid and cover the pan. Simmer steadily for 20 minutes, then strain 300 ml/½ pint (1¼ cups) of the fish liquid and put into a clean pan.

Add the milk, the flaked fish and the mashed potatoes; stir briskly to mix well, then bring to boiling point. Lower the heat and add the butter and cream. Simmer for a few minutes. Adjust the seasoning and serve topped with parsley.

Variations

- Omit the butter and cream and use a little more milk.
- Chop the onion(s) finely. Use only 2 small potatoes, diced and cooked until just tender. Add the chopped onions to the water when cooking the fish and keep them in the fish liquid when making the stock. Remove the skin etc. from this liquid, but retain the onions. Put the stock, with the onions, diced potatoes, flaked fish and milk into the saucepan. Add the butter and cream and heat as instructed in the main recipe.

Luxury Cullen Skink: Omit the potatoes and use a very large finnan haddock or 450 g/1 lb haddock fillet. Skin, cook and flake the haddock. Pound or liquidize with 2 hard-boiled eggs and a little milk until smooth. Stir in 900 ml/1½ pints (3¾ cups) of milk and 300 ml/½ pint (1¼ cups) single (light) cream. Season to taste and heat gently. Top with chopped parsley.

Freezing: The first version of this soup freezes well. Do not freeze the version containing hard-boiled eggs.

COCKLE SOUP

Cooking time: 30 minutes • Serves 4 to 6

My mother had a great fondness for cockles and from time to time used to make the following soup. I now realize that it has a great similarity to an American chowder, but as children we knew it simply as Mother's Soup.

Metric/Imperial	Ingredients	American
1.8 litres/3 pints	cockles	7½ cups
2 medium	onions	2 medium
2 small	leeks	2 small
2 medium	potatoes	2 medium
2 or 3 rashers	bacon	2 or 3 slices
25 g/1 oz	butter	2 tablespoons
900 ml/1½ pints	water	3¾ cups
½ to 1 teaspoon	anchovy essence	½ to 1 teaspoon
2 tablespoons	chopped parsley	2½ tablespoons
1 tablespoon	chopped chives	1¼ tablespoons
to taste	salt and freshly ground black pepper	to taste
300 ml/½ pint	single (light) cream	1¼ cups
	To garnish	
	chopped parsley	

Wash the cockles in plenty of cold water as they are inclined to be sandy; drain well. Peel and neatly dice the onions; slice the leeks, including a little of the tender green part. Peel the potatoes and cut into 1.25 cm/½ inch dice. Remove the rind from the bacon and cut the rashers into neat fingers.

Heat the butter and bacon rinds, add the onions and bacon and cook until the onions become golden brown and the bacon crisp. Pour the water into the pan, bring it to the boil, then add the anchovy essence and remaining vegetables, herbs and a little seasoning.

Cover the pan and simmer for 20 minutes, or until the vegetables are soft, but still a good shape. Remove the bacon rinds. Add the cockles and heat for 4 to 5 minutes – no longer – then serve topped with a generous amount of parsley.

Do not freeze.

CRAB AND AVOCADO SOUP

Cooking time: 30 minutes plus time to make fish stock • Serves 4 to 6

The combination of crabmeat and avocados in this Caribbean soup is a very pleasant one. The soup is beautifully creamy and satisfying. If you do not want the trouble of making stock from the crab shell, see Variations.

Metric/Imperial	Ingredients	American
1 medium	**cooked crab**	1 medium
900 ml/1½ pints	**fish stock (see page 15)**	3¾ cups
1 small	**onion**	1 small
2	**garlic cloves**	2
50 g/2 oz	**butter**	¼ cup
1 tablespoon	**plain (all-purpose) flour**	1¼ tablespoons
2	**ripe avocados**	2
2 teaspoons	**lemon juice**	2 teaspoons
150 ml/¼ pint	**single (light) cream**	⅔ cup
to taste	**salt and freshly ground black pepper**	to taste

Remove all the flesh from the crab; put a little of the white crabmeat on the side for garnishing the soup.

Put the body, shell and claws of the crab into the fish stock and bring to simmering point. Cover the pan and simmer for 15 minutes, then strain the liquid. By this time it should be reduced to 750 ml/1¼ pints (good 3 cups).

Peel and finely chop the onion; peel and crush the garlic. Heat the butter in a saucepan, add the onion and garlic and cook gently for 5 minutes. Stir in the flour then add the crab stock. Stir as the liquid comes to the boil, then add most of the crabmeat and heat for 3 minutes. Do not overcook as this toughens the crab. Halve the avocados, remove the skin and stones and cut the flesh into 6 mm/¼ inch dice. Add to the soup with the lemon juice, cream and seasoning. Heat gently and serve topped with the reserved white crabmeat.

Variations

- Use water instead of fish stock; this provides a less colourful liquid with slightly less flavour.
- If you do not want to use the crab shell, add a few drops of anchovy sauce or essence to give a stronger fish flavour and slightly pink colour to the liquid.
- Canned or defrosted frozen crabmeat can be used in this recipe.

Lobster and Avocado Soup: Use a small lobster in place of the crab. The shell can be simmered in the liquid before making the soup.

Prawn and Avocado Soup: Use about 100 g/4 oz (¼ lb) prawns (shrimp) instead of crabmeat. The weight refers to the prawns when peeled. Simmer the prawn shells in the stock or water to give extra flavour.

Freezing: Do not add the avocado if you plan to freeze this soup; it is best added when the soup is defrosted.

Quick Tip

This soup can be cooked in a microwave. Be very careful about heating the liquid once the shellfish has been added because overcooking toughens all fish.

CRAB AND PRAWN GUMBO

Cooking time: 35 minutes plus time to make stock • Serves 4 to 6

This is another Creole soup in which okra is used to give a special taste and texture. Fresh or frozen crabmeat can be used.

Metric/Imperial	Ingredients	American
1 medium	onion	1 medium
1	red pepper	1
3 medium	tomatoes	3 medium
450 g/1 lb	okra	1 lb
50 g/2 oz	butter	¼ cup
1.2 litres/2 pints	fish stock (see page 15) or water	5 cups
to taste	salt and freshly ground black pepper	to taste
450 g/1 lb	crabmeat and peeled prawn (shrimp)	1 lb
	To garnish	
	4 tablespoons (5 tablespoons) cooked rice, optional	
	chopped parsley	
	lemon segments	

Peel and finely chop the onion; deseed the pepper and cut the flesh into 1.25 cm/½ inch dice; skin and chop the tomatoes. Wipe and slice the okra.

Heat the butter in a pan, add the onion and cook gently for 5 minutes, stirring well so this does not brown. Stir in the pepper and tomatoes, then add the fish stock or water. Bring to the boil and cover the pan. Simmer for 15 minutes. Add the okra and seasoning to taste and continue cooking for a further 10 minutes.

Lastly, add the crabmeat and prawns and stir well. Spoon some of the rice in with the fish. Cook for 5 to 8 minutes, or until the soup is very hot, but take care not to overcook the crab. Garnish and serve.

Do not freeze.

PARTAN BREE

Cooking time: 30 to 35 minutes plus time to make stock • Serves 4 to 6

Meaning literally 'crab broth', Partan Bree is a Scottish recipe and one of the most famous crab soups in the world.

Metric/Imperial	Ingredients	American
1 large	cooked crab	1 large
75 g/3 oz	long-grain rice	½ cup
600 ml/1 pint	fish stock (see page 15)	2½ cups
600 ml/1 pint	milk	2½ cups
½ teaspoon	anchovy essence	½ teaspoon
to taste	salt and freshly ground white pepper	to taste
150 ml/¼ pint	single (light) cream	⅔ cup
	To garnish	
	chopped parsley	
	croûtons (see page 193)	

Remove all the flesh from the body and claws of the crab. Save a little white and dark meat to garnish the soup.

Put the rice and stock into a large saucepan, bring to the boil, then simmer for 20 minutes or until the rice is nearly tender. Add the milk towards the end of the cooking time and heat gently. Stir in the anchovy essence and crabmeat and add seasoning to taste. Avoid using too much salt. Simmer for a few minutes only until the crab is really hot, do not overcook. Stir the cream into the soup before serving and heat gently. Garnish with the reserved crabmeat, parsley and croûtons.

Do not freeze.

CHOWDERS

These soups are extremely popular in Canada and the USA. The word chowder comes from the French word *chaudière*, meaning a fish kettle. The most popular chowders are based on fish, sometimes mixed with pork, but those made with vegetables and meat are excellent.

Chowders should be full of ingredients – almost like a stew. It is important to cut the ingredients into even-sized pieces so that the soup looks attractive. Never overcook them because they should retain texture as well as flavour.

Although it is possible to cook chowders in a large bowl in a microwave, it is important to check the cooking process regularly so that the ingredients do not become too soft.

NEW ENGLAND CLAM CHOWDER

Cooking time: 30 minutes • Serves 4

Although Clam Chowder is a favourite in many parts of America, the New England version is the best known. If fresh clams are not available, use the canned variety or substitute cockles. Most cooks chop or mince the clams, but if they are very small this is not essential. If using fresh clams, save the liquid from the shells. A thick slice of salt pork is traditionally added to the soup but smoked bacon rashers (slices) can be used instead. Never overcook this soup because clams, like all shellfish, become tough.

Metric/Imperial	Ingredients	American
2 medium	onions	2 medium
3 medium	potatoes	3 medium
225 g/8 oz	salt pork or bacon	½ lb
900 ml/1½ pints	water	3¾ cups
900 ml/1½ pints	minced fresh clams and their liquid or equivalent in canned clams	good 4 cups
600 ml/1 pint	milk or half milk and half single (light) cream	2½ cups
to taste	salt and freshly ground white pepper	to taste
	6 to 8 plain crackers	
	To garnish	
	paprika	
	chopped parsley	

Peel and finely chop the onions. Peel the potatoes and cut into 1.25 cm/½ inch cubes. Derind the pork or bacon and dice the meat. Heat the rinds for 2 minutes, add the pork or bacon and cook for 2 to 3 minutes. Mix the onions and potatoes with the meat and stir over a moderate heat until pale golden in colour.

Remove the pork or bacon rinds, add the water and bring to the boil. Cover the pan, lower the heat and cook steadily for 10 to 15 minutes or until the ingredients are tender. Meanwhile, simmer the clams with their liquid for 2 to 3 minutes; if using canned clams, this is not necessary, just tip the clams and liquid into the soup, then pour in the milk or milk and cream. Taste the soup and add seasoning; you may not need salt. Heat thoroughly but do not boil.

Crumble the crackers into the soup bowls, add the hot soup and garnish with paprika and parsley.

Variations

- For a stronger flavour add 2 or 3 crushed garlic cloves to the onions.
- Use chicken or fish stock instead of water (see pages 14 and 15).
- To give more colour and flavour to the soup, add 2 or 3 finely diced celery sticks and ½ finely diced green pepper to the potatoes.

- Omit the milk and/or cream and use tomato juice instead.

White Fish Chowder: Follow the main recipe or incorporate some of the variations on page 123. If possible use fish stock (see page 15) instead of water. Lightly cook and dice 450 to 550 g/1 to 1¼ lb cod or other white fish, making sure it is free from skin and bone. Add to the soup instead of the clams.

Shellfish Chowder: Follow the main recipe or incorporate some of the variations above. If possible, use fish stock made from white fish and shellfish (see page 123). Add the diced flesh of a good-sized cooked lobster or crab, or 350 g/12 oz (2 cups) peeled shrimps, prawns (shrimp) or cooked mussels instead of the clams.

A female lobster containing the roe (coral) gives an especially good colour to the soup.

Do not freeze.

LOBSTER BISQUE

Cooking time: 25 minutes plus time to make stock • Serves 4

A bisque is a rich fish soup that includes cream. The secret of the good flavour is to use the shell of the fish to produce the stock. If you can buy a hen lobster, the red coral (roe) gives the soup a wonderful colour. (The tail of a hen lobster is broader than that of the male.)

Metric/Imperial	Ingredients	American
1 medium	cooked lobster	1 medium
900 ml/1½ pints	water	3¾ cups
1 medium	onion	1 medium
sprig	parsley	sprig
sprig	thyme	sprig
few	fennel leaves	few
to taste	salt and freshly ground white pepper	to taste
40 g/1½ oz	butter	3 tablespoons
25 g/1 oz	plain (all-purpose) flour	¼ cup
225 ml/7½ fl oz	double (heavy) cream	scant 1 cup
	To garnish	
	little double (heavy) cream, optional	
	chopped fennel or basil leaves	

Remove all the flesh and coral from the lobster.

To make the stock, crush the shell and place in a saucepan with the water, the peeled whole onion, herbs and a little seasoning. Cover and simmer for 30 minutes, then strain. You should have 600 ml/1 pint (2½ cups) of stock.

Heat the butter in a saucepan, add the flour and stir over a low heat for 2 or 3 minutes. Add the stock, bring to the boil and stir until thickened.

Flake the lobster flesh very finely; it can be pounded, if you wish, or processed for a very short time. Stir the flesh, coral and cream into the thickened mixture. Heat gently and serve with the garnish.

Variations

- Add 2 tablespoons (2½ tablespoons) brandy or dry sherry to the hot lobster soup: do not allow to boil.
- Another way of thickening a *bisque* is to omit the flour and stir 50 g/ 2 oz (1 cup) fine breadcrumbs into the soup before adding the lobster.

Crab Bisque: Use the flesh from a medium crab instead of the lobster. The colour of this *bisque* is improved by adding 2 to 3 teaspoons tomato purée (paste).

Salmon Bisque: Use 350 g/12 oz (¾ lb) cooked or canned salmon instead of lobster and fish stock (see page 15). The stock can be flavoured with a little chopped fennel and parsley.

Freezing: These soups freeze well provided the lobster and crab are *not* cooked in the hot liquid. Simply blend them into the thickened liquid, then cool and freeze. Add the cream and any alcohol when reheating the soup.

Quick Tip

Instead of making fresh stock, use ready-prepared fish stock.

MUSSEL CREAM SOUP (MOULES À LA CRÈME)

Cooking time: 30 minutes • Serves 4 to 6

This is a really delicious soup, combining mussels with the sharpness of white wine and a creamy sauce.

Metric/Imperial	Ingredients	American
1.8 litres/3 pints	fresh mussels	7½ cups
1 medium	onion	1 medium
300 ml/½ pint	dry white wine	1¼ cups
1 tablespoon	chopped parsley	1¼ tablespoons
50 g/2 oz	butter	¼ cup
50 g/2 oz	plain (all-purpose) flour	½ cup
600 ml/1 pint	milk	2½ cups
to taste	salt and freshly ground black pepper	to taste
150 ml/¼ pint	single (light) cream	⅔ cup
	To garnish	
	chopped parsley	
	lemon slices	

Clean the mussels, as described opposite. Peel and chop the onion; place in a pan with the mussels, wine and parsley. Heat until the mussels open, then strain the liquid and take the mussels off the shells.

Heat the butter in a saucepan, stir in the flour and cook gently for 1 or 2 minutes. Add the milk, stirring as the mixture comes to the boil and thickens. Add a little seasoning, then stir in the cream and mussel liquid. Heat gently, taking care not to boil the soup. Finally, add the mussels and continue cooking gently for 2 or 3 minutes. Top with the parsley and lemon slices.

Variation

Cream of Scallop Soup: Slice 8 medium scallops or halve about 24 queenies (tiny scallops). Poach them in 300 ml/½ pint (1¼ cups) dry white wine for a few minutes only until they turn opaque.

Make the sauce with butter, flour and milk, as in the main recipe. Add the cream. Heat thoroughly, then stir in the scallops and their poaching liquid. Heat for a few minutes without boiling, then serve topped with chopped parsley or fennel leaves and lemon slices.

Do not freeze.

MUSSEL AND TOMATO SOUP

Cooking time: 40 minutes • Serves 4 to 6

The combination of mussels and tomatoes is a very pleasant one, and basil, the perfect herb. I have been fairly generous with the amount of basil, so if it is not your favourite herb, use fewer leaves.

Metric/Imperial	Ingredients	American
1.8 litres/3 pints	fresh mussels	7¹/₂ cups
3 medium	onions	3 medium
300 ml/¹/₂ pint	dry white wine	1¹/₄ cups
1 tablespoon	chopped parsley	1¹/₄ tablespoons
550 g/1¹/₄ lb	tomatoes	1¹/₄ lb
2 tablespoons	olive or sunflower oil	2¹/₂ tablespoons
1.2 litres/2 pints	water	5 cups
to taste	salt and freshly ground black pepper	to taste
12 to 18	basil leaves, or to taste	12 to 18

To cook mussels: scrub shells in cold water, discard any that are open and do not close when tapped sharply. Remove any beards (seaweed-like growth on the shells). Put the mussels into a large pan. Peel and finely chop one of the onions; add to the pan with the white wine and chopped parsley. Place over a medium heat for 5 to 8 minutes, or until the mussels open. Discard any that remain closed. Watch this stage carefully for overcooking will make the fish tough. Cool sufficiently to handle. Remove the mussels and strain the liquid. Discard the shells, then return the mussels and the liquid to the pan.

While the mussels are cooking prepare the rest of the soup. Peel and finely chop the remaining onions; skin and chop the tomatoes. Heat the oil in another saucepan, add the onions and cook for 5 minutes over a low heat, stirring well so the onions do not brown. Add the tomatoes and continue cooking for another 10 minutes over the low heat. Add the water, seasoning and basil. Bring to the boil, lower the heat and cover the pan. Cook for 15 minutes, then add the mussels and the liquid from the second pan. Heat for a few minutes and serve with plenty of fresh crusty bread.

Variations

• To give a slightly crisp texture to the tomato mixture, chop a small celery heart very finely and add to the tomatoes halfway through the cooking period.

Mussel, Tomato and Rice Soup: Follow the main recipe but use 1.5 litres/2¹/₂ pints (6¹/₄ cups) water. Add 50 g/2 oz (4 tablespoons) long-grain rice to the onions and tomatoes, then add the liquid and proceed as the main recipe.

Do not freeze.

OYSTER CREAM SOUP (VELOUTÉ AUX HUÎTRES)

Cooking time: 25 minutes plus time to make stock • Serves 4 to 6

Nowadays oyster soup is considered something of a luxury, but in the nineteenth century oysters were regarded as poor man's food. In fact, Sam Weller in Charles Dickens' Pickwick Papers *stated 'that poverty and oysters always seem to go together'.*

Metric/Imperial	Ingredients	American
18 to 24 small	oysters	18 to 24 small
50 g/2 oz	butter	1/4 cup
50 g/2 oz	plain (all-purpose) flour	1/2 cup
600 ml/1 pint	fish stock (see page 15)	2 1/2 cups
300 ml/1/2 pint	milk	1 1/4 cups
300 ml/1/2 pint	single (light) cream	1 1/4 cups
to taste	salt and freshly ground white pepper	to taste
	To garnish	
	cayenne pepper	
	To serve	
	halved lemons	

When you, or the fishmonger, open the oysters, try to retain as much liquid in the shells as possible. Pour this into a container, then remove the oysters from the shells and cut into neat dice.

Heat the butter in a saucepan, stir in the flour and cook gently for 1 or 2 minutes. Add the fish stock and bring to the boil. Lower the heat, cover the pan and cook gently for 10 to 15 minutes. Add the milk and cream, heat a little and season to taste; remember oysters are very salty.

Add the diced oysters and oyster liquid, heat gently and serve dusted with cayenne pepper. Offer the lemons separately.

Variations

• For a lighter soup omit the milk and use that amount of extra fish stock.

Welsh Oyster Soup (Cawl Wystrys): This is a very unusual soup in that the oysters are combined with meat. You need about 24 small oysters to serve 4 to 6 people.

Peel 2 onions but leave them whole; put into a saucepan with about 225 g/8 oz (1/2 lb) scrag end of mutton or lamb, a few meat bones, 1.8 litres/3 pints (7 1/2 cups) of water and a blade of mace or pinch of ground mace. Bring to the boil and remove any scum. Cover the pan and simmer gently for 1 1/2 hours. Strain the liquid. If not clear, clarify as described on page 49. You should have no more than 900 ml/ 1 1/2 pints (3 3/4 cups) or a little less. If necessary, boil vigorously in an open pan to reduce to this amount.

Heat 50 g/2 oz (1/4 cup) butter in a saucepan, stir in 50 g/2 oz (1/4 cup) plain flour, then add the meat stock. Bring to the boil and cook, stirring well, until it thickens. Tip in the oyster liquid and season to taste. Either add the oysters and cook gently for 2 minutes or put the oysters into soup plates and top with the very hot soup. Garnish with raw, sliced leek and lemon wedges.

Do not freeze.

TROUT SOUP

Cooking time: 35 minutes plus time to make stock • Serves 4 to 6

Metric/Imperial	Ingredients	American
2 medium	**trout**	2 medium
2 medium	**leeks**	2 medium
2 small	**onions**	2 small
50 g/2 oz	**butter**	¼ cup
1 litre/1¾ pints	**fish stock (see page 15)**	scant 4½ cups
1 tablespoon	**lemon juice**	1¼ tablespoons
small bunch	**parsley**	small bunch
to taste	**salt and freshly ground black pepper**	to taste
	To garnish	
	chopped chervil	

Clean the trout, but do not remove the heads as these give extra flavour to the stock. Wash and thinly slice the leeks, using a little of the tender green part to add colour to the soup. Peel and finely chop the onions.

Heat the butter in a saucepan, add the leeks and onions and cook gently for 10 minutes or until pale golden in colour.

Add the fish stock, lemon juice, parsley and a little seasoning. Cover the pan and simmer for 10 minutes. Put in the fish (including the head), this can be chopped into fairly large pieces to fit in the pan. Cook gently for 10 to 15 minutes. Transfer the trout to a plate and flake the flesh discarding bones, skin and head. Remove the bunch of parsley from the stock.

Return the flaked fish to the pan and heat. Serve garnished with chopped chervil.

Variations

• Whiting can be used instead of trout.

Puréed Trout Soup: Make the soup as described above, but sieve or liquidize the finished mixture. Return to the pan and reheat. Do not overcook.

For a richer soup add 3 to 4 tablespoons (3¾ to 5 tablespoons) double (heavy) cream and 1 or 2 teaspoons horseradish cream to the purée.

Freezing: The puréed soup freezes well, but the soup containing the flaked fish does not, because the fish becomes too soft.

PROVENÇAL FISH SOUP

Cooking time: 1 hour 15 minutes • Serves 4 to 6

This is a very popular soup in the South of France, and restaurants in Provence vie with each other to produce the most noteworthy version. Basically it is a clear soup which has small pieces of perfectly cooked fish floating in it. While it can be based on only one type of fish, a mixture of fish greatly improves the flavour. Use whatever is available on the day.

This soup is often served with croûtons, French bread and a small bowl of Rouille or Aïoli (see pages 134 and 131).

Metric/Imperial	Ingredients	American
1 to 1.35 kg/2¼ to 3 lb	assorted fish, such as bream, sole, red mullet, skate, monkfish, cod and whiting	2¼ to 3 lb
1.8 litres/3 pints	water	7½ cups
2	shallots or small onions	2
3 to 4	garlic cloves	3 to 4
to taste	salt and freshly ground black pepper	to taste
few	fennel leaves	few
½ teaspoon	ground saffron or strands	½ teaspoon
1 tablespoon	chopped chervil	1¼ tablespoons
1 tablespoon	chopped fennel leaves	1¼ tablespoons
150 ml/¼ pint	white wine	⅔ cup
To serve		
croûtons (see page 193)		
Rouille or Aïoli (see pages 134 and 131)		

Cut the heads, tails and fins off the fish and place in a pan of water. Peel and chop the shallots or onions and garlic; add to the water with a little seasoning and the whole fennel leaves. Cover the pan and cook steadily for 1 hour.

Strain the stock; you should have about 1 litre/1¾ pints (scant 4½ cups). Cut the fish into neat pieces, add to the stock with the saffron, chervil and chopped fennel leaves. Simmer for 10 to 15 minutes, then remove the fish and flake or dice as much as desired; discard all the skin and bones.

Return the fish to the pan with the wine and heat well, but do not overcook. Adjust the seasoning and serve with croûtons and Rouille or Aïoli.

Variations

• To add more colour and interest to the soup, cook thin slices of carrot with the diced fish. If you have a fancy cutter, use this to give a more attractive shape to the carrots. Diced celeriac or fennel may also be added.

- If you prefer an absolutely clear soup, follow the instructions for Fish Consommé on page 53 instead of the method above.

Fish, Pepper and Tomato Soup: Make the fish stock as described on page 130 or on page 15, then add small pieces of diced, uncooked fish (free from skin and bones), 2 to 3 tablespoons (2½ to 3¾ tablespoons) finely diced red pepper and 4 to 5 tablespoons (5 to 6 tablespoons) diced tomato pulp. Cook for 10 to 15 minutes. Serve garnished with crème fraîche.

● **Freezing:** The clear stock freezes well, but do not freeze the soup with the cooked fish because this becomes over-soft.

AÏOLI (GARLIC MAYONNAISE)

No cooking ● Serves 6 to 8

This mayonnaise, strongly flavoured with garlic, is a pleasing accompaniment to the fish soup on page 130. Although Rouille (see page 134) is often served with it, in Provence, Aïoli makes a pleasant change.

Metric/Imperial	Ingredients	American
4	large garlic cloves	4
2	egg yolks	2
to taste	salt and freshly ground black pepper	to taste
up to 250 ml/8 fl oz	extra virgin olive oil	up to 1 cup
1 tablespoon	lemon juice or white wine vinegar, or to taste	1¼ tablespoons
1 tablespoon	boiling water, see method	1¼ tablespoons

Peel and crush the garlic cloves with 1 of the egg yolks; ideally, this should be done in a pestle and mortar to get a very smooth mixture, but it can be done in a liquidizer. Add the second egg yolk with the seasoning and blend thoroughly.

Gradually add as much oil as necessary to obtain a really thick consistency. Blend in the lemon juice or wine vinegar.

The boiling water is not essential, but it does give a slightly lighter mayonnaise. It should be beaten into the other ingredients very slowly.

Variation

- Use half olive oil and half sunflower oil.

Do not freeze.

BOUILLABAISSE

Cooking time: see method – about 45 minutes • Serves 6 to 8

This is the most popular soup around the French Mediterranean coast. Its name comes from boul abaisso *(boil up and serve). In praising this soup, I cannot do better than quote the words of Henry Smith, the chef and writer, in his book on* Soups *(Practical Press, 1949):*

> This Bouillabaisse a noble dish is,
> A sort of soup, or broth or stew,
> Or hotchpotch of all sorts of fishes,
> That Greenwich never could outdo;
> Green herbs, red peppers, mussels, saffron,
> Soles, onions, garlic, roach and dace,
> All these you eat at Errl's tavern,
> In that one dish of Bouillabaisse.

Although one cannot hope to get a totally authentic flavour when cooking this soup outside the Mediterranean, it can still be a triumph. Remember – the wider the assortment of fish used, the better the dish will be. As it takes quite a time to gather all the ingredients together, I think this is a soup for a large number of people who will delight in its sight, aroma and flavour.

Metric/Imperial	Ingredients	American
1.35 kg/3 lb	assorted fish, see method	3 lb
few	baby crabs or small lobsters	few
about 18	mussels	about 18
about 18	large prawns (shrimp)	about 18
to taste	salt and freshly ground black pepper	to taste
3 large	onions	3 large
3	garlic cloves	3
350 g/12 oz	tomatoes	³/₄ lb
2	red peppers	2
6 tablespoons	olive oil	7¹/₂ tablespoons
3.3 litres/5¹/₂ pints	water or fish stock, see method	scant 14 cups
1 tablespoon	chopped fennel leaves	1¹/₄ tablespoons
1 tablespoon	chopped parsley	1¹/₄ tablespoons
2	fresh bay leaves or 1 dried leaf	2
300 ml/¹/₂ pint	white wine, optional	1¹/₄ cups
¹/₄ teaspoon	ground saffron or strands	¹/₄ teaspoon

Trim the fish, reserving the heads, tails and fins. Mediterranean sole are often very small, so you may like to halve larger soles, or fillet them; keep the bones, tails and heads. Other fish that could be included are bream, red mullet, small pieces of skate wing, monkfish, cod and whiting. The choice depends on what is available and really fresh. The shellfish can be cooked, if not done already (see page 116).

Place the fish trimmings in a pan with just over 3.3 litres/5½ pints (about 14 cups) lightly seasoned water to cover. Simmer for about 25 minutes to extract the flavour, then strain and use the liquid as fish stock.

Peel and finely chop the onions and garlic. Skin, halve, deseed and chop the tomatoes. Deseed the peppers, cut the flesh into neat strips. Heat the oil in a very large pan, add the onions and garlic, cook for 5 minutes. Add the tomatoes and peppers and cook for 10 minutes. Pour in the water or fish stock, add the herbs and boil briskly for about 15 minutes until the amount of liquid is reduced slightly and the stock and onions are well mixed.

Add the selection of fish and cook for about 10 minutes. Put the shellfish in at the end of the cooking time with the white wine, saffron and a little extra seasoning. Heat for another minute. Do not overcook.

Transfer the soup to a large tureen and let everyone help themselves. Rouille (garlic mayonnaise, see opposite) is an excellent accompaniment and you will need plenty of hot rolls or French bread to mop up the delicious liquid.

As the shellfish are served in their shells, provide finger-bowls.

Variation

- If using saffron strands, you may like to infuse them in a little water or fish stock. Strain the liquid and add to the soup, discarding the strands.

Do not freeze.

ROUILLE

No cooking • Serves 4 to 6

In Provence this garlic-flavoured mayonnaise is given extra colour and flavour by adding red pepper. If you like a hot sauce, use a deseeded red chilli pepper; for a sweeter taste use an ordinary pepper. It is possible to make this mayonnaise in a liquidizer or food processor and to use the whole egg rather than just the egg yolk. Adding fine breadcrumbs makes the sauce firmer and ideal to put on soup. Extra virgin oil, which comes from the first pressing of the olives, has the finest flavour.

Metric/Imperial	Ingredients	American
1	red chilli pepper or sweet red pepper	1
3	garlic cloves	3
1	egg yolk	1
up to 300 ml/½ pint	extra virgin olive oil	up to 1¼ cups
3 level tablespoons	fine, soft breadcrumbs	3¾ level tablespoons
to taste	salt and freshly ground black pepper	to taste

Split the chilli pepper or sweet pepper, remove the seeds, then finely chop the flesh; wash your hands carefully after handling chillies because the juice can sting. Peel and finely chop the garlic.

Whisk the egg yolk in a bowl, then gradually whisk in the oil until the desired thickness is achieved. Add the breadcrumbs, garlic and pepper. Season to taste.

Variations

- Instead of breadcrumbs, soak a crustless slice of bread in a little water for 10 minutes, squeeze dry and mash until smooth.
- Add a little lemon juice or wine vinegar for a sharper flavour.
- Add 1 or 2 teaspoons chopped fennel leaves to the mayonnaise.

Liquidizer or Food Processor Mayonnaise: It can be tricky to whisk a single egg or egg yolk in certain machines as they only work efficiently with larger amounts. In most cases it is better to double the quantities and store any excess sauce in the refrigerator for up to one week.

Place the egg yolk(s) or whole egg(s) in a liquidizer or food processor and switch on for a second or two. With the motor running, pour the oil slowly through the funnel or hole in the lid until the desired thickness is achieved. Transfer to a bowl and add the remaining ingredients.

Do not freeze.

Quick Tip

Add the pepper and a few breadcrumbs to ready-made garlic mayonnaise. If the garlic flavour is not sufficiently strong, add 1 or 2 chopped garlic cloves or a little garlic purée.

SPANISH FISHERMEN'S SOUP
(SOPA DE PESCADORES)

Cooking time: 55 minutes plus time to make stock • Serves 4 to 6

This is a sustaining soup which has plenty of flavour. Shellfish should be included if possible, but can be omitted if more white fish is used. Choose a firm white fish such as cod, hake or fresh haddock. Spanish fishermen would use fish readily available on the day and would mix several varieties.

Metric/Imperial	Ingredients	American
1 medium	onion	1 medium
2	garlic cloves	2
450 g/1 lb	tomatoes	1 lb
2 tablespoons	olive oil	2½ tablespoons
1.2 litres/2 pints	fish stock (see page 15)	5 cups
1 teaspoon	grated lemon rind	1 teaspoon
1 to 2 tablespoons	lemon juice, or to taste	1¼ to 2½ tablespoons
2 teaspoons	chopped mixed herbs, or 1 teaspoon dried mixed herbs	2 teaspoons
50 g/2 oz	short-grain rice, see Variation	4 tablespoons
pinch	saffron powder or a few saffron strands	pinch
to taste	salt and freshly ground black pepper	to taste
675 g/1½ lb	white fish	1½ lb
225 g/8 oz	cooked shellfish, crab, prawns, etc.	½ lb
	To garnish	
	diced cucumber	

Peel and dice the onion; peel and crush the garlic. Skin the tomatoes and chop the flesh neatly. Heat the oil in a large saucepan, add the onions, garlic and tomatoes and cook for 5 minutes. Pour in the stock, add the rind and lemon juice and bring to the boil. Stir the herbs, saffron and a little seasoning into the liquid. Cover the pan and cook steadily for 30 minutes, stirring once or twice during this time; this helps the starch in the rice to thicken the soup.

Skin and bone the fish, cut into 2.5 cm/1 inch dice. Add to the soup and simmer for 10 to 15 minutes or until the fish is just tender: do not allow it to break. Add the shellfish and a little of the diced cucumber and heat for a few minutes. Serve garnished with more cucumber.

Variation

• Use long-grain instead of short-grain rice and shorten the cooking time by 15 minutes.

Do not freeze.

6 MEAT SOUPS

Meat soups have been part of family fare for centuries. Their great advantage is that they combine a limited amount of meat with plenty of homely vegetables, thus making a filling meal for hungry folk with the minimum of expenditure. Some of the world's most interesting meat soups come from Britain. For example, it's hard to beat home-made Oxtail Soup, with its succulent flavour and special texture (see page 146).

Serve a meat soup when the main course is based on fish or vegetables, or make it the main dish itself. Follow it with salad and fruit and you have a really satisfying meal.

COOKING MEAT SOUPS

Meat soups can be cooked in various ways. The timings in the recipes assume you are using a saucepan but, if more convenient, any of the methods below can be used.

Oven cooking: Allow about 50 per cent longer cooking time than that given in the recipes. Preheat the oven to 160°/325°F/gas mark 3 or 150°C/300°F/gas mark 2. Use a casserole with a tight-fitting lid so that the liquid in the soup does not evaporate too much. If the lid is loose, put a piece of foil under it to guarantee a good seal.

Microwave cooking: If the meat is tender, you can cook the soup in a large covered bowl. It needs 10 per cent less liquid and will be ready in about half to two-thirds of the time it would take to cook in a saucepan. Microwaves are less efficient for tougher cuts of meat, such as stewing beef. Use the defrost setting but check that the soup is simmering gently. If cooking too quickly, lower the setting. For more about microwaving soups, see page 7.

Pressure cooking: Pressure cookers are excellent for cooking meat because they tenderize even the toughest cuts and the short cooking time helps retain both flavour and texture. The Scotch Broth on page 148, for example, would take only 10 to 12 minutes, depending on the quality of the meat, compared to 2 to 2½ hours in a saucepan.

Never have the pressure cooker more than half-filled with the liquid and ingredients. For further information about pressure cooking soups, see page 7.

Slow cooking: Always bring the ingredients to the boil in a saucepan before putting them in a slow cooker, or add boiling water or boiling stock. Allow 5 to 6 hours cooking time for most meat soups.

GARNISHING MEAT SOUPS

The mixture of vegetables used in a soup often provide sufficient colour; where this is not the case, the recipes suggest a specific garnish.

If you know that the vegetables need lengthy cooking in order to flavour the meat, and will therefore have lost some colour, it is a good idea to hold back a few diced raw vegetables and cook them briefly in stock or seasoned water to garnish the soup. They not only have bright colours but a firm texture and fresh flavour.

ARGENTINE BEEF SOUP (LOCRO DE TRIGO)

Cooking time: 1 hour plus time to make stock • Serves 4 to 6

This meat soup, with its colourful mixture of ingredients, tastes as good as it looks. Canned butter (lima) beans are used to save cooking time, but cooked dried beans could be substituted. Soak and cook these as instructed on page 108.

Metric/Imperial	Ingredients	American
2 medium	onions	2 medium
3 medium	tomatoes	3 medium
1 large	red pepper	1 large
3 rashers	bacon	3 slices
2 tablespoons	olive oil	2½ tablespoons
350 g/12 oz	minced (ground) beef	¾ lb
1 teaspoon	paprika, or to taste	1 teaspoon
1.2 litres/2 pints	brown stock (see page 14)	5 cups
to taste	salt and freshly ground black pepper	to taste
225 g/8 oz	garlic sausage	½ lb
225 g/8 oz	canned butter (lima) beans	½ lb
225 g/8 oz	canned sweetcorn	½ lb

Peel and chop the onions and tomatoes. Deseed the pepper and cut the flesh into neat dice. Remove the rind from the bacon and chop the rashers.

Heat the bacon rinds and oil in a large saucepan, remove the rinds and add the minced beef, bacon and onions. Stir over a low heat for 10 minutes or until the beef is slightly brown. Stir the paprika into the ingredients, add just a little stock to moisten and stir well to ensure the minced beef does not form into lumps. Pour in the remainder of the stock, then add a little seasoning, the pepper and tomatoes. Bring to the boil, stirring briskly. Cover the pan and simmer for 40 minutes, stirring from time to time.

Cut the garlic sausages into neat dice, add to the soup with the well-drained beans and sweetcorn and heat for a further 10 minutes. Taste and adjust the seasoning before serving.

Freezing: The basic soup freezes well, but it is advisable to add the sausage, beans and sweetcorn when reheating.

GOULASH (GULYAS)

Cooking time: 1¼ hours • Serves 4 to 6

Although Hungarian goulash is more often served as a stew, a similar blend of ingredients makes a satisfying soup that is full of flavour. Sweet rather than spicy paprika is used to colour and flavour the dish. Do make sure it is fresh: when stale, it develops an unpleasant, musty taste.

Metric/Imperial	Ingredients	American
3 medium	**onions**	3 medium
2 large	**tomatoes**	2 large
100 g/4 oz	**lean pork**	¼ lb
100 g/4 oz	**veal or tender beef**	¼ lb
40 g/1½ oz	**butter or lard (shortening)**	3 tablespoons
1 tablespoon	**paprika, or to taste**	1¼ tablespoons
1.2 litres/2 pints	**brown stock (see page 14) or water**	5 cups
to taste	**salt and freshly ground black pepper**	to taste
2 medium	**potatoes**	2 medium
	To garnish	
	yoghurt or soured cream	

Peel and finely chop the onions. Skin and chop the tomatoes. Cut the meat into 1.25 cm/½ inch dice. Heat the butter or lard in a saucepan, add the onions and cook gently for 5 minutes. Add the two meats and the paprika and continue cooking slowly, stirring well, for another 5 minutes. Add the tomatoes and stock, season lightly and bring to the boil. Lower the heat, cover the pan and simmer for 45 minutes.

Peel the potatoes and cut into 1.25 cm/½ inch dice. Add to the soup and cook for a further 15 minutes. Serve garnished with the yoghurt or soured cream.

Variation

• Use only one kind of meat instead of several.

Freezing: This soup freezes well.

HARIRA

Cooking time: 50 minutes • Serves 4 to 6

I have visited Morocco on a number of occasions and have a great regard for their imaginative cuisine. A friend of mine, who lived there for many years, gave me this recipe and its variations. Harira is traditionally served after sunset during the holy month of Ramadan when devout Muslims fast between sunrise and sunset.

Metric/Imperial	Ingredients	American
2 medium	onions	2 medium
450 g/1 lb	tomatoes	1 lb
2 or 3	celery sticks	2 or 3
225 g/8 oz	lamb, boned weight	½ lb
225 g/8 oz	chicken, see method	½ lb
50 g/2 oz	butter	¼ cup
2 teaspoons	garam masala, or to taste	2 teaspoons
¼ teaspoon	ground saffron	¼ teaspoon
1 litre/1¾ pints	water	scant 4½ cups
2 tablespoons	couscous	2½ tablespoons
2 tablespoons	lemon juice	2½ tablespoons
to taste	salt and freshly ground black pepper	to taste
	To garnish	
	chopped parsley	
	lemon wedges	

Peel and finely chop the onions. Skin, halve and deseed the tomatoes. Chop the celery finely, and if the leaves are fresh, chop these too. Cut the lamb and chicken into 1.25 cm/½ inch dice; it is quite usual to add chicken wings rather than chicken flesh, in which case be rather more generous with the weight.

Heat the butter, add the onions, lamb, chicken and garam masala and cook slowly for 10 minutes. Take care the ingredients do not become too brown. Add the tomatoes, celery and saffron and cook for a further 5 minutes. Pour in most of the water, bring the liquid to the boil and stir well. Cover the pan, lower the heat and simmer for 20 minutes.

Blend the couscous with the remaining water and lemon juice, add to the soup and stir over the heat for 5 minutes until smooth. Season to taste and simmer for a further 10 minutes, stirring from time to time.

Serve topped with the parsley and lemon wedges.

Variations

- Omit the couscous and add about 75 g/3 oz (⅜ cup) washed split lentils halfway through the cooking period.
- Omit the couscous. Cover 75 g/3 oz (scant ½ cup) chickpeas in water and soak overnight. Drain and rub the skin off the peas. Place the peas in a pan, cover with fresh water, add a little salt and simmer for 1 hour.

Add the peas to the other ingredients in the main recipe after cooking the vegetables and meats in the butter. The liquid in which the peas were cooked can be added as part of the total liquid in the soup.
- If garam masala is not available, flavour the soup with ½ teaspoon ground ginger, ½ to 1 teaspoon ground cinnamon and ½ teaspoon ground coriander instead.
- If saffron is not available, use ½ teaspoon turmeric instead.
- This soup is often flavoured with a generous amount of freshly chopped parsley and a few chopped fresh coriander leaves.

Do not freeze.

HAM CHOWDER

Cooking time: 30 minutes plus time to make stock • Serves 4 to 6

This is an excellent way of serving cooked ham, and the apples really complement the flavour of the meat. This satisfying soup is a complete meal in a bowl.

Metric/Imperial	Ingredients	American
450 g/1 lb	potatoes, peeled weight	1 lb
450 g/1 lb	onions	1 lb
50 g/2 oz	bacon fat or butter	¼ cup
350 g/12 oz	ham	¾ lb
600 ml/1 pint	chicken stock (see page 14)	2½ cups
600 ml/1 pint	milk	2½ cups
to taste	salt and freshly ground black pepper	to taste
2 or 3	sweet eating apples	2 or 3
150 ml/¼ pint	single (light) cream	⅔ cup
	To garnish	
	skinned and diced tomatoes	

Peel the potatoes and grate coarsely or cut into 1.25 cm/½ inch dice. Peel and grate the onions or chop finely.

Heat the bacon fat or butter, add the potatoes and fry gently over a very low heat until golden. Cut the ham into small dice.

Pour the stock and milk over the vegetables, add a little seasoning and bring to the boil. Cover the pan and simmer for 15 minutes. Meanwhile, peel and dice the apples. Add to the soup with the ham and heat for a further 10 minutes. Stir in the cream, heat gently for a few minutes, then taste and adjust the seasoning. Serve topped with the diced tomatoes.

Variations

- For a less filling soup, reduce the amount of potatoes and onions to 350 g/12 oz (¾ lb) and the ham to 225 g/8 oz (½ lb).
- Use all or part bacon stock (see page 14), and boiled bacon instead of chicken stock and ham. Check the flavour of the stock to ensure it is not too salty.

- Omit the apples and cook approximately 225 g/8 oz (½ lb) diced celeriac or celery with the potatoes and onions.
- Use half grated potatoes and half grated carrots.

Ham and Chicken Chowder: Omit the apples from the main recipe and use celeriac or celery as suggested above. Add 225 g/8 oz (½ lb) cooked diced chicken with 100 g/4 oz (¼ lb) diced ham.

Do not freeze.

LAMB BROTH

Cooking time: 1 hour • Serves 4 to 6

Now that minced (ground) lamb is readily available, I make this old-fashioned and sustaining soup with it. Alternatively, dice a slice of lean uncooked lamb from the leg or shoulder and use that instead. The cooking time will be a little longer.

Metric/Imperial	Ingredients	American
1 tablespoon	pearl barley	1¼ tablespoons
2 medium	onions	2 medium
2	garlic cloves	2
4 medium	carrots	4 medium
1 small	turnip	1 small
¼ small	celery heart	¼ small
1 tablespoon	sunflower oil	1¼ tablespoons
450 g/1 lb	minced (ground) lamb	1 lb
1.2 litres/2 pints	water	5 cups
to taste	salt and freshly ground black pepper	to taste
1 tablespoon	chopped parsley, or to taste	1¼ tablespoons
2 teaspoons	chopped mint, or to taste	2 teaspoons
3 medium	tomatoes	3 medium
	To garnish	
	chopped mint and/or chopped parsley	

Place the barley in a saucepan and cover with cold water. Bring to the boil, then strain the barley. This process is known as blanching and it makes the barley whiter.

Peel and chop the onions and garlic. Peel the carrots and turnip and cut into small dice. Chop the celery.

Heat the oil in a pan, add the onions, garlic and lamb and stir over a very low heat for 10 minutes or until the meat is slightly coloured.

Add a little of the water and stir briskly to ensure the meat does not form into lumps. Pour in the rest of the water, add the prepared vegetables, barley, a little seasoning and the herbs. Bring to the boil, cover the pan and lower the heat. Simmer for 30 minutes.

Skin, halve and deseed the tomatoes. Cut the pulp into neat pieces. Add to the broth and continue cooking for 10 minutes. Adjust the seasoning and serve the soup topped with parsley and/or mint.

Freezing: This soup freezes well.

KIDNEY SOUP 1

Cooking time: 1¼ to 1½ hours plus time to make stock • Serves 4 to 6

The recipe below is based on ox kidney, which has a stronger taste than lamb's kidneys, and thus makes a richer-flavoured soup. It does take a fairly long time to cook in a saucepan, so use either a pressure cooker or slow cooker (if available) or cook on a very low heat.

The second version, made with lamb's kidneys, is ready in 30 minutes, so is ideal for busy people. Kidney soup provides a satisfying light meal, especially if a poached egg is added to each bowl of piping hot soup.

Metric/Imperial	Ingredients	American
2 medium	onions	2 medium
350 g/12 oz	ox kidney	¾ lb
2 rashers	streaky bacon	2 slices
50 g/2 oz	butter	¼ cup
1.5 litres/2½ pints	beef stock (see page 13)	6¼ cups
2 tablespoons	chopped parsley	2½ tablespoons
2 or 3	fresh sage leaves or pinch of dried sage	2 or 3
to taste	salt and freshly ground black pepper	to taste
25 g/1 oz	plain (all-purpose) flour	¼ cup
To garnish		
	croûtons (see page 193)	

Peel and chop the onions. Skin the kidney and remove any gristle and fat. Cut the meat into 1.25 cm/½ inch dice. Derind the bacon and chop the rashers into small pieces. Heat the butter with the bacon rinds, add the onions, bacon and kidney and cook gently for 5 minutes. Remove the bacon rinds.

Pour in nearly all the stock, then add the herbs and seasoning. Cover the pan and simmer for 1 hour, or until the kidney is tender.

Blend the flour with the remaining stock, whisk into the soup and stir over the heat until thickened. Simmer for a further 5 to 10 minutes. Take out the sage leaves and add any extra seasoning required. Garnish with croûtons just before serving.

Variations

• Use a little less stock and add Madeira or port wine to soups 1 or 2.

Puréed Kidney Soup: Remove a little cooked kidney and chop this finely for garnish. Prepare the soup as above, and when thickened, sieve or liquidize. The sage leaves do not need removing in this case. Garnish with the chopped kidney and croûtons. Chopped hard-boiled egg makes an interesting garnish.

Kidney Soup 2: Peel and chop 1 medium onion and 2 bacon rashers, save the rinds. Dice 225 g/8 oz (½ lb) skinned lamb's kidneys. Coat in 1 tablespoon (1¼ tablespoons) seasoned flour. Heat 25 g/1 oz (2 tablespoons) butter and the bacon rinds, add the onion and bacon and cook gently for 5 minutes. Remove the bacon rinds. Put the kidneys into the pan with the onions and bacon and cook for a further 5 minutes.

Add 900 ml/1½ pints (3¾ cups) brown stock, preferably made from lamb bones (see page 14) and bring to the boil. Cover the pan and simmer for 15 minutes, then serve the soup. If preferred, sieve or liquidize the soup, then reheat. Garnish as above.

Freezing: All these soups freeze well.

MEATBALL SOUP (JOU WANTZE T'ANG)

Cooking time: 5 minutes plus time to make stock • Serves 4

This Chinese clear soup depends a great deal on having a well-flavoured chicken or meat stock (see page 14). Use very good-quality, lean pork for the meatballs and do not overcook them.

Metric/Imperial	Ingredients	American
750 ml/1¼ pints	beef or chicken stock (see pages 13 and 14)	good 3 cups
	For the meatballs	
100 g/4 oz	lean pork fillet	¼ lb
1 teaspoon	chopped spring onions (scallions)	1 teaspoon
½ to 1 teaspoon	finely chopped root ginger	½ to 1 teaspoon
1 tablespoon	soy sauce	1¼ tablespoons
1 tablespoon	rice wine or dry sherry	1¼ tablespoons
to taste	salt and freshly ground black pepper	to taste

Strain the stock into a saucepan, make quite sure it has no fat (see page 12 for details of skimming stock).

Mince or finely chop the pork, blend with the remaining ingredients and form into balls 2 to 2.5 cm/¾ to 1 inch in diameter. If the mixture seems a little soft, chill it well for a time before shaping. Bring the stock to the boil, add the meatballs, simmer for 3 to 5 minutes, then serve.

Variations

- Mix 1 tablespoon (1½ tablespoons) finely chopped water chestnuts and/or the same amount of beansprouts with the pork and other ingredients.

Freezing: The soup and meatballs freeze well.

MEXICAN SOUP (SOPA MEXICANA)

Cooking time: 40 minutes plus time to make stock • Serves 4 to 6

This is a satisfying meat soup which has much the same ingredients as Chilli con Carne. The amount of chilli powder used is generous, so add it gradually to achieve a flavour you like. Makes of chilli powder vary a great deal in their strength – another reason for adding it gradually.

Metric/Imperial	Ingredients	American
2 medium	onions	2 medium
2	garlic cloves	2
2	celery sticks	2
1	green pepper	1
2 medium	tomatoes	2 medium
2 tablespoons	olive oil	2½ tablespoons
1 to 1½ teaspoons	chilli powder	1 to 1½ teaspoons
750 ml/1¼ pints	beef stock (see page 13)	good 3 cups
2 tablespoons	tomato purée (paste)	2½ tablespoons
175 to 225 g/6 to 8 oz	raw minced (ground) beef	¾ to 1 cup firmly pressed down
to taste	salt and freshly ground black pepper	to taste
175 g/6 oz	canned red kidney beans, weight when drained	1 cup
	To garnish	
	chopped parsley	

Peel and chop the onions and garlic. Cut the celery into thin strips. Deseed the pepper and cut into small dice. Skin and finely chop the tomatoes: there is no need to remove the seeds. Heat the oil, add the onion and garlic and cook gently for 5 minutes. Put in the celery, pepper, tomatoes and chilli powder. If you have not made this soup before, use only ½ teaspoon of the powder at this stage, then taste the soup when it is nearly cooked and whisk in any extra chilli powder you require.

Stir well and add the stock, tomato purée and minced beef. Bring to the boil, stir briskly and add a little seasoning. Cover the pan and simmer gently for 20 minutes. Put in the beans and simmer for a further 10 minutes. Add any extra seasoning required. Serve topped with parsley.

Variation

- Vegetarians can make this soup using vegetable stock (see page 14) and canned or cooked sweetcorn or chickpeas instead of the beef (Add these with the beans.) The total cooking time of this variation would be about 25 minutes.

Freezing: This soup freezes well.

MULLIGATAWNY SOUP

Cooking time: 1 hour plus time to make stock • Serves 6

Here is my favourite recipe for this popular curried soup. It has a good mixture of savoury and sweet ingredients. Old recipes for making the stock suggest it is based on boiling a sheep's head in water, but lamb bones produce an excellent result. Mutton bones give a stronger taste to the stock, but this meat is somewhat scarce nowadays. A chicken version of this soup appears on page 161.

If you would rather use a mixture of spices instead of curry powder, see the recipe on page 21.

Metric/Imperial	Ingredients	American
1 medium	dessert apple	1 medium
1 large	carrot	1 large
2 medium	onions	2 medium
50 g/2 oz	lamb or mutton dripping or butter	¼ cup
25 g/1 oz	plain (all-purpose) flour	¼ cup
1 tablespoon	curry powder, or to taste	1¼ tablespoons
1.2 litres/2 pints	lamb or mutton stock (see page 14)	5 cups
1 tablespoon	sweet chutney	1¼ tablespoons
25 g/1 oz	sultanas (seedless white raisins)	3 tablespoons
1 teaspoon	sugar or to taste	1 teaspoon
to taste	salt and freshly ground black pepper	to taste
1 to 2 teaspoons	lemon juice or vinegar	1 to 2 teaspoons

Peel and neatly dice the apple, carrot and onions. Heat the dripping or butter and fry these ingredients gently for 5 minutes. Stir in the flour and curry powder and cook for 2 minutes, stirring well. Pour in the stock, stirring as it comes to the boil and thickens slightly.

Add the chutney, sultanas, sugar and seasoning to taste. Simmer gently for 45 minutes. Serve the soup as it is, or sieved or liquidized to make a smooth purée. Add the lemon juice or vinegar just before serving.

Variations

- Mince (grind) 225 g/8 oz (½ lb) uncooked lean lamb or mutton and cook with the apple, carrot and onion in the dripping or butter.
- Add a little finely-cooked lamb or mutton just before serving or puréeing the soup.
- Beef stock (see page 13) makes a pleasing alternative to lamb stock. Minced (ground) uncooked or cooked beef can be added in place of the lamb or mutton suggested above.
- Add 1 tablespoon (1¼ tablespoons) long-grain rice when the stock comes to the boil and the mixture thickens slightly.

Freezing: This soup freezes well.

OXTAIL SOUP

Cooking time: 2½ to 3 hours plus time to make stock • Serves 4 to 6

It is not only the British who esteem oxtail – it is a great favourite in other countries too. The ingredients stipulate 900 g/2 lb oxtail, which is about 5 large pieces, 7 to 8 medium ones, or 10 to 12 small pieces. The cooking time depends on the tenderness of the meat. Whatever version of the soup you cook, allow it to cool overnight so the fat can be easily removed the next day.

Metric/Imperial	Ingredients	American
900 g/2 lb	oxtail	2 lb
1 large	onion	1 large
350 g/12 oz	root vegetables, see method	¾ lb
50 g/2 oz	beef dripping or butter	¼ cup
1.8 litres/3 pints	beef stock (see page 13)	7½ cups
1	bouquet garni*	1
to taste	salt and freshly ground black pepper	to taste
50 g/2 oz	plain (all-purpose) flour	½ cup
	To garnish	
	chopped parsley	

* In this recipe use parsley, rosemary, sage and thyme.

Cut the oxtail into joints if this has not already been done by the butcher. Soak in cold water for 30 minutes, then drain well. Peel and chop the onion. Prepare the vegetables and cut into bite-sized pieces. (Use mostly carrots, a small amount of turnip, swede or parsnip plus a little celeriac or celery.) If you intend sieving or liquidizing the soup, use a generous amount of vegetables and then you can omit the flour for thickening.

Heat the dripping or butter, add the onion and other vegetables and cook gently for about 10 minutes or until they are golden in colour. Add most of the stock together with the herbs, oxtail and seasoning. Cover the pan and simmer gently for 2½ to 3 hours or until the meat is tender. Remove the bouquet garni and the oxtail. Cut the meat from the bones and discard any surplus fat.

Blend the flour with the remaining stock, whisk or stir into the hot soup. Continue stirring until thickened. Return the oxtail to the pan and heat, then garnish and serve.

If possible leave the soup overnight. When cold store in the refrigerator. Next day remove all the fat from the top of the soup and thoroughly reheat.

Variations

- Add several tablespoons port or red wine to the soup.
- Omit 300 ml/½ pint (1¼ cups) stock and use that amount of strong beer.
- Add 2 to 3 tablespoons (2½ to 3¾ tablespoons) tomato purée (paste) or 3 skinned and deseeded tomatoes to the other ingredients.

Puréed Oxtail Soup: Remove the meat from the bones, then sieve or liquidize with the other ingredients and reheat. If you prefer, you can sieve or liquidize the soup without the oxtail. Chop the meat finely and return to the soup. Take great care when using a liquidizer or food processor that no splinters of bone are left in the liquid, as these could damage the appliance.

American-Style Oxtail Soup: Coat the oxtail in seasoned flour and fry in the dripping or butter. Add 1.5 litres/2½ pints (6¼ cups) stock, a little seasoning, a generous pinch of cayenne pepper, 2 teaspoons Worcestershire sauce and 6 juniper berries. Cover the pan and simmer for the time stated in the main recipe. Remove the oxtail, cut the meat from the bones and discard any surplus fat.

Strain the stock and return to the pan. Add 3 medium, neatly diced carrots, 2 small, thinly sliced leeks, 3 diced celery sticks and the oxtail. Cook for about 15 minutes or until the vegetables are tender.

Italian-Style Oxtail Soup: This is based on a delicious Italian recipe – *coda di bue alla vaccarinara*. Fry the onion plus a crushed garlic clove, as in the main recipe. Add 1.2 litres/2 pints (5 cups) brown stock, plus 300 ml/½ pint (1¼ cups) white wine, the oxtail, 1 sliced leek and 1 sliced carrot, the bouquet garni and seasoning. Cook as before. When tender, remove the oxtail from the stock. Chop the meat finely and discard any fat. Strain the stock and return to the pan with 3 sieved tomatoes or 3 tablespoons (3¾ tablespoons) tomato purée (paste) and ½ a small, finely chopped celery heart. Heat for 10 minutes, then add 100 g/4 oz (¼ lb) chopped prosciutto, 2 tablespoons (2½ tablespoons) pinenuts and the chopped oxtail. Heat for 5 minutes and serve.

Oxtail Consommé: It is essential to use a well-flavoured beef stock for cooking the oxtail. Follow the main recipe, but omit the flour. When the oxtail is cooked, strain the stock through fine muslin or a fine sieve. Cut the oxtail from the bones and discard any fat. Return the meat to the stock with a little Madeira and reheat. Garnish with thinly sliced fried mushrooms and cooked green peas.

Freezing: The puréed version of this soup freezes best. The tiny pieces of oxtail in other versions tend to lose texture and flavour.

SCOTCH BROTH

Cooking time: 2 to 24 hours • Serves 4 to 6

Sometimes called Barley Broth, this is one of the best-known Scottish recipes and makes splendid cold-weather food. Instead of using lamb, you could substitute stewing beef.

Metric/Imperial	Ingredients	American
50 g/2 oz	pearl barley	good ¼ cup
675 g/1½ lb	scrag end of lamb	1½ lb
1.5 litres/2½ pints	water	6¼ cups
to taste	salt and freshly ground black pepper	to taste
to taste	faggot of herbs*	to taste
450 g/1 lb	mixed root vegetables	1 lb
¼	small cabbage heart	¼
To garnish		
chopped parsley		

* 'Faggot' is the Scottish word for bouquet garni. Tie a mixture of parsley, chives and thyme with cotton or in a muslin bag.

Blanch the barley as described on page 141 and strain it.

Remove any surplus fat from the meat and place in the saucepan with the water, barley, seasoning and herbs. Bring to the boil, remove any scum that forms on the surface, then lower the heat and simmer for 1¼ hours.

Lift the meat from the liquid, cut into small, neat pieces and return it to the pan. If very tender, leave the meat on one side and return it to the liquid when adding the cabbage.

Peel and dice the root vegetables, add to the liquid in the pan and cook steadily for 25 to 30 minutes. Shred the cabbage, add to the rest of the ingredients and cook for 5 to 10 minutes only. Remove the herbs and garnish the soup with parsley.

Freezing: This soup freezes well.

SOUR-HOT SOUP (SUAN LA T'ANG)

Cooking time: 15 minutes plus time to make stock • Serves 4

This Chinese soup makes an excellent first course, but could also be served as a light main dish because of its high protein content.

Metric/Imperial	Ingredients	American
4	**dried mushrooms**	4
175 g/6 oz	**lean pork fillet**	³/₄ cup when chopped
25 g/1 oz	**bean curd (tofu)**	¹/₄ cup when chopped
900 ml/1¹/₂ pints	**beef stock (see page 13)**	3³/₄ cups
1 tablespoon	**brown malt or red wine vinegar**	1¹/₄ tablespoons
1 tablespoon	**soy sauce**	1¹/₄ tablespoons
2 tablespoons	**rice wine or dry sherry**	2¹/₂ tablespoons
2 teaspoons	**cornflour (cornstarch)**	2 teaspoons
2 tablespoons	**water**	2¹/₂ tablespoons
to taste	**salt and freshly ground black pepper**	to taste

Soak the mushrooms as directed on the packet, then drain and thinly slice or chop them. Finely chop the meat by hand or in a food processor. Chop the bean curd into very small pieces.

Bring the stock to the boil, add the mushrooms and pork and simmer for 10 minutes. Put in the bean curd, vinegar, soy sauce and wine. Blend the cornflour with the cold water, stir into the soup and simmer for 5 minutes, stirring well until slightly thickened. Season to taste.

Variations

- The authentic Chinese recipe adds about ¹/₄ teaspoon monosodium glutamate to the other ingredients. Many people do not like to use this, but it is obtainable from shops specializing in Chinese foods.
- Omit the cornflour (cornstarch) thickening and leave the meat in larger pieces.

Freezing: This soup freezes well but it is advisable to add the wine when reheating, as much of the alcohol flavour is lost in freezing.

7 POULTRY AND GAME SOUPS

In this chapter you will find that many of the recipes are based upon chicken. This is because chicken soups are a great favourite and there are so many different flavours that can be added to the chicken to increase its versatility. Chicken has become one of our most economical protein foods, so chicken soups are far from being a luxury. If you want to ring the changes, many of these soups can be made with alternative ingredients, such as turkey, guinea fowl, quail or pheasant. Duck and goose are not as usual in a soup as chicken or turkey but one of my favourite soups, using duck, with goose as an alternative, is on page 162.

Farmed and wild venison are becoming better known as they are increasingly available from supermarkets and good butchers. You could use this meat to give a robust flavour in the Game Soup on page 163 or in some of the meat soups in Chapter 6.

Poultry and game soups can be cooked in the same ways as those based on meat (see pages 136 to 149). Modern chickens, however, are easily overcooked, so it is important to time cooking carefully. This is particularly true of traditional Chicken Soup (see right), where a whole bird is used.

LOWERING THE CALORIE CONTENT

Like other soups in this book, some of the chicken recipes contain cream, which is delicious but does add to the calorific content of a dish.
To reduce this you can substitute low-fat yoghurt or fromage frais.
Take care, though, not to boil the soup or it will curdle, just as it would with cream. Simmer gently and whisk well while the soup is heating.

GARNISHES FOR POULTRY AND GAME SOUPS

If you would like to change the garnishes recommended in the recipes, consider a good colour contrast. Soups based on chicken or turkey or game birds often are creamy in flavour, which is delicious, but inclined to look a little pallid. Herbs, browned nuts, particularly almonds, finely chopped or sliced vegetables or slices of lemon or orange add both colour and flavour to pale soups.

Game soups are generally brown, so a little cream or sprinkling of herbs would be an excellent garnish.

Crisp croûtons make a pleasant contrast in texture to the soft consistency of the soups.

CHICKEN SOUP

Cooking time: 1¾ hours • Serves 6 to 8

The cooking timing for chicken soup has varied over the years. In the days when it was made with an elderly fowl who was past laying eggs, the bird would have been rather fatty and taken probably 3 hours to tenderize. Modern chickens are younger and leaner, and therefore quicker to cook, but they have less flavour. None the less, the soup still tastes good.

Metric/Imperial	Ingredients	American
1	**chicken weighing about 1.8 kg/4 lb when trussed, without giblets**	1
2.4 litres/4 pints	**water**	10 cups
to taste	**salt and freshly ground black pepper**	to taste
450 g/1 lb	**mixed root vegetables, see method**	1 lb
1	**bouquet garni***	1
1 large	**onion**	1 large
3 or 4	**cloves, optional**	3 or 4
75 g/3 oz	**long-grain rice**	scant ½ cup

* Sprigs of parsley, thyme and rosemary tied with cotton or in muslin.

Put the chicken and water into a large saucepan and add seasoning. Peel and chop the vegetables: use small onions, carrots, turnip, swede (rutabaga) and celery. Put about a quarter of the vegetables, plus the bouquet garni, into the pan with the chicken. Peel the onion, press in the cloves and add to the pan. Bring to the boil, remove any scum and lower the heat so the liquid is simmering steadily. Cover the pan and cook for 1 hour or until the chicken is just tender. Remove the chicken and cut about half the flesh, or the amount required, into neat pieces. Save the remainder for another dish.

Boil the liquid in an open pan for 15 minutes or until reduced to 1.8 litres/3 pints (7½ cups). Strain, return to the saucepan and bring to the boil again. Add the remaining vegetables plus the rice and any extra seasoning required. Cook steadily for 15 minutes. Return the diced chicken to the soup and heat for 10 minutes.

Variations

- In summertime add fresh peas and/or young broad (fava) beans to the selection of vegetables.

Creamy Chicken Soup: Follow the main method, but allow only 1.2 litres/2 pints (5 cups) of stock in which to cook the rice and vegetables and heat the chicken. In a separate pan melt 50 g/2 oz (¼ cup) butter or chicken fat, stir in 50 g/2 oz (½ cup) plain (all-purpose) flour, cook for 1 to 2 minutes, then add 450 ml/¾ pint (scant

2 cups) milk. Bring to the boil and cook steadily until thickened. Add 150 ml/¼ pint (⅔ cup) double (heavy) cream. Warm gently for 2 or 3 minutes. Whisk this hot sauce into the very hot soup just before serving. Taste and adjust the seasoning. Serve garnished with parsley.

Freezing: This soup freezes well if the second batch of vegetables, rice and chicken are not overcooked.

CHICKEN AND WATERMELON SOUP

Cooking time: 25 to 30 minutes plus time to make stock • Serves 4 to 6

This is an unusual mixture of chicken and fruit. As the ingredients suggest, it is based on an Oriental recipe.

Metric/Imperial	Ingredients	American
25 g/1 oz	dried mushrooms	¼ cup when chopped
150 ml/¼ pint	boiling water	⅔ cup
225 g/8 oz	chicken breast	½ lb
100 g/4 oz	lean pork	¼ lb
750 ml/1¼ pints	chicken stock (see page 14)	good 3 cups
to taste	salt and freshly ground black pepper	to taste
100 g/4 oz	shelled fresh or frozen peas	¾ cup
100 g/4 oz	canned bamboo shoots	¼ lb
350 g/12 oz	watermelon pulp, weight without skin and seeds	¾ lb

Chop the dried mushrooms into small pieces, cover with the boiling water and leave to soak for 1 hour. Cut the chicken and pork into neat pieces, discard the skin from the chicken.

Heat the stock, add the pork and mushrooms and bring to simmering point. Add a little seasoning, cover the pan and simmer for 10 minutes only. Put in the chicken and fresh peas, and simmer for a further 10 minutes. If using frozen peas, add them with the bamboo shoots.

Cut the bamboo shoots into matchstick pieces and dice the watermelon pulp. Do this on a plate, so no juice is wasted. If preferred, the fruit can be cut into small balls using a vegetable scoop.

Add the bamboo shoots and watermelon, plus any juice from the fruit, to the soup, simmer for a further 5 minutes, then add any extra seasoning required and serve.

Variations

- About 1 tablespoon (1¼ tablespoons) lemon or lime juice can be added with the watermelon.
- The stock can be flavoured with 1 to 2 teaspoons finely grated root ginger or ¼ to ½ teaspoon ground ginger.

Do not freeze.

COCK-A-LEEKIE

Cooking time: 1½ hours plus time to make stock, if using • Serves 4 to 6

This dish is frequently the basis for two meals, as only a small amount of chicken is used in the soup, leaving the rest of the bird for another day. It is one of Scotland's most famous soups.

Metric/Imperial	Ingredients	American
12 large	prunes, ready-to-eat if possible	12 large
450 g/1 lb	leeks	1 lb
1.2 litres/2 pints	chicken stock (see page 14) or water	5 cups
1 small	chicken	1 small
to taste	sprigs of parsley and thyme	to taste
to taste	salt and freshly ground black pepper	to taste
	To garnish	
	chopped parsley	

If not ready-to-eat, soak the prunes in water overnight or for several hours. For soft prunes, cook steadily in the soaking water until they reach the texture you like. This process can be omitted if you like firmer prunes.

Cut the leeks into thin rings. Put the chicken stock or water into a saucepan, then add the chicken, herbs and seasoning to taste. Cover the pan and cook steadily for 1 hour, or until the chicken is tender. Lift the bird out of the pan. Strain the stock, measure and, if necessary, boil rapidly in an open pan until reduced to 900 ml/1½ pints (3¾ cups).

Add the leeks and prunes to the stock, cover the pan and cook for 20 or 30 minutes or until tender.

If adding only a little chicken to the soup, dice approximately 225 g/8 oz (½ lb) breast meat and add to the pan. Heat the soup and garnish with chopped parsley.

Variations

- Use beef stock instead of chicken stock or water to give a stronger flavoured soup.
- To give a more pronounced vegetable flavour to the soup, add a few chopped leeks, an onion and a little diced bacon with the chicken and herbs, then strain. These ingredients are not served in the soup but they add an excellent flavour to the stock, particularly if you are using water.
- Instead of cooking a whole chicken, cook one chicken portion, or as many as required, to give a satisfying soup.

CURRIED CHICKEN SOUP

Cooking time: 40 minutes plus time to make stock • Serves 4 to 6

This is a splendid soup in which to use up leftover chicken. The carcass could be used to make the stock. The amount of curry powder in the recipe gives a moderately hot flavour, which is beautifully balanced by the addition of cream.

Metric/Imperial	Ingredients	American
2 large	onions	2 large
1 medium	sweet apple	1 medium
50 g/2 oz	butter or chicken fat	1/4 cup
1 tablespoon	curry paste or powder	1 1/4 tablespoons
1 tablespoon	cornflour (cornstarch)	1 1/4 tablespoons
900 ml/1 1/2 pints	chicken stock (see page 14)	3 3/4 cups
1 tablespoon	lemon juice	1 1/2 tablespoons
to taste	salt and freshly ground black pepper	to taste
225 g/8 oz	cooked chicken	1/2 lb
150 ml/1/4 pint	milk	2/3 cup
150 ml/1/4 pint	single (light) cream	2/3 cup
2	egg yolks	2
	To garnish	
	watercress	
	diced red pepper or diced cooked bacon or ham	

Peel and finely chop the onions and apple. Heat the butter or chicken fat and gently fry the onions and apple for 5 minutes. Add the curry paste or powder and cornflour, mix well and cook for 1 to 2 minutes. Add the stock and lemon juice and bring to the boil. Season lightly, then lower the heat, cover the pan and simmer for 20 minutes. Dice the cooked chicken, add to the stock, then sieve or liquidize to give a smooth mixture.

Return to the pan and add the milk. Blend the cream and egg yolks together, whisk into the hot, but not boiling, soup and cook gently for 5 to 10 minutes. Adjust the seasoning and serve topped with the garnish.

Variations

- For a slightly thicker soup, add 1 or 2 peeled and diced potatoes to the onions and apple, or increase the amount of chicken to 350 g/12 oz (3/4 lb).
- Use cooked turkey instead of chicken.

Freezing: The puréed mixture freezes well. Add the milk, cream and egg yolks only when reheating the soup.

INDONESIAN CHICKEN SOUP (SOTO AJAM)

Cooking time: 45 minutes plus time to make stock • Serves 4 to 6

A pleasant mixture of European and Far Eastern influences, this soup requires a strongly flavoured chicken stock.

Metric/Imperial	Ingredients	American
2 medium	onions	2 medium
2	garlic cloves	2
2 small	leeks	2 small
2 small	potatoes, preferably new	2 small
225 to 350 g/8 to 12 oz	chicken breast or leg meat, boned weight	½ to ¾ lb
1 tablespoon	sunflower oil	1¼ tablespoons
1.5 litres/2½ pints	chicken stock (see page 14)	6½ cups
1 to 2 teaspoons	grated root ginger	1 to 2 teaspoons
to taste	salt and freshly ground black pepper	to taste
2	eggs	2
4 tablespoons	chopped canned bamboo shoots	5 tablespoons
6 tablespoons	chopped canned water chestnuts	7½ tablespoons

Peel and finely chop the onions and garlic. Slice the leeks thinly, including a little of the tender green stalks. Scrape the potatoes and cut into thin matchsticks. Remove the skin from the chicken and dice the meat.

Heat the oil in a pan, add the onions and garlic and cook gently for 10 minutes, or until nearly tender. Stir well so they do not colour. Pour in the stock, add the ginger and bring to the boil. Season lightly, then cover the pan, lower the heat and simmer for 15 minutes. Add the chicken, potatoes and leeks and continue simmering for a further 15 minutes.

Hard-boil, shell and chop the eggs while the soup is cooking. Add to the pan with the bamboo shoots and water chestnuts. Continue cooking for a further 5 minutes. Taste the soup, adjust the seasoning and serve.

Variation

• Add 2 teaspoons light soy sauce towards the end of the cooking period.

Do not freeze.

LORRAINE SOUP

Cooking time: 20 minutes plus time to make stock • Serves 4 to 6

Often known as La Reine Soup, this dish dates back to the 16th century and reflects the culinary links between France and Scotland in the days of Mary Queen of Scots. It is undoubtedly my favourite chicken soup; I love the subtle thickening given to the stock by almonds. The chicken stock must be very well flavoured – almost like a Chicken Consommé (see page 51).

Metric/Imperial	Ingredients	American
2	eggs	2
50 g/2 oz	almonds	generous ½ cup
225 g/8 oz	cooked chicken breast	½ lb
900 ml/1½ pints	chicken stock or consommé (see pages 14 and 51)	3¾ cups
25 g/1 oz	soft breadcrumbs	½ cup
150 ml/¼ pint	single (light) cream	⅔ cup
to taste	salt and freshly ground black pepper	to taste
	To garnish	
	chopped parsley	

Hard-boil the eggs, shell them and remove the yolks. Chop the yolks and whites separately. Reserve whites for garnish. Blanch and finely chop the almonds, unless you plan to liquidize or process the soup, in which case they can be left whole. Cut the cooked chicken into very small dice.

To prepare the soup by hand, put the egg yolks, almonds and chicken breast into a bowl, add a little chicken stock, then pound the mixture until smooth. Alternatively, liquidize or process the ingredients with some of the stock to a smooth purée.

Pour the remaining chicken stock into a saucepan, add the chicken purée with the breadcrumbs, cream and seasoning. Heat thoroughly but do not allow the soup to boil. Garnish each portion with the chopped egg whites and parsley.

Do not freeze.

QUEEN SOUP (DRONNING SUPPE)

Cooking time: 20 minutes plus time to make stock • Serves 4

Egg yolks and cream give this Norwegian soup a lovely rich taste, but take care not to overheat it or the mixture will curdle. The traditional garnish is small Chicken Balls (see page 198), but the quick tip offers an alternative to these.

Metric/Imperial	Ingredients	American
1.2 litres/2 pints	chicken stock (see page 14)	5 cups
3	egg yolks	3
150 ml/¼ pint	single (light) cream	²/₃ cup
3 tablespoons	dry sherry	3³/₄ tablespoons
to taste	salt and freshly ground white pepper	to taste
	To garnish	
	diced chicken or ham	

In this recipe it is important that the stock is free from any fat; page 12 explains how to clarify stock. Put the egg yolks, cream and sherry into a really large bowl and place over a pan of hot, but not boiling, water. Whisk briskly until the mixture thickens.

Heat the stock to simmering point, then gradually whisk into the egg yolk mixture. Season to taste and serve topped with the chicken or ham.

Variations

• Instead of cream, use ordinary or skimmed milk.

Vegetarian Queen Soup: Use vegetable stock and garnish the soup with very small diced, cooked carrots and grated cheese.

Freezing: This soup is better freshly made as it is inclined to separate during freezing. Defrosted chicken stock could be used.

Quick Tip

Heat the stock in the microwave on full power, then whisk into the thickened egg mixture. If not sufficiently hot, return to the microwave for 1 to 2 minutes on a low setting, whisking every ½ minute.
Let it stand for 1 to 2 minutes before serving.

ROYAL SOUP (SOPA REAL)

Cooking time: 15 minutes plus time to make stock • Serves 4

This quickly-made and interesting Spanish soup needs a really well-flavoured chicken stock. The eggs and other ingredients are not heated, so the soup must be very hot.

Metric/Imperial	Ingredients	American
2	eggs	2
100 g/4 oz	cooked ham	¼ lb
100 g/4 oz	cooked chicken breast, weight without bone and skin	¼ lb
1 slice	bread	1 slice
1.2 litres/2 pints	chicken stock (see page 14)	5 cups
to taste	salt and freshly ground white pepper	to taste
1 wine glass	dry sherry, or to taste	1 wine glass

Make sure the soup bowls are thoroughly warmed. Hard-boil, shell and chop the eggs; dice the ham and chicken, and cut the bread into small neat pieces. Divide all these ingredients between the bowls. Heat the stock, taste and adjust the seasoning, then stir in the sherry and warm for 1 minute. Pour over the cold ingredients and serve immediately.

Variation

• Heat 1 tablespoon (1¼ tablespoons) olive oil in a frying pan, fry the diced bread until crisp, add the chopped eggs, diced ham and chicken. Fry in the oil for a few minutes, then place in the bowls. Add the heated stock and sherry.

Do not freeze.

THAI LEMON AND CORIANDER SOUP

Cooking time: 15 minutes plus time to make stock • Serves 4 to 6

I have based this recipe on one I found in a delightful small book entitled Herbs *by Marilyn Bright (Appletree Press, 1995). Although I love a curry flavour, I found the original amount of 2 tablespoons (2½ tablespoons) hot curry paste rather overwhelmed the delicious taste of lemon and coriander, so I have reduced this. To emphasize the lemon in the soup, I have added a little chopped lemon grass to the original recipe.*

Metric/Imperial	Ingredients	American
1	uncooked chicken breast	1
1	red chilli pepper	1
1 or 2 stems	lemon grass	1 or 2 stems
small bunch	coriander leaves	small bunch
900 ml/1½ pints	chicken stock (see page 14)	3¾ cups
1 tablespoon	hot curry paste, or to taste	1¼ tablespoons
2 tablespoons	lemon juice, or to taste	2½ tablespoons
to taste	salt	to taste

Skin the chicken and cut the flesh into thin shreds. Slit the pepper, remove the seeds and thinly slice the pod. (Wash your hands after doing this because chilli juice can sting sensitive skin and be very painful, especially near your eyes.)

Chop the lemon grass and coriander leaves finely. Put the stock and curry paste into a saucepan, heat until the paste has dissolved, then add the chicken, lemon juice and lemon grass. Bring just to the boil, lower the heat and cover the pan. Simmer for 8 minutes or until the chicken is tender.

Add the chilli pepper and coriander, heat for 2 to 3 minutes only, then add salt to taste. It is unlikely you will need to add any pepper. Serve hot.

Do not freeze.

TURKEY AND CHESTNUT SOUP

Cooking time: 40 minutes • Serves 4 to 6

The combination of turkey and chestnuts is a traditional one, and extremely good too. The recipe below uses uncooked turkey, but it is also possible to use cooked poultry. The turkey carcass can be used to make stock.

Metric/Imperial	Ingredients	American
350 g/12 oz	chestnuts	¾ lb
2 medium	onions	2 medium
¼	celery heart	¼
350 g/12 oz	uncooked turkey portion	¾ lb
25 g/1 oz	turkey fat or butter	2 tablespoons
1.2 litres/2 pints	chicken or turkey stock (see page 14)	5 cups
1 tablespoon	chopped parsley	1¼ tablespoons
1 teaspoon	chopped thyme or ½ teaspoon dried thyme	1 teaspoon
to taste	salt and freshly ground black pepper	to taste

Slit the chestnuts in a cross at the rounded end. Place into a little boiling water and cook for 10 minutes. Cool sufficiently to handle, then remove the outer shells and brown skins.

Peel and chop the onions and dice the celery. Cut the turkey flesh into small dice. Heat the fat or butter and cook the onions and turkey for 10 minutes, or until golden in colour, stirring often.

Add the stock, chestnuts, herbs and seasoning. Simmer for 25 to 30 minutes, then serve.

Variations

- If using cooked turkey, add rather more vegetables, such as sliced carrots and a little diced celeriac, to give the soup more flavour. Add the diced cooked turkey towards the end of the cooking time.

Puréed Turkey and Chestnut Soup: Cook the soup as instructed above. Take out a few chestnuts and a little turkey for garnish, then sieve or liquidize the soup. Reheat and top with crème fraîche or soured cream, chopped chestnuts and turkey.

Turkey Giblet Soup: Cook turkey giblets with 1.8 litres/3 pints (7½ cups) of water and about 225 g/8 oz (½ lb) mixed diced vegetables. When tender, strain the stock. Pour 900 ml/1½ pints (3¾ cups) of the stock into a saucepan, add 350 g/12 oz (¾ lb) neatly diced vegetables and cook until the vegetables are tender. Add a little of the diced liver from the giblets to the soup and stir in 300 ml/½ pint (1¼ cups) single (light) cream. Heat gently and top with chopped parsley.

The remainder of the stock can be frozen or used to make gravy.

After Christmas Soup: Remove any cooked turkey clinging to the carcass and set aside. Use the carcass to make turkey stock (see page 14). Liquidize the amount of stock required with any suitable leftover vegetables, the reserved turkey flesh and any leftover stuffing. Heat and serve.

Freezing: The Turkey and Chestnut Soup and stock freezes well.

CHICKEN MULLIGATAWNY SOUP

Cooking time: 1¾ hours • Serves 6

The following recipe comes from Australia, where it appears in The Early Settler's Book of Household Lore *(Raphael Arts Pty Ltd, 1977), originally published in 1809. Most of the measurements in the recipe are those I have added, since the original instructions are somewhat vague. If using the suggested quantity of curry powder, use a mild variety.*

Although this is a very satisfying soup, the original recipe states that it should be served with a dish of cooked rice 'if you can get it' – an indication that rice was something of a luxury in early 19th-century Australia.

Metric/Imperial	Ingredients	American
4 medium	**onions**	4 medium
1 small head	**garlic**	1 small head
50 g/2 oz	**butter**	¼ cup
1 small	**chicken**	1 small
3 tablespoons	**curry powder or to taste**	3¾ tablespoons
2 tablespoons	**plain (all-purpose) flour**	2½ tablespoons
1 tablespoon	**lemon juice**	1¼ tablespoons
to taste	**salt and cayenne pepper**	to taste
600 ml/1 pint	**water**	2½ cups
600 ml/1 pint	**chicken stock, see method**	2½ cups

Peel and chop the onions and garlic. Heat the butter in a saucepan and gently cook the onions and garlic until light brown. Cut all the flesh from the chicken. Make stock from the carcass by simmering it in a covered pan of water. Meanwhile, cut the chicken flesh into small pieces.

Blend the curry powder and flour with the onions and garlic. Add the chicken, mix well, then add the lemon juice, a little salt and cayenne pepper and the water. Cover the pan and simmer for 30 minutes. Add the chicken stock, cover the pan tightly, simmer for 1 hour, then serve.

The original recipe makes no mention of sieving the soup, but you can sieve or liquidize it if you wish. This will produce a thick purée, in which case you will need to add more stock to give the desired consistency.

Variations

- A cold version of Mulligatawny Soup appears on page 183.
- A meat version of Mulligatawny Soup appears on page 145.

Freezing: This soup freezes well, but the texture is better if the chicken is only lightly cooked, especially if you serve the soup without sieving or liquidizing it.

DUCK SOUP

Cooking time: 15 minutes plus time to cook the duck and
make the stock • Serves 4 to 6

*This recipe, inspired by Peking Duck, arose from an experiment I made
one day when I had part of a cooked duck left over. The skin of the bird
must be very crisp and the duck flesh free from fat. The duck stock, made
from the carcass, must be full of flavour and fat-free.*

Metric/Imperial	Ingredients	American
1.2 litres/2 pints	duck stock (see page 14)	5 cups
2	garlic cloves	2
½ small	cucumber	½ small
225 g/8 oz	cooked duck	½ lb
5 tablespoons	sliced spring onions (scallions)	6 tablespoons
2 tablespoons	rice wine or dry sherry	2½ tablespoons
1 tablespoon	soy sauce, or to taste	1¼ tablespoons
to taste	salt and freshly ground black pepper	to taste
	To garnish	
	crisp duck skin, see Note	

Heat the duck stock. Peel, but do not chop, the garlic cloves, add to the
stock and simmer for 5 minutes. Peel the cucumber and cut the pulp into
matchstick-sized pieces. Finely dice the duck flesh. Add the cucumber,
duck and spring onions to the stock and simmer for 5 minutes.

Gradually pour in the rice wine or sherry and soy sauce, tasting the
soup as you do so. Heat for a few minutes, then add any seasoning
required. Remove the garlic cloves. Cut the duck skin into narrow shreds
and add to the soup immediately before serving.

Note: If the duck skin is not as crisp as you would wish, heat it for a few
seconds in a microwave or under a grill.

Variation

• For an even better soup, use the recipe for Duck Consommé (see page
  51) instead of the stock. Add 1 or 2 teaspoons of sugar to the soup if
  you wish.

Freezing: The soup does not freeze well, but the stock or consommé can
be frozen.

Duck Broth: Lightly roast a small duck and save about 450 g/1 lb of the
flesh. Use the remaining duck, plus the bones and giblets, to make a very
well-flavoured stock. Boil briskly to reduce to 1.2 litres/2 pints (5 cups).
Strain, allow to cool and remove all the fat.

Return the stock to the pan with 2 medium, finely-diced onions,
2 medium, skinned, deseeded tomatoes, several tablespoons finely-diced
celery and a small sprig of sage. Simmer for 10 minutes.

Add 225 g/8 oz (½ lb) diced potatoes and continue cooking for

15 minutes. Remove the sage and add the finely-diced duck with
2 tablespoons (2½ tablespoons) port or Madeira wine. Simmer until the
duck is hot, then serve.

Freezing: The broth does not freeze well, but the stock can be frozen.

GAME SOUP

Cooking time: see method • Serves 4 to 6

*The flavour of this soup depends upon the particular type of game used.
Whatever you choose, always taste game soup critically, for a little
sweetening in the form of redcurrant, apple or cranberry jelly often
greatly improves the flavour. After this recipe you will find specific hints
to add an individual flavour to the particular game being used.*

Metric/Imperial	Ingredients	American
1 large	grouse or pheasant or small rabbit	1 large
2 medium	onions	2 medium
2 medium	carrots	2 medium
¼	celery heart	¼
50 g/2 oz	butter	¼ cup
1.8 litres/3 pints	water	7½ cups
1	bouquet garni*	1
1 teaspoon	juniper berries	1 teaspoon
to taste	salt and freshly ground black pepper	to taste
300 ml/½ pint	red wine	1¼ cups

* Use a sprig of thyme, a sprig of parsley and 1 blade of mace tied in
muslin.

Cut the grouse, pheasant or rabbit into joints. If using game birds, the
giblets can also be cooked to give a stronger-flavoured soup. If using
rabbit, the offal can also be included. Wash the giblets or offal in plenty
of cold water to which a few drops of vinegar have been added.
  Peel and chop the onions and carrots; dice the celery. Heat the butter
and add the game birds or rabbit. Cook steadily for 10 to 15 minutes, or
until golden brown. Add the onions after 10 minutes' cooking. Pour the
water into the pan, then add the carrots, celery, bouquet garni, juniper
berries and a little seasoning. Bring to the boil, remove any scum that
comes to the top of the liquid. Cover the pan, lower the heat and simmer
gently until the bird or rabbit is tender. If these are young, the cooking
time will be 1 to 1¼ hours; if older and tougher, allow 1¾ to 2 hours.
  Strain and reserve the stock, then remove the vegetables and the bird or
rabbit. Take the flesh off the bones if you wish, mix with the giblets or
offal. Sieve, process or liquidize the meat and vegetables with a little of
the stock. Return the purée to the pan with the red wine and enough
stock to make a good, creamy consistency. Add extra seasoning if

required and reheat. If the flavour of the soup is a little bitter, stir in 1 or 2 tablespoons (1¼ or 2½ tablespoons) redcurrant, apple or cranberry jelly and heat until dissolved.

Many garnishes, including croûtons (see page 193), can be added to this soup.

Variations

- Use 3 to 4 quails or other small game birds instead of the game suggested.
- Add 2 tablespoons (2½ tablespoons) glacé cherries or raisins to the soup and heat for a few minutes.

Creamy Game Soup: Omit the giblets or offal in making the basic soup. Save a little cooked breast from the game birds or rabbit, dice neatly and put on one side for garnish. Sieve or liquidize the soup as on page 163, then return to the pan with 300 ml/½ pint (1¼ cups) double (heavy) cream instead of the red wine. Heat gently, then stir in a little dry sherry just before serving. Top with the diced game.

Hare Soup: Follow the main recipe, but use just the legs of a hare: the back (saddle) can be roasted for a main course.

Use the blood of the hare as part of the 1.8 litres/3 pints (7½ cups) of liquid. Cook as per main recipe but allow 2 hours or until the legs are tender. Remove all the flesh, dice a little for garnish and sieve or liquidize the rest with the vegetables.

Return the purée to the saucepan with enough stock to give the desired consistency. Flavour the soup with port rather than red wine, and add several tablespoons redcurrant or crab apple jelly to give a faintly sweet taste.

Garnish the soup with the diced hare.

Venison Soup: Use 550 g/1¼ lb stewing venison in the main recipe. Add several bacon rashers (slices) and simmer until the venison is tender. Sieve or liquidize all the meat with the vegetables and bacon. Return to the pan with the strained stock and a little port or Madeira wine. Reheat and flavour with a small amount of French or English mustard and any extra seasoning required.

You may like to add 1 to 2 tablespoons (1¼ to 2½ tablespoons) redcurrant jelly.

Freezing: Game soups freeze well, but add any alcohol or cream only when reheating.

8 FRUIT SOUPS

People sometimes express surprise at my enthusiasm for fruit soups as they are not traditional British fare. In fact, you are far more likely to encounter them in Scandinavia or Germany. It was my sister, who lives in Norway, who first introduced me to fruit soup, and since then I have experimented with many different varieties of fruit and been delighted with the results.

If you have any doubt as to the suitability of fruit for soups, consider tomatoes: although we treat them as a vegetable, they are just as much a fruit as apples, bananas and strawberries – all of which form the basis of very pleasant soups. It is, of course, essential to choose the fruits and their accompanying ingredients with care so that the mixture does not taste like a runny dessert. In some recipes I have used chicken stock, which gives a delicate savoury taste. Vegetarians could easily substitute a mellow vegetable stock. A savoury flavour is also achieved in some recipes by combining fruit and vegetables, e.g. Orange and Carrot Soup (see pages 175 and 176).

Take care not to make fruit soups too sweet: they should be refreshing and stimulate the palate for the rest of the meal.

Nuts are a fruit too, and you will find two recipes based on them in this chapter. The Almond Soup (see page 166) is a good basic recipe which lends itself to many variations. Before serving nut soup, do ask your guests if they can tolerate nuts in order to avoid any allergic reactions.

USING FRUIT JUICE

If the recipe ingredients include fruit juice, this can be obtained in two ways. Rub ripe fruit through a hair or nylon sieve, or liquidize it, then strain through a jelly bag or fine muslin to obtain the juice. If the fruit is not very ripe, cook it lightly with a little, if any, water, then rub it through the sieve or liquidize it and strain as before.

Modern electric mixers have attachments to extract juice from fruit, so if you have this appliance, do make use of it.

GARNISHING FRUIT SOUPS

Herbs, such as mint, rosemary or thyme, make a pleasing garnish and one which adds a little flavour too.

Nuts may also be used, but some of the prettiest decorations on colourful fruit soups are flowers. Use edible ones like rose petals, apple and cherry blossom, borage flowers and primroses. Never use flowers from bulbs with food.

ALMOND SOUP (SOPA DE ALMENDRAS)

Cooking time: 20 minutes plus time to make stock • Serves 4 to 6

A soup based on almonds is made in both Spain and Portugal; it has a delicate flavour and is ideal for a light first course.

Metric/Imperial	Ingredients	American
150 g/5 oz	almonds	1 cup
25 g/1 oz	butter	2 tablespoons
25 g/1 oz	plain (all-purpose) flour	1/4 cup
600 ml/1 pint	chicken stock (see page 14)	2 1/2 cups
300 ml/1/2 pint	milk	1 1/4 cups
1/4 teaspoon	ground cinnamon or grated nutmeg	1/4 teaspoon
pinch	allspice	pinch
to taste	salt and freshly ground white pepper	to taste
5 tablespoons	dry white wine	6 1/4 tablespoons

Blanch (skin) the almonds, reserve a few whole ones or slivered almonds (strips) for garnish, then chop the remainder very finely. Heat the butter in a saucepan, stir in the flour, then gradually add the chicken stock and milk. Stir as the liquid comes to the boil and thickens slightly, then add the chopped almonds and cook gently for 5 minutes. Stir in the spices and seasoning. Make sure the soup is no longer boiling, then whisk in the wine. Heat gently, garnish with the reserved almonds and serve.

Do not freeze.

Quick Tip

Buy ready-chopped almonds or use 100 g/4 oz (1 cup) ground almonds instead of whole nuts. In this case, garnish the soup with paprika.

APPLE SOUP

Cooking time: 35 to 40 minutes plus time to make stock • Serves 4 to 6

Refreshing apple soups are among the most suitable fruit mixtures to serve at the start of a meal. Apples are a splendid partner to other fruits as they can give a slight 'bite' to fruits that are too bland to serve by themselves. Choose cooking apples with a sharp flavour and add any of the numerous flavourings suggested.

The use of white stock gives a slight savoury flavour to the soup, but this can be changed as you will see under variations. The stock must be free from any fat.

Metric/Imperial	Ingredients	American
450 g/1 lb	**cooking apples, prepared weight**	1 lb
1 medium	**onion**	1 medium
25 g/1 oz	**butter**	2 tablespoons
1 tablespoon	**cornflour (cornstarch)**	1¼ tablespoons
900 ml/1½ pints	**white stock (see page 14)**	3¾ cups
1 tablespoon	**lemon juice, or to taste**	1¼ tablespoons
to taste	**salt and freshly ground black pepper**	to taste
1 tablespoon	**soft brown sugar, or to taste**	1¼ tablespoons
150 ml/¼ pint	**double (heavy) cream**	⅔ cup
	To garnish	
	1 or 2 red-skinned eating apples	

Peel and core the cooking apples, then cut into dice or slices. Peel and chop the onion. Heat the butter in a pan, mix in the cornflour and stir over a low heat for 2 minutes. Add the stock and lemon juice. Whisk or stir as the liquid comes to the boil. Add the apples and onion with a little seasoning and the sugar. Lower the heat, cover the pan and simmer for 20 minutes. Sieve or liquidize the soup.

If serving hot, return the soup to the saucepan and reheat, but do not allow to boil. Whisk in the cream, then adjust the seasoning and sweetness of the soup. Serve garnished with finely diced unpeeled eating apples and/or croûtons (see page 193).

If serving cold, allow the soup to become completely cold. Whisk in the cream, taste and adjust the seasoning and sweetness. Garnish with the apple and serve with semi-sweet biscuits.

Variations

• Instead of stock, use half white wine or dry cider and half water.

Curried Apple Soup: Add ½ to 1 teaspoon curry powder, ½ teaspoon ground cinnamon and ¼ teaspoon ground cloves to the main recipe.

Ginger Apple Soup: Add 1 teaspoon grated root ginger to the soup and omit the lemon juice.

Spiced Apple Soup: Add ½ to 1 teaspoon ground cinnamon and ¼ to
½ teaspoon ground cloves to the ingredients in the main recipe.
The lemon can be retained or omitted.

Apple and Apricot Soup: Omit the onion in the main recipe.
Use 350 g/12 oz (¾ lb) apples (weight when peeled and cored) and
225 g/8 oz (½ lb) halved fresh apricots. Use water, or half water and half
white wine, instead of stock.

Apple and Elderberry Soup: Use 350 g/12 oz (¾ lb) apples (weight when
peeled and cored) and 100 g/4 oz (¼ lb) elderberries in the main recipe.
The white stock blends well with this mixture of fruits, but you can also
use water or three-quarters water and a quarter red wine.
   The main recipe is delicious flavoured with a spray of elderflowers.
Cook these with the apples and liquid but remove them before sieving or
liquidizing the soup.

Apple and Melon Soup: Follow the main recipe, but omit the onion and
use water or half water and half white wine instead of stock. Use 225 g/
8 oz (½ lb) apples (weight when peeled and cored) and 350 g/12 oz
(¾ lb) diced melon. You may like to increase the amount of lemon juice
slightly or flavour this soup with a little ground ginger or grated root
ginger.

Apple and Orange Soup: Use 350 g/12 oz (¾ lb) apples (weight when
peeled and cored) plus 1 tablespoon (1¼ tablespoons) finely grated
orange zest. Add the zest to the liquid when cooking the soup. Sieve or
liquidize the pulp of 2 large oranges with the apple mixture. Garnish with
orange segments.
   Alternatively, sieve the flesh of 2 large oranges with the cooked apples.

Freezing: All these soups freeze well, but do not add the cream until
reheating the soup, or until it has defrosted if serving cold.

APRICOT AND APPLE SOUP

Cooking time: 25 minutes • Serves 4 to 6

This is an interesting combination of flavours which produces a most refreshing cold soup, although it can be served hot (see Variations).

Metric/Imperial	Ingredients	American
350 g/12 oz	**fresh apricots, prepared weight**	¾ lb
225 g/8 oz	**cooking apples, prepared weight**	½ lb
1 tablespoon	**lemon juice**	1¼ tablespoons
600 ml/1 pint	**water**	2½ cups
to taste	**sugar**	to taste
	To garnish	
	1 dessert apple	
	soured cream	

Halve the apricots and remove the stones. Peel, core and thinly slice the apples. Put the two fruits into a saucepan with the lemon juice and water. Cover the pan and simmer steadily until the fruit is tender. Remove a few apricot halves and thinly slice these for garnish. Add sugar to taste to the fruit mixture. Sieve or liquidize and chill well.

Dice the apple finely and add to the soup with the sliced apricots. Top with the soured cream.

Variations

- The recipe above produces a soup that has a fairly thick consistency, although this will vary with the juiciness of the fruits. The amount of liquid can be increased but it is better to add this after sieving or liquidizing the mixture.
- If the soup is to be served hot, it tastes better with a stronger-flavoured liquid. Use fat-free chicken stock (see page 14) or half white wine or cider and half water instead of all water.

Creamy Apricot and Apple Soup: Follow the main recipe but use only 450 ml/¾ pint (scant 2 cups) water in which to cook the fruits. Liquidize the soup with 300 ml/½ pint (1¼ cups) single (light) cream or soured cream. These proportions can also be used with the variations that follow.

If serving hot, heat the ingredients with great care so that the soup does not curdle. Never allow it to boil.

Curried Apricot and Apple Soup: Add 1 teaspoon curry paste to the ingredients in the main recipe or the variations below.

Apricot Soup: Follow the main recipe, but use 450 g/1 lb apricots (weight when stoned) and omit the apples.

This soup has more flavour if 450 ml/¾ pint (scant 2 cups) of water is mixed with 150 ml/¼ pint (⅔ cup) white wine.

Apricot and Orange Soup: Omit the apples in the main recipe and use the pulp of 3 large oranges instead. These should be free from any pips, skin or pith.

Garnish the soup with the soured cream and fine shreds of orange peel.

Freezing: All these soups freeze well, but do not freeze the garnish.

AVOCADO SOUP 2

Cooking time: 10 minutes plus time to make stock • Serves 4 to 6

Avocados have long been popular as a first course, but little known as a soup. Their distinctive flavour makes them an ideal fruit for this purpose. The chicken stock must be free of fat (see page 12). Take care if using chicken stock cubes as their flavour must not overpower the fruit.

Metric/Imperial	Ingredients	American
2 tablespoons	**lemon juice**	2½ tablespoons
2 large	ripe avocados	2 large
450 ml/¾ pint	**chicken stock (see page 14)**	scant 2 cups
150 ml/¼ pint	single (light) cream	⅔ cup
150 ml/¼ pint	yoghurt	⅔ cup
to taste	salt and freshly ground black pepper	to taste
few drops	Tabasco sauce	few drops
few drops	soy sauce (optional)	few drops
	To garnish	
	finely chopped tomato	

Put the lemon juice into a basin. Halve the avocados, remove the skin and stones, and mash the pulp with the lemon juice. Sieve the mixture and mix with the stock. (This may be done in a liquidizer or food processor.)

Bring the soup to boiling point, remove from the heat and whisk in the cream and yoghurt. Heat gently without boiling, then add the seasoning and two sauces.

Garnish with the tomato and serve at once.

Variations

• To serve cold, add the cold stock, cream, yoghurt and flavouring to the mashed avocados. Chill and garnish just before serving.

Avocado and Prawn Soup: Use either fish stock or delicately flavoured chicken stock in the main recipe. Add about 100 g/4 oz (⅔ cup) small or finely-chopped prawns (shrimp) to the soup with the cream and yoghurt. Flaked white crabmeat could be used instead of prawns.

Do not freeze.

MEXICAN BANANA SOUP (SOPA DE PLATANO)

Cooking time: 25 minutes plus time to make stock • Serves 4 to 6

Knowing my fondness for bananas, a friend told me about an interesting soup based on this fruit that she had tasted in Mexico. Her description was vague but inspired me to experiment, and this is the result. I cannot claim it is a classic Mexican recipe, but it tastes good. One thing my friend stressed was that the bananas must be very firm, certainly not over-ripe.

Metric/Imperial	Ingredients	American
1 large	green pepper	1 large
1 medium	onion	1 medium
4 medium	tomatoes	4 medium
1 tablespoon	olive oil	1¼ tablespoons
1 litre/1¾ pints	chicken stock (see page 14)	scant 4½ cups
225 g/8 oz	bananas, weight when peeled	½ lb
2 tablespoons	lemon juice, or to taste	2½ tablespoons
few drops	Tabasco sauce, or to taste	few drops
to taste	salt and freshly ground white pepper	to taste
	To garnish	
	whipped cream	

Halve the pepper lengthwise and remove the core and seeds. Place rounded side uppermost, under a preheated grill until the skin becomes black (see page 97). Peel, then finely dice the flesh. Peel and finely dice the onion. Skin, halve and deseed the tomatoes, then chop the pulp into small neat pieces.

Heat the olive oil in a pan, add the onion and cook gently for 5 minutes. Add the stock and bring to the boil. Mash the bananas with the lemon juice until perfectly smooth. Stir into the stock and heat well. Add the diced pepper, tomatoes, Tabasco and a little seasoning. Simmer for 10 minutes. Serve the soup hot or cold topped with a little whipped cream.

Variation

• Add 1 teaspoon curry paste or powder to the soup instead of the Tabasco sauce.

Do not freeze.

CHESTNUT CREAM SOUP

Cooking time: 40 minutes plus time to make stock • Serves 4 to 6

There are many ways of using chestnuts in a soup. This particular recipe gives a rich, creamy mixture.

Metric/Imperial	Ingredients	American
450 g/1 lb	chestnuts	1 lb
2 medium	onions	2 medium
50 g/2 oz	butter	1/4 cup
900 ml/1½ pints	chicken stock (see page 14)	3¾ cups
to taste	salt and freshly ground black pepper	to taste
150 ml/¼ pint	milk	2/3 cup
150 ml/¼ pint	single (light) cream	2/3 cup
2 tablespoons	dry sherry	2½ tablespoons
	To garnish	
	paprika	
	chopped parsley	
	croûtons (see page 193)	

Wash the chestnuts and cut a cross into the rounded end. Put into water, boil for 8 to 10 minutes, then strain. Remove the outer shells and brown skins when sufficiently cool to handle.

Peel and roughly chop the onions. Heat the butter, add the onions and cook for 5 minutes. Add the chicken stock and chestnuts with a little seasoning, cover the pan and simmer for 15 minutes. Sieve or liquidize the mixture and return to the pan with the milk and cream. Bring to simmering point and cook for 10 minutes. Whisk the sherry into the hot, but not boiling, soup, simmer for 1 minute only, then garnish and serve.

Variation

• For a richer soup, use 300 ml/½ pint (1¼ cups) single (light) cream and omit the milk.

Freezing: This soup freezes well, but do not add cream or sherry until the soup is being reheated.

Quick Tip

Use 350 g/12 oz (¾ lb) canned unsweetened chestnut purée instead of fresh chestnuts. Simmer the onions in the stock for 10 minutes, then sieve or liquidize the mixture for an absolutely smooth soup (this is not essential). Add the chestnut purée, milk and cream. Season to taste and heat well, then whisk in the sherry as above.

NORWEGIAN FRUIT SOUP (FRUGT SUPPE)

Cooking time: 30 minutes or 1 hour • Serves 4 to 6

This is one of the most interesting hot fruit soups. The juice can be made from any fruit, but those with a sharp flavour, such as cooking apples, oranges or grapefruit, dark plums or berry fruits, are the nicest because they make a good contrast to the oats and prunes. Details of making fruit juice appear on page 165.

Metric/Imperial	Ingredients	American
100 g/4 oz	dried prunes	¼ lb
900 ml/1½ pints or 1.2 litres/2 pints	water, see method	3¾ cups or 5 cups
50 g/2 oz	rolled oats	good ½ cup
450 ml/¾ pint	unsweetened fruit juice	scant 2 cups
2 tablespoons	caster sugar	2½ tablespoons

If using ready-to-eat prunes, place them in 900 ml/1½ pints (3¾ cups) of water and simmer for 20 minutes. If using non ready-to-eat prunes, place them in 1.2 litres/2 pints (5 cups) of water, soak overnight, then simmer for about 50 minutes.

Lift the prunes from the liquid, remove the stones, then return the fruit to the liquid. Place the pan over the heat, add the rolled oats and stir as the soup comes to the boil. Cook for 5 minutes, stirring briskly until thickened. Add the fruit juice and sugar, stir until the sugar has dissolved, then heat for a few minutes only and serve.

Freezing: This soup freezes well. Do not overcook the oats, as they continue cooking when the soup is reheated.

ORANGE SOUP

Cooking time: 15 minutes plus time to make stock • Serves 4

This rather unusual and very simple soup is equally good served hot or well chilled. A fat-free chicken stock is essential for this recipe.

Metric/Imperial	Ingredients	American
1 medium	onion	1 medium
450 ml/³/₄ pint	chicken stock (see page 14)	scant 2 cups
½ teaspoon	ground cinnamon, optional	½ teaspoon
450 ml/³/₄ pint	orange juice	scant 2 cups
150 ml/¹/₄ pint	dry white wine	²/₃ cup
to taste	salt and freshly ground black pepper	to taste
	To garnish	
	1 orange	

Peel and finely chop the onion. Place in a saucepan with the stock and cinnamon, then cover and simmer for 10 to 15 minutes, or until the onion is very soft.

If serving hot, strain the stock and return to the pan. Add the orange juice and wine, together with any seasoning required, and bring just to boiling point. Meanwhile, cut away the skin and pith from the orange and chop the pulp into neat pieces, free from skin and pips. Add to the soup just before serving.

If serving cold, strain the stock, allow it to become completely cold, then mix with the orange juice and wine. Garnish as above.

Variations

• Pare the rind from 2 large oranges, avoiding the bitter white pith. Squeeze the juice from the fruit. Increase the amount of stock to 600 ml/1 pint (2½ cups). Simmer the rind in the stock with the onion for 15 minutes, then strain and blend with the juice of the oranges.
• To make a vegetarian soup use water or vegetable stock instead of chicken stock.

Orange and Mint Soup: Add a sprig of mint to the stock instead of cinnamon. Garnish the soup with orange pieces and a little finely chopped mint.

Orange and Tomato Soup: Use tomato juice instead of chicken stock in the main recipe.

Orange and Yoghurt Soup: Follow the main recipe or either of the variations, but blend 150 ml/¹/₄ pint (²/₃ cup) yoghurt with the mixture just before adding the white wine.

Do not freeze: This soup is better freshly made, but frozen orange juice could be used.

ORANGE AND CARROT SOUP

Cooking time: 15 minutes • Serves 4

This soup, and the variations that follow, are based on a mixture of fruit and vegetables. Use young tender carrots and grate or dice them finely to shorten the cooking time.

Metric/Imperial	Ingredients	American
350 g/12 oz	carrots, peeled weight	³/4 lb
1 medium	onion	1 medium
600 ml/1 pint	water	2¹/2 cups
to taste	salt and freshly ground white pepper	to taste
1 tablespoon	finely grated orange rind	1¹/4 tablespoons
300 ml/¹/2 pint	orange juice	1¹/4 cups
	To garnish	
	orange segments	
	yoghurt	
	watercress or mint leaves	

Peel and grate or dice the carrots; peel and finely chop the onion. Bring the water to the boil, add the carrots and onion with a very little seasoning and the orange rind. Cover the pan and cook steadily for 10 minutes or until the vegetables are tender. Sieve or liquidize the ingredients.

If serving hot, return the ingredients to the pan, add the orange juice and heat quickly. Adjust the seasoning and serve garnished with very small pieces of orange segment, a little yoghurt and watercress leaves.

If serving cold, allow the carrot mixture to become completely cold, then add the chilled orange juice. Season to taste and garnish as above, using mint instead of watercress leaves. Chill well before serving.

Variations

- To give a stronger flavour to the soup use fat-free chicken stock (see page 14) or add a small sprig of thyme or lemon thyme when cooking the carrots.

Citrus Carrot Soup: Follow the main recipe, but use only 1 teaspoon grated orange rind with 2 teaspoons grated lemon rind. Use 2 tablespoons (2¹/2 tablespoons) lemon juice and only 250 ml/8 fl oz (1 cup) orange juice.

Serve hot or cold and garnish as above.

Melon and Carrot Soup: Use only 225 g/8 oz (¹/2 lb) carrots and the pulp of a medium-sized melon. Cook the carrots and onion with the same amount of water as in the main recipe. Sieve or liquidize the mixture with most of the melon, then add 2 tablespoons (2¹/2 tablespoons) lemon juice and 150 ml/¹/4 pint (²/3 cup) dry white wine or orange juice, or a mixture of the two.

Serve hot or cold garnished with small, neat pieces of melon and watercress or mint leaves, but no yoghurt.

Freezing: The vegetable purée can be frozen without the orange juice, so this is added freshly, when the carrot mixture has defrosted. The purée may separate during freezing, so whisk well or liquidize again before using.

Quick Tip

These soups can be cooked on full power in a microwave. As the cooking time is short, the amount of liquid need not be reduced.

STRAWBERRY SOUP

No cooking • Serves 4 to 6

Strawberries may seem an unlikely basis for a soup, but the flavour is excellent. The fruit should be ripe, but not over-ripe, and a minimal amount of sugar is added.

If you have access to wild strawberries, do use them as they have an especially delicious taste.

Metric/Imperial	Ingredients	American
450 g/1 lb	strawberries	1 lb
900 ml/1½ pints	milk	3¾ cups
to taste	sugar	to taste
	To garnish	
	small strawberries or lemon slices	

Hull the fruit, then sieve it, mix with the cold milk and add sugar to taste. Alternatively, liquidize or process the fruit with the milk, then add the sugar. Chill well before serving. Float small strawberries or lemon slices on the soup just before serving. Serve with plain biscuits or crackers.

Variations

• Use half milk and half white wine or cider.

Frosted Strawberry Soup: Pour the mixture into freezing trays or a suitable container. Freeze lightly, then stir well and return to the freezer. Always remove from the freezer about 15 minutes before serving.

Freezing: It is better to freeze the strawberry purée alone and mix it with the milk after defrosting.

SUMMER BERRY SOUP

Cooking time: 30 minutes • Serves 4 to 6

In the past many savoury soups were thickened with tapioca or sago, which are unfashionable products these days. The sago in this Danish recipe goes well with the lovely mixture of summer fruits, but you can use rice if you prefer.

Metric/Imperial	Ingredients	American
450 g/1 lb	mixed berry fruits, see method	1 lb
600 ml/1 pint	water	2½ cups
600 ml/1 pint	rosé wine	2½ cups
50 g/2 oz	caster sugar, or to taste	¼ cup
2 tablespoons	lemon juice, or to taste	2½ tablespoons
50 g/2 oz	sago	⅓ cup

Prepare a selection of raspberries, strawberries and loganberries with a few redcurrants or blackcurrants.

Bring the water and wine to the boil, add the sugar and lemon juice, then tip in the sago. Stir well and simmer for 15 to 20 minutes, or until the sago is almost cooked. Add the fruits and continue cooking for 5 minutes or until the fruits are softened but still a good shape. Chill well before serving.

Variation

• Use long-grain rice instead of sago.

Do not freeze.

9 COLD SOUPS

There is something very inviting about hot soup, particularly on a cold day. People smile in anticipation of its warming effect and comforting flavour. Mention cold soups, however, and the reaction is rather different. People may express polite interest, but rarely enthusiasm.

If you are among the sceptics, I hope the recipes in this chapter will change your mind. Cold soups are not just for hot weather, although they are very appropriate at that time; they can be served throughout the year and are invaluable to busy cooks as they can be prepared well in advance.

Cold soups must have a really good flavour or they risk being insipid. Think of colourful Spanish Gazpacho and its exciting combination of ingredients, or cool Vichyssoise with its delicate flavour. Both are captivating dishes, whatever the weather.

Consommés, although delicious hot, are wonderfully refreshing cold, or even jellied and lightly frosted. Suggestions for making and serving these appear on pages 189 to 192.

The consistency of cold soups is important. In those that are equally good hot or cold, it may be necessary to adapt the consistency slightly. It may be perfect when the soup is hot but if it has been thickened by making a purée or adding flour, soups become slightly thicker when cold. You may therefore have to add a little extra stock, milk or wine. Taste and judge what is the best ingredient to incorporate into the soup.

Just as it is important to serve a hot soup really hot, it is equally important to ensure that cold soups are served really cold in well-chilled containers.

CHILLED CUCUMBER AND CHEESE SOUP

No cooking • Serves 4 to 6

Delicately flavoured cheese is best for this cold soup. A recipe for a hot version appears on page 73.

Metric/Imperial	Ingredients	American
½ large	cucumber	½ large
100 g/4 oz	soft cream cheese	¼ lb
1 teaspoon	chopped mint	1 teaspoon
300 ml/½ pint	milk	1¼ cups
450 ml/¾ pint	yoghurt	scant 2 cups
to taste	salt and freshly ground white pepper	to taste
to taste	little English or French mustard	to taste
	To garnish	
	chopped parsley or chervil	
	chopped chives	

Remove most of the peel from the cucumber, but retain about 5 cm/ 2 inches to give a delicate green colour to the soup. Slice the cucumber, place in a liquidizer or food processor with the rest of the ingredients and purée until smooth. Chill and serve garnished in chilled soup cups.

Variations

- For a stronger taste, increase the amount of cheese to 225 g/8 oz (½ lb).
- Camembert cheese is an excellent alternative to cream cheese.

Chilled Celery and Cheese Soup: The mint can be omitted from the main recipe. Use the heart from a medium-sized head of celery instead of cucumber. Chop and use raw, or steam until just tender, then leave until cold. Liquidize with the other ingredients. Garnish with a few celery leaves and finely chopped chives.

- Use 225 g/8 oz (½ lb) diced celeriac (weight when peeled) instead of celery.

Chilled Courgette Soup: Omit the mint in the main recipe. Use 350 g/ 12 oz (¾ lb) young courgettes (zucchini) instead of cucumber. Cut away the tough ends of the washed courgettes but do not peel. Use raw, or slice and steam until just tender, then leave until cold.

A stronger-flavoured cheese is required with courgettes. Use grated Cheddar or Gruyère cheese, or crumbled Stilton and liquidize with the other ingredients. Garnish with small pieces of tomato and chopped chives.

Chilled Fennel and Cheese Soup: Omit the mint in the first recipe. Use 1 good-sized fennel bulb or 2 smaller ones instead of cucumber, together with the cream cheese and the other ingredients. Liquidize until smooth, then chill. Garnish with chopped fennel leaves.

Fennel has a very distinct flavour, and a creamy goat's cheese makes a good partner to the vegetable.

Freezing: Do not freeze any of these recipes.

GAZPACHO

No cooking • Serves 4 to 6

This famous Spanish soup is delicious throughout the year, but is at its best when the tomatoes are beautifully fresh. Like many classic recipes, there are several versions, and each area of Spain feels that its version is the best. The recipe below is one I have used for many years, and includes some of the variations I have enjoyed. It contains less olive oil than many versions, but do use best quality extra virgin olive oil nonetheless.

Metric/Imperial	Ingredients	American
900 ml/1½ pints	water	3¾ cups
675 g/1½ lb	ripe tomatoes	1½ lb
1 medium	cucumber	1 medium
2 medium	Spanish or red onions	2 medium
2	garlic cloves	2
2 tablespoons	extra virgin olive oil	2½ tablespoons
1 tablespoon	lemon juice, or to taste	1¼ tablespoons
to taste	salt and freshly ground black pepper	to taste
	To top the soup	
	½ small cucumber	
	2 small Spanish or red onions	
	1 small red pepper	
	1 small green pepper	
	100 g/4 oz (¼ lb) bread	

Chill the water until required. If you intend sieving the soup, you can use the tomatoes whole. If using a liquidizer or food processor and you want a completely smooth soup, it is advisable to skin, halve and deseed (concass) the tomatoes, then chop the pulp. Peel the cucumber, onions and garlic and chop into small pieces.

Sieve all these ingredients, pound until smooth, or liquidize or process until smooth. Gradually blend in the olive oil, lemon juice and seasoning, then add sufficient chilled water to make a flowing consistency. The soup should not be too thick, for the rest of the ingredients add bulk. Pour into a tureen or glass bowl and refrigerate until required.

Meanwhile, peel and finely dice the cucumber and onions. Deseed and dice the peppers. Trim the crusts from the bread and cut the crumb into neat dice. These ingredients can be placed in small bowls around the tureen, or sprinkled on top of the soup immediately before serving.

Variations

- The onions chosen have a fairly mild flavour but spring onions (scallions) could be substituted.
- To emphasize the tomato flavour add 2 tablespoons (2½ tablespoons) tomato purée (paste).
- Chicken or veal stock, absolutely free from fat (see page 14), could be used instead of water.
- Instead of diced bread, top the soup with crisp croûtons (see page 193).
- Add ½ to 1 teaspoon cumin powder and/or a few drops of Tabasco sauce to the other ingredients.
- Sieve or liquidize ½ a green and ½ a red pepper with the rest of the ingredients.
- A less classic version of this soup includes a ripe avocado sieved or liquidized with the other ingredients.

Malaga Gazpacho: Simmer 1 chopped onion and 2 chopped garlic cloves in 1.2 litres/2 pints (5 cups) good white stock (see page 14) for 30 minutes. Strain the stock and cool. Mix with 450 g/1 lb peeled, seeded and chopped tomatoes, 1 peeled and finely diced small cucumber, 1 diced red pepper, 1 diced green pepper and 5 tablespoons (6¼ tablespoons) cooked rice. A small amount of finely chopped spring onions (scallions) could also be added. Season well and flavour with lemon juice. Olive oil is not necessary in this soup, but a little could be incorporated. Chill very well before serving. No topping ingredients are added to this soup.

Freezing: The puréed tomatoes and other ingredients can be frozen, but the topping ingredients in the classic soup should be freshly prepared so that they keep their firm texture. The Malaga Gazpacho should not be frozen.

Quick Tip

Prepare the cucumber and onions as in the main recipe, then pound, sieve or liquidize and blend with enough tomato juice to make a flowing consistency. Gradually add a little lemon juice and seasoning, plus a little olive oil, if you wish. Some of the ingredients suggested in the variations would improve this particular version of gazpacho.

GUACAMOLE SOUP

No cooking • Serves 4

This soup, based on the famous Mexican dip, contains avocados, garlic, tomatoes and peppers to make a piquant and refreshing cold soup. If the ingredients are liquidized, the peppers and onions need not be diced very finely, except those used for garnish. If pounded or sieved, it is easier to obtain a smooth mixture if the ingredients are cut into very small pieces. If soya milk is used, this becomes a vegan soup.

Metric/Imperial	Ingredients	American
3 or 4	garlic cloves	3 or 4
½	red pepper	½
½	green pepper	½
2 large	tomatoes	2 large
2 tablespoons	lemon juice	2½ tablespoons
2 large	ripe avocados	2 large
3 tablespoons	chopped spring onions (scallions)	3¾ tablespoons
750 ml/1¼ pints	milk or soya milk	good 3 cups
few drops	Tabasco sauce	few drops
to taste	salt and freshly ground black pepper	to taste

Peel and chop the garlic cloves; deseed and dice the peppers; skin, deseed and chop the tomatoes. Put the lemon juice into a bowl, then halve the avocados, remove the stones and scoop the flesh into the lemon juice to prevent discoloration. Sieve, pound or liquidize the garlic, half the peppers, the tomatoes, avocados and lemon juice and half the spring onions. Gradually mix in the milk, Tabasco sauce and seasoning.

Chill well. Serve topped with the remaining peppers and spring onions.

Do not freeze.

COLD MULLIGATAWNY SOUP

Cooking time: as specific recipe, see below • Serves 4 to 6

This is one of my favourite cold soups. The hot spicy flavour is lessened slightly by adding cream or yoghurt, and the colourful garnish makes it look most inviting.

Metric/Imperial	Ingredients	American
	as Mulligatawny Soups	
	(see pages 145 and 161)	
300 ml/½ pint	*single or double (light or*	*1¼ cups*
	heavy) cream or yoghurt	
	To garnish	
	1 red pepper	
	1 green pepper	
	1 yellow pepper	

Prepare either of the soups and allow to become completely cold. Sieve or liquidize the soup and mix with the cream or yoghurt. Chill well.

Deseed the peppers and cut into very small pieces. Sprinkle a little on each portion of soup immediately before serving and place the remainder in a dish so everyone can add more if wanted.

Freezing: This soup freezes well, but add the cream or yoghurt only when defrosted.

RUSSIAN CUCUMBER SOUP (OKROCHKA)

Cooking time: 10 minutes plus time to make stock • Serves 4 to 6

This is a sustaining cold soup, which would be ideal for a light meal in summertime. The mixture of two different stocks may sound troublesome but they and the wine make a good alternative to the kvass *(a drink produced from fermented rye bread) which would be used in Russia. If using stock cubes, be sparing with them so that their flavour does not overpower the other ingredients.*

Metric/Imperial	Ingredients	American
300 ml/½ pint	chicken stock (see page 14)	1¼ cups
300 ml/½ pint	beef stock (see page 13)	1¼ cups
300 ml/½ pint	white wine	1¼ cups
1 small	bunch mint	1 small
2	eggs	2
1 medium	cucumber	1 medium
2 small	pickled gherkins	2 small
225 g/8 oz	cooked chicken	½ lb
1 teaspoon	French mustard	1 teaspoon
to taste	salt and freshly ground black pepper	to taste
150 ml/¼ pint	yoghurt or soured cream	⅔ cup
4 tablespoons	sliced spring onions (scallions)	5 tablespoons
	To garnish	
	chopped dill	

Chill the two stocks well, then mix with the white wine and add the mint. Place in the refrigerator. Hard-boil, shell and chop the eggs. Peel the cucumber and cut into 6 mm/¼ inch dice. Thinly slice the gherkins. Cut the chicken into small, neat pieces. Blend the mustard and a little seasoning with the yoghurt.

Remove the mint from the stock, gently mix all the ingredients together and chill well. Garnish with the dill just before serving.

Variation

- Diced cooked meat could be used instead of chicken; try salted silverside or brisket of beef.

Do not freeze.

COLD TOMATO SOUPS

The Tomato Soup recipe on page 101 and the Lentil and Tomato Soup variation on page 112 may both be served cold as well as hot.
The other variations on pages 102 to 103 are excellent as hot soups but less successful when cold.

TOMATO AND APPLE SOUP

Cooking time: 30 minutes • Serves 4 to 6

Choose a really good cooking apple with a pronounced bite for this soup.

Metric/Imperial	Ingredients	American
450 g/1 lb	tomatoes	1 lb
450 g/1 lb	cooking apples, prepared weight	1 lb
1 medium	onion	1 medium
1	garlic clove	1
450 ml/³/4 pint	water	scant 2 cups
150 ml/¹/4 pint	white wine or dry cider	²/3 cup
to taste	salt and freshly ground black pepper	to taste
2 teaspoons	caster sugar, or to taste	2 teaspoons
150 ml/¹/4 pint	single (light) cream	²/3 cup
	To garnish	
	mint or parsley leaves and croûtons (see page 193)	

Skin, seed and chop the tomatoes if you plan to liquidize the soup, but not if you intend to sieve it. Peel, core and slice the apples. Peel the onion and garlic but leave whole. Put the tomatoes, apples, onion and garlic into a pan with the water and wine or cider. Add a very little seasoning and the sugar. Bring to boiling point, lower the heat, then cover the pan and simmer for 20 minutes.

Remove the onion and garlic, which will have imparted a delicate taste to the mixture, then sieve or liquidize the soup. Cool, then add the cream and any extra seasoning or sugar required. Chill and serve topped with the garnish.

Variations

- Although fresh tomatoes, especially the plum variety, are best in this soup, you can substitute 350 g/12 oz (³/4 lb) canned tomatoes or Italian pomodori.
- Slimmers can omit the cream in the recipe and use low-fat yoghurt instead.

Tomato and Apricot Soup: Substitute 450 g/1 lb ripe apricots for the apples in the main recipe. Halve and stone the fruit. Add 1 tablespoon (1¹/4 tablespoons) lemon juice to sharpen the taste of the soup. Follow the main recipe. Garnish with crème fraîche or fromage frais and lemon slices.

When fresh apricots are not available, use 350 g/12 oz (¾ lb) canned apricots in natural juice. Use the juice from the can plus enough water to give 450 ml/¾ pint (scant 2 cups).

Ready-to-eat dried apricots can also be used. Simmer 175 g/6 oz (1½ cups) sliced apricots in 300 ml/½ pint (1¼ cups) water until soft; most of this liquid will evaporate. Add to the tomatoes and other ingredients in the main recipe and cook as directed.

Tomato and Beetroot Soup: Follow the main recipe, but add 1 small peeled and diced, cooked beetroot to the other ingredients. Garnish with soured cream or yoghurt and chopped chives. The amount of apples can be reduced to 350 g/12 oz (¾ lb).

Tomato and Carrot Soup: Omit the apples in the main recipe and add 450 g/1 lb young carrots instead. Peel and slice thinly or grate them so that they cook in the same time as the tomatoes. In this variation the onion and garlic can be peeled and chopped, then sieved or liquidized with the other ingredients.

A sprig of chervil and one of rosemary can be added to the other ingredients, but these should be removed before sieving or liquidizing the soup. Garnish with cream or curd cheese plus chopped chives and chervil.

Freezing: All these soups freeze well, but do so without adding the cream. Whisk this into the ingredients when these are defrosted.

VICHYSSOISE

Cooking time: 20 to 25 minutes plus time to make stock • Serves 4 to 6

This is one of the best known and most delicious cold soups. In order to preserve the fine flavour, it is essential not to overcook the vegetables. Old rather than new potatoes give a better texture to the soup.

Metric/Imperial	Ingredients	American
8 medium	**leeks**	8 medium
2 medium	**potatoes**	2 medium
50 g/2 oz	**butter**	¼ cup
750 ml/1¼ pints	**chicken stock (see page 14)**	good 3 cups
to taste	**salt and freshly ground white pepper**	to taste
150 ml/¼ pint	**dry white wine**	⅔ cup
150 ml/¼ pint	**double (heavy) or whipping cream**	⅔ cup
	To garnish	
	chopped chives	

Wash and thinly slice the leeks. Peel and dice the potatoes. Heat the butter in a saucepan, add the vegetables and stir for 4 minutes without browning. Pour in the stock, add seasoning and bring to the boil. Lower the heat, cover the pan and simmer gently for 15 to 20 minutes. Allow to become completely cold, then sieve or liquidize with the wine and cream. Chill very well and serve garnished with the chives.

Variations

- For a vegetarian soup use water or vegetable stock.
- Omit the wine and use 150 ml/¼ pint (⅔ cup) extra stock with a squeeze of lemon juice, or use milk without lemon juice.

Apple Vichyssoise: Omit half the leeks and use a large peeled and diced cooking apple instead.

Chicken and Coconut Vichyssoise: Use only 5 medium-sized leeks and 1 potato. Make certain the chicken stock has a strong flavour. Add 100 g/ 4 oz (¼ lb) cooked, skinned chicken breast and 50 g/2 oz (¼ cup) creamed coconut to the other ingredients. Melt the coconut and heat the chicken in the stock just before the vegetables are cooked. Sieve or liquidize and garnish with chopped chives.

Cucumber Vichyssoise: Omit the leeks and use a large peeled and diced cucumber instead. A better flavour is given to the soup if several finely chopped spring onions (scallions) are added.

You can use 4 leeks in the main recipe and add just half a peeled and diced large cucumber. Garnish with chives as before.

Green Pea Vichyssoise: Use only 6 leeks and 1 potato in the main recipe, and add 100 g/4 oz (¾ cup) shelled peas plus a sprig of mint half way through the cooking period. Remove the mint before sieving or liquidizing the soup. Garnish with chives as before.

Prawn Vichyssoise: Use fish stock (see page 15) instead of chicken stock. Add 100 g/4 oz (¼ lb) peeled prawns (shrimp) to the other ingredients when the vegetables are almost cooked. Garnish with whole prawns.

White crabmeat makes an excellent alternative to the prawns.

Cream of Leek Soup (Potage Crème de Poireaux): This classic hot French soup uses much the same ingredients as Vichyssoise, but substitute milk for the wine and add 1 medium, finely-chopped onion. Cook the soup as above, then sieve or liquidize the ingredients. Reheat, whisk in the cream and heat gently for another few minutes. Garnish as before.

Welsh Green Milk Soup: This is a traditional recipe which uses somewhat similar ingredients to Vichyssoise. It is generally served hot. Use only 4 leeks and 2 small potatoes plus 2 small onions. Dice the onions, leeks and potatoes finely and neatly, as this soup is not sieved or liquidized. Simmer in 450 ml/¾ pint (scant 2 cups) lamb or mutton stock (see page 14) until tender. Meanwhile, make 600 ml/1 pint (2½ cups) White Sauce (see page 24). Gradually mix the vegetables and stock into the sauce, then add a few tablespoons single (light) cream and season to taste. Garnish with chopped parsley.

Freezing: All the versions of Vichyssoise freeze well, except the last soup, which tends to lose texture when frozen. Whisk or liquidize the soups after defrosting to make sure they are velvety smooth.

Quick Tip

This is an ideal soup for cooking in the microwave.

JELLIED SOUPS

The recipes that follow should be set lightly and not be sufficiently firm to turn out.

Powdered gelatine, which appears in all these recipes, is easy to use: simply sprinkle it on to the cold liquid, allow it to stand for a short time to soften, then dissolve over a pan of hot water or in the microwave. Do not stir the gelatine while it is standing or early in the process of dissolving; doing so tends to move the undissolved powder to the edges of the bowl, where it will harden. Stir briskly when the gelatine appears dissolved to check that the liquid is quite clear, then blend with the remaining ingredients in the recipe.

If you buy gelatine in bulk rather than in sachets (envelopes), use 1 level tablespoon (1¼ level tablespoons) instead of 1 sachet.

JELLIED CONSOMMÉS

Cooking time: as recipes • Serve as recipes

Metric/Imperial	*Ingredients*	*American*
	selected consommé(s)	
	gelatine, as required, see method	

Make one or two consommés. It is interesting to use two flavours rather than just one, e.g. Beef or Chicken with Tomato Consommé (pages 49, 51 and 54).

If the consommé shows no sign of natural setting, allow 11 g/0.4 oz (1 sachet) to each 900 ml/1½ pints (3¾ cups).

If there are signs of light setting, allow 11 g/0.4 oz (1 sachet) to 1.2 litres/2 pints (5 cups).

If the consommé is almost sufficiently stiff, allow 1 teaspoon gelatine to each 900 ml/1½ pints (3¾ cups).

Soften the gelatine in a little cold consommé, allow to stand for 3 minutes, then dissolve over a pan of hot water or in the microwave. Blend with the remaining warm consommé, then add any extra seasoning and flavouring such as sherry or brandy. Chill well before serving.

Freezing: Always allow the jelly to set before freezing.

Serving Jellied Consommés

Spoon into chilled soup cups and allow to set lightly. Garnish with small pieces of tomato, cucumber, diced hard-boiled eggs or chopped herbs, slices of lemon or orange, crème fraîche, mayonnaise or cream cheese. If using two consommés, allow one consommé to set lightly, then spoon over the second one.

Set in a basin, then whisk until frothy. Spoon into soup cups and garnish.

Allow to set in a shallow dish, then cut into squares with a sharp knife dipped in hot water. Two kinds of consommé look attractive served this way.

JELLIED GAZPACHO

No cooking • Serves 6 to 8

This jellied form of Gazpacho (see page 180) makes a very refreshing start to a summer meal. If you have a juice extractor, it would be far nicer to use fresh tomato juice than bottled or canned.

Metric/Imperial	Ingredients	American
900 ml/1½ pints	bottled or canned tomato juice	3¾ cups
2 sachets (22 g/0.8 oz)	gelatine (see page 189)	3 envelopes
1 tablespoon	lemon juice, or to taste	1¼ tablespoons
to taste	salt and freshly ground black pepper	to taste
1 bunch	spring onions (scallions)	1 bunch
1	green pepper	1
½ medium	cucumber	½ medium
2 medium	tomatoes	2 medium

Pour 4 tablespoons (5 tablespoons) of the cold tomato juice into a bowl. Sprinkle the gelatine on top and allow to stand for 3 minutes. Place the bowl over a pan of very hot water or heat in the microwave until the gelatine has completely dissolved. Add to the rest of the tomato juice with the lemon juice and a little seasoning. Put on one side until the mixture becomes like a thick syrup.

Trim and slice the white bulbs of the spring onions; deseed the pepper and chop the pulp into very small dice. Skin half the cucumber and cut the pulp into matchstick pieces; dice the remainder. Skin, halve and deseed the tomatoes, then dice the pulp.

Stir half the chopped spring onions, half the diced pepper, the matchstick pieces of cucumber and half the diced tomatoes into the jelly. Spoon into 6 to 8 glasses or bowls. Leave until lightly set. Top each portion with the reminder of the vegetables. Chill well before serving.

Do not freeze.

ICED SOUPS

A surprising number of soups can be iced, rather than served cold or hot. Take care that they are lightly frozen rather than firm. It is generally wise to bring them out of the freezer about 15 minutes before serving: spoon into the chilled containers and stand these in the refrigerator.

Serving Iced Soups

Serve in tall, chilled sundae glasses rather than soup bowls. Make them look more colourful by adding a rim of finely chopped parsley. Simply brush the rim of the empty container with a little unwhisked egg white, then invert over a bed of chopped parsley: this will adhere to the rim. Chill until ready to add the iced soup.

Garnishes for iced soups should be well chilled but not iced, unless specified in the recipe.

ICED CUCUMBER SOUP

No cooking • Serves 4 to 6

This is a wonderfully refreshing soup. The chopped herbs add a pale green colour to the mixture, so the cucumber skin, which can taste rather bitter when the soup is iced, can be discarded.

Metric/Imperial	Ingredients	American
1 large	cucumber	1 large
600 ml/1 pint	yoghurt, see Note	2½ cups
1 tablespoon	lemon juice	1¼ tablespoons
3 tablespoons	finely chopped chives	3¾ tablespoons
2 teaspoons	chopped mint	2 teaspoons
1 tablespoon	chopped chervil or parsley	1¼ tablespoons
to taste	salt and freshly ground white pepper	to taste
	To garnish	
	yoghurt	
	mixed chopped herbs	

Peel and slice the cucumber, then sieve or liquidize until smooth. Mix with all the other ingredients. Spoon into a suitable container and freeze slightly. Stir to redistribute the herbs through the cucumber mixture (they may have sunk to the bottom). Freeze again lightly, then serve in chilled bowls, topped with the yoghurt and herbs.

Variation

• Slimmers can use low-fat yoghurt or fromage frais.

Note: This soup will not keep well in the freezer for more than 48 hours if low-fat yoghurt or fromage frais is used. Full-cream yoghurt is necessary for longer storage up to one month.

ICED ORANGE SOUP

Cooking time: 10 minutes • Serves 4 to 6

Despite the large quantity of oranges, this soup has a distinctly savoury taste. It can be kept in the freezer for up to 3 months and is ideal for slimmers.

Metric/Imperial	Ingredients	American
4	*very large oranges*	4
or 6	*moderately large oranges*	or 6
450 ml/³/₄ pint	*water*	scant 2 cups
¹/₂	*chicken stock cube*	¹/₂
3 tablespoons	*chopped spring onions (scallions)*	3³/₄ tablespoons
2 or 3 drops	*Tabasco sauce*	2 or 3 drops
1 small	*sprig thyme or lemon thyme*	1 small
	To garnish	
	orange and lemon slices	

Pare enough zest from the oranges to give 3 level tablespoons (3³/₄ tablespoons); do not use any bitter white pith. Place in a saucepan with the water, bring to the boil, then lower the heat and simmer for 7 minutes. Do not cover the saucepan; the liquid should evaporate to leave barely 300 ml/¹/₂ pint (1¹/₄ cups) of orange-flavoured stock. Remove the zest, then dissolve the stock cube in the hot liquid.

Halve the oranges, scoop out all the flesh and add to the liquid with the other ingredients. Sieve or liquidize the soup. When completely cold, pour into a suitable container and freeze lightly (see page 191). Spoon into serving bowls and garnish with the orange and lemon slices.

GARNISHES AND ACCOMPANIMENTS TO SOUPS

The garnishes added to soup should give instant eye-appeal, so choose them carefully to add contrast in colour and texture. Suggestions about suitable garnishes appear at the end of recipes in this book. Crisp toppings, such as croûtons and Melba toast, are familiar accompaniments to soup, but there are many others. Some of my favourites include Bruschetta and Crostini, which are flavoured with garlic and olive oil.

In my opinion nothing is nicer with soup than delicious home-made bread or rolls, or for a change scones, muffins or cornbread. Recipes for all these can be found in my **Basic Basics Baking Handbook** (Grub Street).

CROÛTONS

Cooking time: 5 to 6 minutes • Serves 4 to 6

The quantities below will make enough for 4 to 6 servings. Since croûtons store or freeze very well, it is worth making a large batch.

White bread makes more attractive-looking croûtons, but those made from brown or wholemeal bread have a very good flavour. If anxious to avoid fried foods, bake or toast the croûtons instead, see below.

Metric/Imperial	Ingredients	American
2 large	**slices of bread**	2 large
	For frying	
40 g/1½ oz	*butter*	3 tablespoons
1 tablespoon	**sunflower or olive oil**	1¼ tablespoons

Trim off the crusts and cut the crumb into 6 mm/¼ inch dice. Heat the butter and oil in a frying pan, add the diced bread and fry steadily, turning frequently, until golden brown on all sides. Drain on kitchen paper and use immediately, or cool and freeze (see over).

Variations

Deep-Fried Croûtons: Heat the oil in a deep fryer to 190°C/375°F. Put the diced bread into a fine-meshed frying basket and cook for 2 minutes or until crisp and golden brown. Drain on kitchen paper and serve immediately or freeze (see page 194).

Baked Croûtons 1: Dice the bread and place on ungreased baking trays. Preheat the oven to 180°C/350°F/gas mark 4 and bake the bread for about 12 minutes, or until crisp and golden in colour. If more convenient, cook for about 30 minutes at 150°C/300°F/gas mark 2. There is no need to drain these croûtons. If really dry and crisp, they can be stored in tins or airtight jars.

Baked Croûtons 2: Toss the diced bread in 1 tablespoon oil or melted butter, then place on baking trays and bake in the oven preheated to 180°C/350°F/gas mark 4. Drain on kitchen paper and serve immediately or freeze (see below).

Toasted Croûtons: Toast the slices of bread until brown and crisp then cut into small dice. These toasted croûtons are better freshly made.

Garlic Croûtons: Follow the main recipe or the first variation but add 1 or 2 crushed garlic cloves to the butter and oil.

Another way to incorporate a garlic flavour is to toss the cooked croûtons in a very little garlic salt before serving.

Freezing: Put the croûtons on flat plates or trays and open-freeze until firm. Pack and use within 3 months.

CHEESE CROÛTONS

Cooking time: 25 to 30 minutes • Serves 8 to 10

These make an excellent garnish on a variety of soups, especially vegetable soups. It is advisable to use Parmesan cheese because it sticks to the buttered bread better than any other cheese, and its strong flavour means that only a small amount is necessary.

Metric/Imperial	Ingredients	American
5 large	slices of bread, about 1.25 to 2 cm/½ to ¾ inch thick	5 large
75 g/3 oz	butter	⅜ cup
50 g/2 oz	Parmesan cheese, see method	½ cup

Trim off the crusts, then cut the crumb into 1.25 to 2 cm/½ to ¾ inch squares. Melt the butter and finely grate the cheese. Carefully turn the bread in the melted butter, then roll in the grated cheese. If you want a really thick coating, use at least 50 per cent more cheese.

Preheat the baking trays and the oven to 150°C/300°F/gas mark 2. This ensures that the croûtons do not stick to the trays. Arrange the croûtons in a single layer on the trays and bake until golden. Allow to cool.

Freezing: Open-freeze the croûtons on flat trays, then pack into bags or boxes. (Open-freezing ensures they do not stick together.)

MELBA TOAST

The orthodox way of making Melba toast is to toast slices of bread on both sides, then split them horizontally to give ultra-thin slices. The untoasted sides are then toasted until crisp and brown.

I find this process somewhat dangerous, even with a good sharp knife and a steady hand. My preferred method is to cut wafer-thin slices of bread and bake them on baking trays in the oven preheated to 180°C/350°F/gas mark 4. After about 10 minutes the slices are really crisp and brown. Serve with butter.

FLAVOURED TOAST

Fingers of savoury toast combine well with many soups. The toast must be freshly made, then spread with butter and topping and served at once.

Anchovy Toast: Spread the hot toast with a little butter and some anchovy paste.

Instead of anchovy paste, use canned anchovies in oil. Drain and chop the fish and blend with a little unsalted butter. Spread on the bread, cut into fingers and top with chopped parsley.

Cooked fresh anchovies can be used in the same way as the canned variety.

Serve with fish soups.

Cheese on Toast: Spread hot toast with a little butter, then add thin slices of Cheddar, Gruyère or other good cooking cheese. Put under a preheated grill for just a few minutes until the cheese melts, then cut into neat fingers.

Herb-flavoured cream cheese can be used instead of sliced cheese, but do not heat this: simply spread on hot toast.

Serve particularly with vegetable soups.

Pâté on Toast: Soft liver pâté or fish pâté can be spread neatly on hot, buttered toast, then garnished with small pieces of lemon, orange or tomato. If the pâté is firm, cut in slices to fit the toast.

Tapenade, the anchovy and olive spread from Provence, and similar mixtures, such as Gentleman's Relish, make good toppings on hot toast. They can also be used on fingers of bread and butter.

BRUSCHETTA (GRILLED ITALIAN BREAD)

Cooking time: a few minutes

This is a simple but delicious Italian delicacy, in which bread is grilled and flavoured with garlic and olive oil.

Metric/Imperial	Ingredients	American
1	Italian loaf	1
1	garlic clove	1
several tablespoons	**extra virgin olive oil**	several tablespoons

Slice and toast the bread, or prepare it in the oven, as described in Melba Toast (see page 195). Peel the garlic clove, cut across the middle, then rub the cut ends over the hot bread. Drizzle with olive oil and eat at once.

Variations

- The toasted or oven-baked crisp bread can be topped with the ingredients suggested on page 195. I also like to use finely chopped mixed peppers fried in a little olive oil as a topping. Ricotta cheese is an excellent topping, by itself or under the cooked peppers.

Crostini: is another name given to these slices of toast. Crostini can be flavoured with garlic and oil too or topped with various savoury ingredients.

Do not freeze.

GARLIC BREAD

Cooking time: 10 to 15 minutes • Serves 4 to 6

Metric/Imperial	Ingredients	American
1	long French loaf (baguette)	1
	For the filling	
85 g/3 oz	butter	3/8 cup
2 to 3	garlic cloves, to taste	2 to 3
little	salt	little

Preheat the oven to 200°C/400°F/gas mark 6. Make several slits in the loaf at regular intervals, but do not cut right the way through.

Cream the butter. Peel and crush the garlic cloves. Blend the garlic with the butter, then insert in the slits in the loaf. Wrap in foil and bake for 10 minutes. For a crustier finish, leave unwrapped and heat for 15 minutes.

Variations

Anchovy Bread: Blend the 85 g/3 oz (3/8 cup) butter with 1 teaspoon anchovy essence or several finely chopped anchovies. Insert into the loaf and bake as above.

Garlic Cheese Bread: Blend 50 g/2 oz (1/2 cup) butter, 50 g/2 oz (1/2 cup) grated Gruyère or other cheese with the crushed garlic. Insert into the loaf and bake as above.

Savoury Cream Cheese Bread: Mix 100 g/4 oz (1/2 cup) cream cheese with 1 tablespoon (1 1/4 tablespoons) chopped gherkins, 2 teaspoons chopped capers and 1 tablespoon (1 1/4 tablespoons) chopped parsley. Insert into the loaf and bake as above.

Tomato Butter: Blend 85 g/3 oz (3/8 cup) butter with 1 to 2 tablespoons (1 1/4 to 2 1/2 tablespoons) tomato purée (paste). Insert into the loaf and bake as above.

Quick Tip

The filled bread can be heated for approximately 1 1/2 minutes on defrost setting in the microwave. Using a higher setting makes the bread hard.

Freezing: All except the garlic filling freeze well. Do not freeze the filled and baked loaf.

CHICKEN BALLS

Cooking time: 8 to 10 minutes • Serves 4 to 8, depending upon the recipe

A speciality of Norwegian cuisine, these chicken balls are an excellent garnish for chicken and other soups. It is important to use uncooked chicken to give the maximum flavour to the mixture.

Metric/Imperial	Ingredients	American
225 g/8 oz	**uncooked chicken breast, weight without skin and bone**	*½ lb*
2	**egg yolks or 1 egg**	2
75 g/3 oz	**butter, chicken fat or margarine**	*⅜ cup*
2 tablespoons	**double (heavy) cream, or amount needed, see method**	*2½ tablespoons*
to taste	**salt and freshly ground black pepper**	to taste

Finely mince or process the chicken breast. Add the egg yolks or egg, the unmelted butter or other fat and mix very well. Stir in the cream, using a little extra if the chicken flesh is very lean. Season to taste and form into balls about the size of a small olive with the help of a teaspoon.

Fill a deep frying pan with water, bring to the boil and add a little salt. Drop in the balls, cook for 8 to 10 minutes and drain well.

Freezing: Place the uncooked or cooked balls on a flat tray, freeze until hard, then pack. There is no need to defrost the mixture before cooking or heating. If uncooked, simmer as directed in the main recipe, or poach for about 12 minutes in the very hot soup. If cooked poach for 3 or 4 minutes only.

Quick tip

Mix all the ingredients in a food processor; take care not to over-process or the ingredients will become too sticky.

PUT IT RIGHT

Q What can be done if a soup has been over-salted?

A Add a little cream or milk. If this makes the soup too thin, mix a little milk with flour or cornflour (cornstarch), as suggested on page 8, add to the soup and stir over the heat until thickened to the correct consistency.

An egg or eggs can also help to counteract saltiness. Beat the egg(s) with a little cold liquid, add several ladlesful of hot soup, tip into the pan and cook slowly, stirring or whisking all the time.

A combination of egg(s) and cream can work miracles in reducing a salty taste.

Another alternative is to add raw potato. If time permits, peel and dice the potato. If the soup is already cooked and time is short, peel and grate at least one good-sized potato, add to the other ingredients and cook for a time, then taste.

Yet another alternative is to add rice or pasta to the soup, as both of these will absorb some of the salt.

Q Are there any last-minute additions to improve the flavour of a soup?

A Yes, there are many, some of which are listed below.

Herbs: add a fairly generous amount of freshly chopped herbs (see pages 17 to 19) or dried herbs.

Spices: stir in ground spice (see pages 19 to 20).

Seasonings: add more salt and pepper. These condiments help to bring out the taste if used judiciously.

Add other seasonings, such as celery salt, garlic salt and mustard. (If using powdered mustard, mix it with a little water, wine or milk if adding to a ready-cooked soup.) Many excellent mustards are now available.

Sauces: soy sauce is extremely good in many soups, but add carefully so that it does not overwhelm the flavour and colour.

Worcestershire sauce is a good addition to fish, meat and poultry soups.

Tabasco sauce is made from hot peppers and adds a real kick to many dishes. Use only a few drops.

Flavourings: tomato ketchup, tomato purée (paste) or sun-dried tomatoes add instant flavour.

Lemon or orange juice adds a refreshing taste.

Sherry or other alcohol immediately gives more flavour.

Q What causes soup to curdle and how can it be rectified?

A Soups curdle when they have been overheated, particularly if they contain an acid ingredient such as wine or lemon juice plus eggs and/or cream or milk. Always heat such mixtures with great care and do not allow to reach boiling point.

If soup has curdled, try one or more of the following techniques to rectify it.

- Whisk briskly with a hand whisk, preferably a balloon type.
- Liquidize the ingredients; this generally produces a smooth texture.
- Strain the soup through a sieve, but do not rub it through if you want to leave the curdled lumps behind.

After liquidizing, you will find that the soup appears somewhat thinner. Do not try to thicken it: just heat it very gently or, if suitable, serve as a cold soup.

Sieving also makes the soup considerably thinner; simply reheat it very gently and serve topped with whipped cream, cream cheese or thick yoghurt, or serve it cold.

SOUPS FOR SLIMMERS

If you are slimming, or trying to keep your weight down, soups can form a useful part of your diet, as they can be both sustaining and filling. To make them suitable for a well-balanced slimming diet:

• Have smaller portions. Most recipes in this book make 4 to 6 servings, so allow yourself one-sixth of the total amount, unless serving the soups as a main dish.
• Where 50 g/2 oz (½ cup) of fat is specified in the recipe, reduce to 25 g/1 oz (2 tablespoons). This is quite feasible, particularly if cooking the soup in a microwave or non-stick pan.
• Use semi-skimmed milk where full-cream milk is specified.
• Substitute fromage frais or low-fat yoghurt for cream or full-fat yoghurt in the recipes. Remember that all these ingredients must be heated carefully and not allowed to boil or the soup will curdle.

The following are the best soups for slimmers:

INDEX